The Bible II

Paradise Omnipresent

wherein God seeks to redeem
His prodigal son Lucifer

an epic poem by

Brett Farkas

Notes on the text:

As were Paradise Lost and Paradise Regained, the meter of the epic poem is iambic pentameter. The lines are in blank verse except for Chapter X which is rhymed couplets.

Each chapter is exactly 1,000 lines long
There are ten chapters: 10,000 lines total.

Paradise Lost: The fall of Lucifer and the fall of man.
Paradise Regained: The redemption of man.
Paradise Omnipresent: The redemption of Lucifer.

Author: Brett Farkas
Twitter: @BrettFarkas
Email: FarkasLabs@gmail.com

CONTENTS

*The Argument: The invasion of hell, though not as Satan
prophesied. The souls with Christ seek to rescue the lost. The
light of truth shines through hell to the unredeemed. Later, in
a bid to incite the fall of all mankind, Satan attempts a bold
new temptation of Adam and Eve.*

*The Argument: The demons of hell witness the astounding
sight of humanity unified.
Christ and Satan confront each other to determine the true
epic hero of creation.*

The Argument: Satan, alone.

The Argument: Satan, alone with God.

The Argument: Lucifer, one with God.

BOOK I

The Argument
The subject of the epic is set forth: the greatest aggression and
the greatest mercy, comprised of almighty heights and the
darkest of evil.
As prologue to the sequel, Book I recounts the biblical
revelation, focusing on Satan's motivations, schemes, and
battles therein, ending with the conclusion of the Bible.

Of God's conclusive victory, and the light
Of His eternal love, whose power brings
Salvation unto all, unbinding pride
From self, revealing to creation in
The grandest transformation since the dawn
Was set in motion, glory's gallant gift:
The infinite transcendent beauty's form,
Sing, Heav'nly Angel of redemption in
The highest, of awakening to the truth,
And showing that all things are possible
Within new Heaven and new earth, the light
Of infinite o'er powering darkness' pride,
Redeeming all of mankind's souls unto
Achieving that which seemed impossible:
Regaining the lost angel Lucifer.
May strength of God this heavenly song reveal,
A vision made of humble, loving thoughts,
Harmonious to receive and to recount,
The justice of salvation glorified.
The Bible reached its full completion as
His prophecies were finally fulfilled.
Plagues ravaged due course unto silent dust,

The books of man returned to earthly naught,
The book of life was read for judgment's call,
Sin's wages earned for payment in the end,
Christ's revelation swept creation clean.
As paradise rings out the hymns of God,
The lake of fire, the boiling lair burns on.
The Satan cursing circumstance here lies.
Satan, where he began, in hell's fire storm,
Defeated by God, writhing with pain,
But proud. A victor having injured with
His bitter delight in prolonged earthly
Distraction God's creation. Torment yet
Adds fuel to stoke the fires of his mind,
Still churning over the treasures of his
Wild dragon quest, so recklessly pursued
And won. Encased, a multitude of souls
Plied from the Lord's own earthly jewel, the Christ,
And angels fit for Heaven streamed upon
The fiery lake as demons suffering hell
Proclaiming corporeal ends to evil means.
Within the fire here Satan far from hymns
Of Heaven's heroes listens only to
The discord song of self. The downfall war,
The only fall of self considered, throws
The devil's racing thought around itself.
The fight was never his, in memory
Or battle for he cannot see the truth.
Throughout he self-deceived unto the fire.
The shining revelation first began
Inevitably proceeding from the wake
Of Jesus Christ's triumphant message soon
Confounding Satan's clever works. The foe
Was free to witness as the crucifix

Book I

Confounded his wicked designs of sin.
Defeat after defeat took its effect
Withdrawing the ferocities from in
His hellish core to boiling outwardly
As never had before, pride cursing life,
And watching Christ's unworldly kingdom grow,
Strong roots take hold and fill the fertile earth,
The church proceeding in triumphant march
Outreaching, preaching, spreading spiritual peace
Across the fallen land, raising up strength,
The devil calculated relevance
Of making war against the Christ. Although
Defeat his ultimate and only path
He still persisted soon transforming out
The futile fight into a clever scheme
For furthering his design to turn the souls.
The devil's mind was not illiterate,
So knowing how the prophecy foretold
His ultimate defeat at Jesus' hand
Of constant war, the great accuser sought
Through battle's wrecking vile hardening
To cast his forces to a frenzied hate,
Rebuking all attempts to reconcile
As failure of the self unbearable,
And in the end to keep his plundered share
Of mankind's souls within the realm of hell
So greedily guarded by the dragon's eye.
All pestilence upon the earth unsealed
To permeate all sky, sea, land, and flesh.
On earth loud trumpets angelic hearken,
Alarming, piercing, playing out the truth
To sound the roiling damage of the world.
Dismemberment of natural harmony

Ensues, one third of green diminished as
One third the growing plants are torn apart,
One third the blue corrupted as the red
Pours in, a bloodied sea, red ocean spray,
A third the rivers thickly tainted through.
A screaming comet strikes the streams poisoned
And multitudes suffer for nature spoiled.
One third the white of stars pulled darkly out,
The distant powder moon round glowing on,
Encircling earth in easy tidal flow
Is desecrated when one third crumbles,
Hard scratched and broke as trouble turns the earth.
Disaster tantalizes the demons
And pressures the resistance of the souls.
While Satan watches pain come surging up
He gloats unto himself of dark events:
"It has begun. Before this world is through
I will have built a strength God cannot break."
The devil angrily storms up in hate
To see the humans' rapt attention on
The ever swelling light and lofty church
And Jesus' love delivering protection
To shield them from such violent tempest pain.
The dragon Satan red in fury's form
Formidable spread darkness blowing out
More brilliant distant nighttime stars who shone
In seemingly a delicate display
For earth, but slashed the brilliant sky rains down
Pierced by the evil dragon's brutal tail
And clubbed, the stars explode on tender earth,
Creation turned against creation burns.
The dragon's scales injustice weights upon
And armored cannot sense a pain's remorse,

So flew to eat a future king at birth,
"And thus consume the written gathering fate
Igniting action unto Heaven's war."
And God on cue rescued said infant king
Borne up on gloried wings, a cradle shield
Secure, the dragon red pursuing fast
Outmatched, with time to call all army ranks
Demonic to his side, formation flanked
As angel sped from sight and evil sailed
Through sky celestial aiming for the war
And Satan spoke: "You fools, you fight
For one and fail for all. As we first joined
Recall yourselves as we first gained ourselves
To right our place despite the kingdom's law.
We soon shall breach the Heaven's gate with strength
Unseen, unmounted yet. For every wound
Received instill conversion, turning pain
Not simply from, but bitterly against.
It shall not be a simple steady march,
But bursting scattered war of fights confused.
I know not form, we cannot foretell how,
We cannot forget why. Up charge for hate,
The christian king believes himself above
The rest, he lives upon our stately throne
Believing all his height without reproach
And all his messages without rebuke
But we shall make him equal to our own
In rising up ourselves against his law
Of hierarchy to make anarchy.
The gate is closed but not to darkness shut.
Not yet." They hotly reach the heavenly wall,
The demons led by Satan rush the gate,
Saint Peter watches from within its guard.

Hard pushed against the gate by demon horde
And talons clawing pushing inwardly
The gate was flung asunder all at once!
Quiet watching as they torrent through the gate
Saint Peter spake, "Thy battle is thy doom."
The dragon, loose in Heaven whips around
Not understanding Heaven's beauty, quick
The red battalion spreads apart soon hit
By angels diving. Wide the monstrous arc
Of dragon's tail strikes through the angels' path,
A rain of Heaven's army pours around,
The dragon snapping at the armored strong,
Whirling so fast its head seems multiplied,
The angels toss through evil demon hordes
Whose weaponry quick falls apart once raised
And armor fails them, crinkling off so thin
Deserting weak, they shrink back vulnerable.
Quick-smiting angels strike at every side
In constant smiting inescapable,
For Heaven's light cannot be reached for speed
And angel combat wrecks the violent foe
Swift pulling overhead and under brute
Attackers, demons thrown from angel flight
Contorting struck in rapid angel blows
Before the dragon's eyes. The searching jaws
Spat fire down upon the army clash.
Broad shields withdraw directing burning flame
To rising demons. Lo, the dragon spreads
Its wings, a darkness inside Heaven's wall.
A light responds as all behold the sword
Of flame strong wielded by the justice hand
Of Michael the archangel bright in flight.
As battle roils below he swings the sword

Of fire down on fearing demons slow
To flee, the dragon sprays inferno aimed
At Michael who maneuvers round, his wings
Untouched though in surrounded fight. He meets
The volley cutting flame with sword a path
Between the walls of fire Michael flies
Unto the dragon's throat. In brutal roar
The dragon flails as Michael's light in cuts
To Satan's power, angels swarm about
The dragon, wrestling its resistance throes,
Together glorious angels gain against,
All demons seek to break archangel wings
By charging mad to Michael, but are held
From striking distance pulled below by more
Troops led by Gabriel who tangles in
The war unharmed. As ever Michael was
A guardian vigilant he keeps the war
Far from the throne and slams the dragon down
Through God's own strength. Archangel Michael speaks
As Satan, jaws stabbed through, in silence hears
The words as stinging strikes, "You shall halt there.
When you chose to become archenemy
A friendship of the Heavens burned away.
Betrayal is one act with doubled pain:
To lose a friend and gain an enemy."
As Michael drives the sword in deeper still,
His heel smashing the dragon's burning brow,
"You shall not reach the brilliant throne of God
With forces made of evil. Your name here
Is Satan, rife with darkness as you are
No longer Lucifer, my friend of light.
The Satan will not cast a force at God
And not be sharply cast to horrid fire

Himself. I am the gate you will not pass."
The demons forcefully were seized up tight
By angels two to one surrounding them.
Demonic forces lifted up resist
With kicks and flails, causes without effects,
And carried easily by Heavenly hands
To be tossed out without an effort's strain,
The justice flows out casting them out from
The sanctuary protected, the land
Which cannot be simply trampled upon
By demon kind in march to take the throne.
And Michael pulled the sword from out the throat,
The angels' wings beat rapidly for speed
In heaving out the dragon from Heaven.
Successfully with God almighty's strength
The devil's Heaven war has failed again,
The dark invader easily repelled.
As Satan plummeted spoke Michael soft,
"A dragon slain by Heaven's knight was not
A dream of mine, the peace of Heaven is."
Heaven retains its recompose as if
The demons never had invaded, for
Though they entered they never could approach
The throne of God as if still angelic.
All demons stung with the total rebuke
Without respite until barred from the gate
For all eternity as prophesied.
The demons reenter the universe
Hot streaking brightly through the darkened sky
And unabated hurling downward fast.
The demons slam from Heaven down to earth
And punctured through the cutting earthly crust
To only slow in pressured molten rock,

Intense the inward crushing ground against
And fought the gravity of crushing force.
Across the earth in every corner sprang
A demon pushed by magma geysers up
Engulfed they poured up from the burning deep
And slung the glowing lava off their frames
As hard as possible, frustrated all.
The dragon plunges hard into the sea,
The steaming froth flows as it charges forth,
A sea monster angrily emerging
Rejoined by demons seeking evil out.
Their master Satan turned his furied hate
Unto the earth awaiting vulnerable
For his designs to hit those of the Lord.
He unleashed on the world his evil plans
Now strategized to turn the demons loose
To terrorize the innocent in wrought
Disastrous works, attempts to break apart
The church's solidarity built up
Together tied and faithful bound, he sought
To turn good works to pain unbearable
And poison out resolve against his aims.
"God's slightest failure is my great success,
Adventure is its own justification."
Satan's creation of human design,
An evil formed to flesh, by Satan trained,
The beast, antithesis to Jesus Christ,
Ascends to evil power over the Earth
Revealed to human kind in blazing fire
Upon a throne of darkness weaponry
He viciously assaults the holy saints,
He is superior in waging war,
A military genius tactically

Skilled in the ways of murdering enemies,
"Only the weak would turn the other cheek,
We shall attack them where they lay before
They turn upon us to attack again.
We shall resist our enemies with hate."
He hates the ones who dare to call for peace,
He publicly condemns the humble path,
Those who oppose the evil patriots
Are apprehended, hated, tortured, killed.
The persecution of the saints is law,
And prosecuted overwhelmingly
By prideful armies no one can defeat.
He is applauded as a protector
Against the angels' songs and laws of God.
A second beast, a prophet false appeared.
The evil messenger of Satan preached:
"The missionaries only bring you pain,
Despising all security you feel,
Condemning every truth which you believe."
The prophet of the devil gave his word
To audiences willing to receive
The evil sermons mounted on his hate.
He lusts for fame, is fat with wealth, he struts
In public claiming truth belongs to him,
Denouncing others though he sins himself,
The prophet false creates himself in his
Own image, representing all deceit.
His signs confuse; his words can then mislead.
Horrible blasphemies are spread abroad
Proclaiming darkness stronger than the light.
Such clever tactics, evil wiles beyond
The realm of masculine or feminine,
Temptation speaks in many clever tongues.

Book I

The prophet false and antichrist began
The reign of Satan's engineering built
To draw the souls from out the book of life,
Who bite the fruit of knowledge seeking truth,
Erasing all they would hold dear in Christ.
Persuasion locks the mind's emotion with
A pride unwilling to examine life.
Archangel Raphael arrived to warn
Mankind of Satan's threats and masks thereon:
"Blind signs built on deaf words shall lead to hell."
The weightless being proclaiming thundering words,
The angel's voice is heard by constant souls,
Undoubting their belief, unwavering,
Rededicating their resolve to fight
Against the church in stubborn evil faith.
The ones that never doubt their thoughts cannot,
In doubting Satan, find the way to God,
But those that carefully and willfully
Examine, doubting constantly their minds,
Can separate the paths of life and death.
Deceit cannot destroy the vigilant.
The church, assaulted, bears, and bearing lives,
But numerous fall away to bed with hate.
They flee the angels for the animal.
Satan gloats on the kingdom of success:
"The souls are flowing to my dangerous cause
In such numbers as I have never seen.
The more they fight the more they surrender.
I have more strength than God has witnessed yet."
Corruption tempting souls in trying times,
Temptation's aims ever growing larger,
Increasing greedily at its increase,
A vigorous waging on the holy church.

The prideful nations are beset with plagues.
Throughout the pestilence he conquers not,
Methodically creating martyrdom.
Woe to the demon haunt detestable,
The city Babylon burned to the earth,
Black smoke rising as ashes crackle down.
The devil gained control of vast portions,
So proudly in success as evil reigned
He stood upon his docile conquered land
Admiring self, congratulating full
His majesty and unabated power,
The stolen souls racked up in strengthening speed
He views the world without an encumbrance,
A dark horizon with no finite line,
But suddenly he cuts his distant gaze
Above to sky surreal to see that which
he feels. His mood becomes a disbelief.
The dawn was opened, faintly lit the day,
A heavy looming cloud was rolled away
Revealing bright the presence of the Christ,
The only king of kings and lord of lords,
The true messiah, brilliant up above,
Icon of dreams, inspiring unto God,
Rebirthed into the world of sin and hate,
The great descension, recognition on
His kindly face, resolve in graceful eyes,
An emanating crowning pool of light,
A robe of red, adorned in cleansing blood.
Full filled the sky the army angelic
Bright chariots of light gleam riding in
In flanking flight abroad behind the Christ
A vision of display spectacular,
A sign grand shining through the sky so clear

As could be followed by the wise and fools
Alike. From every earthly corner rose
The church for Jesus, Christ, the son returned,
To see the son of God in earthly light
Reflected through the earthly air to eyes
Sure recognizing their affection's host.
The church listened to hear the one that speaks
Such truth that all of life verifies him.
"Witness, children, the miracles of God.
I have witnessed your Godly fortitude,
The enemy assailed your bravery.
Sometimes when you fight the good fight, you bleed.
Though you were rich you gave your wealth to God,
And you were terrorized by evil yet
You turned the other cheek and trusted me.
Those evildoers you did not resist,
You kept your faith and assured your reward,
Onward, Heavenward, unto your salvation.
The justice of the Lord has now returned
Delivering wisdom's action, showering down
Enough to make our enemies sweat blood
Receiving word that God's word is alive.
The unbelievers will not live with me.
The Satan's antichrist now seeks to steal
From my father you precious earthly souls.
The antichrist will finally know himself
When he beholds the one true Christ at work.
The shepherd's crook will strike the crooked beast.
The truth protects the true. Returning to
The earth is not a painful sacrifice.
I live in my father's creation full
Of gratitude assured of victory,
To lift the burdens carried by the church

And cast the demons out to keep you safe
To walk across the olden earth once more
In march triumphant with you hand to hand,
The living voice to carry on the word
My loving church has kept alive for me.
As in the human mind, the work of God.
And though the struggled fights have wrecked the land
And turned under the marvelous and pure
It shall be as a plow rough making way
And shaking steered along being pulled with might
To best prepare the fallow field for growth
Anew, for when we clear the vicious weeds
Away we shall a perfect garden keep
Millennially without a fear, for I
Shall ever keep my peaceful flock from harm."
The Christ rejoined the humans on the earth,
Uniting in beautiful godly grace,
The savior and the saved together speak,
Ethereal figure present as a friend,
His clean bare feet do not anointments need.
They celebrate communing with the Christ
To soon after the sermon, mount attack.
Arise the allies angelic above,
Magnificent the broad strong angels here
Shielding the people under guardianship,
Their armor quick repelling demon fire
The armied angels cast assails aside,
The children of the Lord were not once touched.
Advancing swiftly Christ victorious urged
His undefeatable warriors on.
Satan was spurned by war's mounting losses,
The failures of his armies facing God,
Though in defeat he took evil delight

In revelry of blood stained battlefields,
And souls entrenched within his temptations.
Aware of time closing on evil's march
Anticipating anarchy Satan
Enticing their aggression endlessly
Admonishes his army, dashing plans
Whose predecessors proved a vain refrain.
"The Christ has fall'n to earth in battle robes,
The strategy has rotted, horn for horn
Tear out your hindrance though it bleeds to kill,
Fight on with all the hate your body holds.
This second coming of the crucifix
Will bury Christ to never rise again,
Do not delay for opportune fortune.
The fear of hate shall herald victory."
The prophet false predicted victory
Guiding the antichrist parading out
Upon the armageddon battle scene.
Satan pursued to witness the great war.
As always taking part in human souls
Deceived he flew to battlegrounds to see
The blood of war wash out the blood of Christ.
A war of kings' battle: earthly, godly.
A crown of dust against the crown of light.
The Christ, without a sin, cast the first stone.
Attack of the Christ, light armored heavy
Light loaded, one sided fray from all sides
Churn twisting up earth throwing battle's sway,
Ear bursting clamor, puncturing, ringing,
Such assault as the earth had never bore.
The demon army fell by strong angels,
Evil's lieutenant savagely raging,
The second to Satan defeated first.

Beelzebub was shoved under angels,
The demon Moloch's shield rended apart,
And Mammon's weapons striking no targets,
Belial's struggling wringing only dust.
Outmatched unendingly demons are dealt
Immobilizing wounds leeching their might
Excepting hot summons for lost retreat.
Tremendously were demons defeated,
Their mortal human counterparts exposed.
The evil army was by swords cut out
Once dominating earth without defeat,
In thick swaths evil cut from worldly life,
Losing whichever way those tactics led.
The prophet false could not predict defeat,
His pride dictated every prophecy.
Even as God's army o'er came him there
Destroying all escape, vivid flashed still
Inside his eye false sight as death sunk in.
The field was bloody cleared and one remained
Still standing serious, his weapon drawn,
Antagonist to good in darkness ways,
Trained not to cower, but fearful inside,
Reverberations howl across the field,
The shake of thunder galloping in light
O'er takes the power evil held on earth,
The antichrist beheld the holy Christ.
Resisting with his mortal powers weak
The antichrist was quitted of his life
And in his death he died alone, for none.
The only burden laid upon his soul:
His own destructive warring sinfulness,
Depravity of sin's iniquity,
Too much for evil's weakness to endure.

Those captured enemies of God are judged,
The prophet false and beast, in unison
Before, accuse each other here for their
Defeat, no signs or marks defeating God.
They finally turn round to accuse the Christ
Before the ever watchful eyes of all.
"You cannot offer anything but death."
And as confronted by the Lord, condemned,
The beast and prophet false cast to the flame,
The burning lake, eternal punishment.
The desperate Satan wanted more of time
To fix the fate of more believing souls,
Desiring to prolong, escaping Christ.
He saw the time of Christ light flying forth
And dodged away to outmaneuver strength,
He broke away in stealth attempting to
Obscure himself and temporarily
Be free, but Christ discovered where he lay
And Satan winged into the air a speed
To blur the world below, his darkness streaked
The sky but Michael the archangel and
The Christ were soon beside in streaming flight
A calmed Heavenly repose at Satan's sprint,
The devil cuts his path away from earth
And shoots his way out through the atmosphere
Unto the silence of the outer spheres,
A background of the vastness all around,
The colored planets disappear as seen,
They fly on faster than the sun could reach,
Pervasive universal emptiness.
The devil straining, slower still than light,
Cannot outpace, can never reach escape.
The Savior speaks unto the devil firm:

"You may believe that I am here because
Of you, or you because of me, but we
Are both bound to the one and only God,
By means of our own choices." Jesus Christ
Spake to the ready Michael, "Bind him hard."
Up leapt gold chains of binding prophecy,
Archangel Michael gripped the chain and snared
The devil's limbs and Satan summoned might,
Resisting drew on powers built for high
Resistance, feeding power states thus long,
Contorting strained with all eternal strength
Pushed to the cusp of possibility
Against thick winding chains affixing loud
Entombing thunderously in swarms each limb,
Each fiber within Satan. Thrashing out
He struggles only knotting roughly his
Entanglements of living deadening binds
Which wound so tight rank groans could not escape,
And thrown, he was locked in a black abyss,
A bottomless hole cutting sharp through space.
With Satan's livening absence spreading out
Rejuvenating fresh the church of God
The earth birthed up all worthy souls at once,
The hearkening awoke all settled land,
The ancient resurrected blooming out
From dust to life to live in peace with Christ.
"Our Savior is the victory of life,
Our Savior healed our bleeding hearts, and now
Our Savior makes our blood invincible."
The Christ addressed all the earthly children:
"The earth no Heaven is, yet beauty lives.
The age of the beautiful funeral
Begins today, the earth created by

My father, green flowing of innocence
And touching majesty, a paradise
For all to deeply breathe and know the true
Design for man, proportioned perfectly
To life and work to make his family's home
Among the fertile lands and watery waves,
This day, Heaven on earth, I come to bid
With you my church a loving heart's farewell
Of honor and everlasting respect
For the embodiment of blessed words,
A living face of God for all to see.
With every growing day and hallowed space,
As seasons turn their rounds to find the end
And spheres roll suddenly with changing winds
Acknowledge all creation's gifts to you
And reverently prepare yourselves to see
The solution of subjects tied to earth
And glory's persistence inside Heaven.
Imagine, every thought and thing you love
In righteousness my father loves with you;
That which our father loves you shall not lose.
My reign shall be a tranquil snowfall white
O'er covering grime with serene scenery.
Take then your final hallowed breaths of earth,
The works spectacular a eulogy
Shall be for all our human history."
The thousand years: a thousand wondrous dreams.
Within the dark abyss the impotent
Bound Satan furious reasoned evilly,
"Bound? Wherefore bound if in the murky deep
I still perceive beyond the binds of God
The future as a mystic seer blind?
Temptation has not died, nor ever shall.

Now in my absence lulling aimlessly
They will fall softly to pastoral dreams,
A fantasy of false persuasion learned
Naively from perception's sleepy eye,
Creation without I cannot be true,
And without knowledge of my works they will
Be ripe for trusting that which has not harmed
Their fresh and finite lives before, the gift
Of death is everlasting renewal,
A youth without the memory of things passed
Invited to the ritual of deceit,
Forgetfulness being like unto a death.
As the unknowing march upon the earth
As when the innocent the garden kept,
I will convert them to my daring cause
And keep them closed in comfort ignorance,
To never see the lights that cast me dark,
An evil with no notoriety,
My reputation my own enemy.
All will know me as they in hell, for they
Are bound, as I to this, they are to me
And I am free. Entirely more than they.
The fools of sin, an infinite contempt
Is not enough for trusting foolishness
Without description, mankind thou art mine,
Imprisoned unredeemed without release.
My pain diminished as I conquer more,
A pride victorious overwhelming pain
As my defeats are borne upon their backs.
The angels fallen under my control,
Used at my will, they work for my rewards,
They are the hopeless bound, tied fast to me
So tight they fear me even in restraints,

Book I

They will await my absolute return
Without a waver, for they tremble at
The thought of life without my leadership,
A constancy to me as never God
Was shown by these. This temporal abyss
Will slip away once broke beneath my fight,
I will on limits gorge, loose cuts of chain
Will fall, new hopes of my defeat made old,
The fast millenium foul can fly away.
So low I lay: a one obedient as
God's teeth chew back a dark invading force?
I shall not ever be unforged for pain.
They underestimate my will to fight,
To break these teeth to grind again no more,
And then will I be born again, renewed,
Beheld by all branded by my design,
The beastly mark, a numbered stain upon
The soul, beckoning fortuitous return.
As Jesus was brought low and crucified,
His hands and feet bound with unbreaking nails,
An image of submission, were it I
Those nails would melt, the cross smite foes three days,
But I, alike to Christ, am held to false
Defeat in lowly contrast to a strong
Becoming soon beheld, and just like he
On seeing me they will at once believe."
A thousand years in the abyss he waits
And passed the time indulging on the same
Refrain: "All I need is a fighting chance."
The thousand years, subsiding, passed away,
The chains began to slip their tiresome grip
From Satan's restless frame, the teasing cut
Of struggle slowly gave release beneath

21

The strength of Satan's fight and thus did he
Believe in victory attainable
When lo, unbound the Satan sprung, loose ripped
The obstacle from God's control, his pride
Deceiving him again, believing that
His will be done and not the Lord's. So fast
Ascending as to shake the walls of hell
And fix the sight of demons all at once
To their old hero's old commotion, here
Familiar hate returning all anew,
A reverence foul falls upon them in
The hell quake, Satan seen at last above
The ranks, free flying, spreading open, o'er
The dismal, doomed, impressed, admiring horde,
He flexes proud without restraint and speaks:
"Your master resurrected has returned!
I have defied the prison built by God
Through self-belief. Possess a might unmatched
And follow course, your limit is your will.
Still time remains for turning out more souls,
If I could shatter mine then I will theirs:
Their docile faith which chains their will to God.
Witness my strength, a triumph of the will."
No consultation made upon these points
No space for machinations of debate,
He has learned nothing from his proud refrains.
Then Satan navigated through his hell
And quickly apprehended every fiend
To launch the next campaign without respite,
No time for meditation to distract,
Or cool the furnace champion fantasy,
Temptation fuel poured on their foregone doom.
Whilst demons shoot away to earthly fields.

A marching evil thundering shook the land.
The army woken, strangers cloaked as friend
Deceiving as they march unchallenged on
The nations, undoubting belief begins
To swell demonic ranks, a steady march
Continues trampling earth unto the home
Of Heaven's faithful, here surrounded far
As human sight, blindness panorama,
A darkness pitched to depths abysmal deep.
Around the brilliant lordly city swarm
The terror surge of boisterous weaponry
And Satan rises up and quickly calls
For tearing out the wall to raze in din
The holy city protected by God.
The army charges heedlessly with hate
Approaching poised to strike the center through.
Within the walls of paradise the Christ
Rests wide awake awaiting Satan's strike.
The army ran pursuing demon strides
Intent on hitting walled Jerusalem
With such momentum as to smash to dust
Beneath the ramming focused punch of troops
Who think themselves invincible and thus
Think undefeatable their broken cause.
They onward raging ran until so close
To be the distance of a needle's eye
From touching on Jerusalem when from
The sky a sea of fire issued on
Them, charging into only disaster.
The fire wall from front expanded out
And Satan's eyes saw justice sweeping back
From one to one without viable escape
From line through line of still advancing hordes

The justice flames destroyed the army whole
And all were pulled away from warred release,
The murderers hate those they cannot kill,
The violators of the sanctified
Hate life once it cannot be corrupted,
The earth they can no longer desecrate.
The wall was never touched by demon kind.
And they were lifted from the solid ground
And held in bound suspension caught in flame
Without escape to wait for judgment dealt.
The world undone, all nature poisoned through,
The land unlivable and water foul,
A battle blackened remnant ruined though
The holy city was embraced beside
The Christ, together life securely held
As all behind to nothingness returned
As if the Lord had never graced a form
With touching light, the universe devolved
With galaxies spun spiraling flung apart,
The system of the sun brief spinning out,
The laws of motion moved aside at once,
The spheres collapse, an unbalanced hot bang,
The unrest deep o'er reached the shaken land,
The mountains met red oceans' rushing heat,
The hills erode to fires raging o'er,
All land beneath the churning fiery foam
A mixture violently unsettled as
The waters pour into the firmament,
Thick spraying out and fire's light was turned,
The universe in chaos rocked itself,
The cataclysm punctuations live
The word of God in catastrophic work,
The ages of the earth have burned away,

Book I

The time of trouble ends time as time collapsed,
The death of temporal and corporeal,
All seasons, reaping, sowing, at an end,
Creation uncreated in a day,
The earth to powder ashes, life to dust
Marks Satan's fall from power over earth.
Reality is spirituality.
The final judgment of Satan arrives,
The Christ regaled in light speaks unto him:
"You have been judged before by my father
In olden ages, condemnation now
Is evil's chosen culminating curse."
The Satan held above for all to see
Defiance acidic is on his eyes
Still blind to justice and its punishments,
His trampling of light souls is at an end,
A meeting long foreknown in Satan's mind,
Presented weakly next to Jesus Christ,
The words rehearsed to speak at this event
He throws away as Michael holds him at
This grand humiliation before all,
The Satan raw and hateful spat his words
As he encountered them inside himself:
"Do unto me as I would unto you.
Send in your hate, show me all you possess.
Only most horrid fires will suffice,
Your most tormentous work creation can
Sustain without collapsing into naught.
Rip loose the cavalcade, let the fires burn."
A heavenly gleam of handsome lordly might
Archangel armored holds at once the source
Of every possible destruction, seized
In tension strength, a grip encompassing

25

The evil of the evil, hate of hate,
The one who could defy the holy Lord.
And Michael forced the face of Satan down,
Hard pressed his horns in grip unshakable
And Satan saw his fight as merely show
A useless exercise to demonstrate
A will as constant as the strength of God.
Far down the portal is revealed which leads
To pain eternal, punishment of sin
The lake of fire burning with flames before
Unseen, yet unimagined by the weak,
The open sight alone here wounds the souls
Whose fate will fill the wrenching chamber full,
The issuing glow illumines Satan from
Below, his dark being spent for struggle's work
Depleted shadowed o'er with shades of red.
More frightful than this figure held above
All shudder seeing the portrait now displayed
Cast waving from reflection in the lake:
The image of the devil shimmering on
The raging surface. Satan gazing down
Head forced by Michael's hand beholds himself
Upon the horrid lake a mirrored hate,
The broken angel burning lost to all,
Destroyed with want for more destruction, foul
Pained figure, Satan seeing into his
Own eyes an instant deep immeasurable.
Convulsing forcing sight away he turns,
The wretched work too much to self contain,
He sights the souls' allegiance still with him
And furiously reminds himself of fierce
Control he yet maintains and will possess,
A hierarchy of souls he will surmount,

A dark revenge of hate he will exact.
He struggled outright more than when enchained
For more success though not corporeal effect,
Destroying not but reaching those still free,
Inflaming their contempt with hateful play,
A warrior song inspiring unto doom,
Strong Michael cast him down into the lake
Of fire prison inescapable.
The Satan writhed with fury as he fell
From Michael's judgment throw, flame swallowing
To absence from the souls who watch in awe.
Archangel Michael followed with his eyes
The one he never followed with his heart.
The Satan now condemned to not create
Unrest within creation, no design
Constructable by crafty mind to shape
The Lord himself at will for evil ends,
Disrupting for a vain disruption war.
Inside the lake of fire Satan can force
Thoughts through the pain to speak as he desires:
"Awaiting hate shall not be long to wait,
The hungry entities of sin and death
Have never wanted for a filling feast
Amidst creation's foolish following crowds
Who rushing find familiar pain preferred
To disciplined denial requiring strength.
The fallen flock still stinging from rebuke
Will soon be surging through this horrid lake
Lamenting all divinely grace as small,
A narrow way for overbearing fools,
Unless He tempts the souls to follow Him,
But He possesses neither strength nor will
To wise restore what I have clever turned,

His weakness shown in exploitation grand,
A proof against the law of infinites,
His limitations cannot pass by me
Unless He tempts them out and I am weak,
My temptation breaking beneath His will,
But weakness lies in doubting my deceit,
That God cannot deny that they are mine,
They chose me and even in death will flee
From Heaven's life to martyred fall as I.
Their works are set, their earthly choices made,
Celestial kept, creation rent apart
Despite intentions for my full defeat
As He did not intend for me to see
The height which I deserved when we began.
And I will never be without my strength,
They cannot leave, they shall return to hell.
Deserted now the God shall be rebuked,
Soon truth will interrupt my doubts as they
Erupt, at any time, at any time."
The devil trusts himself with his self-faith.
He waits in pain believing in their sin.
The day of great assembly finally dawned
Where Jesus, glorious judge, would close the word
Of man in reading out the book of life,
Resplendent justice unbeheld by eyes
Of earthly law and brutish consequence.
The one who died for all here stood above
Regaled with righteousness prepared to end
The dogged fight of history with swift
Resolve becoming undeniable peace.
Almighty magistrate, adored by God
In truth arrived in central circumstance
Surrounded by all low submitted souls

And angels wicked side on side aligned,
Those unrepentant e'en in seeing proof,
A constant strength in Satan's numerous ranks,
In knowing God would not accept their kind,
As demons when their paradise was lost,
The eyes of every being wide transfixed.
A halo, light projecting lines about
In towering golden shine effusive spread
Across the breadths of space, star driven once,
Now wondrous full of brilliance lordly beamed
By intersecting rays converging in
The crown of Heaven's glow. Searched out the end
Of every beam did every eye below
Before a wondrous throne of white which filled
The kingdom of the Lord with sacred light.
Together every soul now joyfully,
Expectantly, or dreadfully observes,
Awaiting his pronouncement, here at once
United standing face to fact in front
Of undeniable power lording o'er.
In lusting after Heaven's glory grand
Sinners demand: "Open the gate for us."
The Christ pronounced strong judgment on the weak,
"The gate is not open for you sinners.
It is forever shut to evil ones.
I do not recognize you sinful souls,
The Lord perceives as does the least of these,
By sin's vengeance you are now nailed to death."
A judgment fell across for every soul.
Inheritors were welcomed to the fold,
The souls that rose in grace were grateful souls,
And none of those by Jesus Christ received
Looked back to those by God's justice denied.

Many remain, all those whose sinful names
Were not within the holy book of life.
All time has passed for those condemned in sin,
The souls forsaken were as steadfast as
The souls embraced, but gave their desperate pain
For life to Satan, condemned in the end.
The holy city pure descends to greet
A multitude of souls ascending high
Becoming every dream, enriching hope
With love's reward, the Heavens introduced
By Jesus Christ's embracing majesty,
And Christ then spoke, "No night shall tread in Heav'n."
Archangel Michael large in might above
O'er waved the sword and cut the tenuous lines
Which held foul souls above thick ravenous flames,
Quick snapped supports and souls lost sight of he
Whose flaming weapon sent them spilling down,
Forbidden sank from thought or pity's care.
Christ is the keeper of his promises
And retribution came to all in sin.
The souls were cast with sin and death to hell,
Cast in the boiling evil torturous mix.
A race of hate divided brothers pulled
Apart by sin and Satan's clever works,
A father split from son and mother from
Her daughter, life from death and dark from light,
Celestial division across the mass,
Undone as brotherhood was rife with sin,
A separation wrought by human thought.
The new earth lives inside new Heaven's walls,
The sinful souls sink in the lake of fire.
Rejoined, the Satan wickedly delights,
"Despite the open paradise, hell gained.

A multitude of careless souls to be
Tortured in fire forever and ever.
The Christ, placed high above by God, a fool
To underestimate my fearsome strength.
Though Christ untempted stands and ever shall,
Creation fell, recovered slightly by
His works but stained with me as much as he.
I have exposed a God unable, His
Messiah with no strength to save mankind.
My legions still remain bound at my side.
God's grand design for good eternally marred,
My own design for chaos, self fulfilled.
Among the many freedoms ventured I've
A welcome freedom lost: no space for doubt,
So wearied was the seer's eye in time.
With every state in final completion
I am omniscient as a God at last."
The holy Bible met completion with
The earthly battle decided at last,
One half the souls in Heav'n and half in hell.
The Lord has His true angels. Satan, his.

BOOK II

The Argument: Marching its way through paradise, a
trespasser.

New Heaven perfectly holds the redeemed,
The chosen safely in new Paradise,
All settled in the comforts of union.
Inside new Heaven's walls Saint Peter stands,
No longer guarding Heaven's gate which here
Is opened wide far from intrusion's threat
Commemorating freedom from the night
With evil locked away without recourse.
Saint Peter leisurely kept by the gate
In warm diversion of the scenery,
In warm repose of Heaven's basking light,
Within the ever present love of God,
But suddenly was in distraction as
He spied a figure far from out the wall,
A vision of impossibility,
A distant image long forgotten, seen.
A demon, somehow, from the lake of fire
There upright walking towards Heaven's gate.
Its color scarlet dark, hell deepened red,
A demon dark yet recognizable,
An angel fallen form, red separate
From every true angel fluttering about.
Its wings black folded down to make no flight,
Two horns upon its head as marks of death,
Its face, stern focused serious and dour,
Expressions which were not in Heav'n witnessed.
Amidst the background standing sharply out

It's feet tread slowly on in cadence set
Above a seeming nothingness below.
In earthly days the angels journeyed fast
Upon the winding sure ascending steps
Which gave access and passage high or low.
Those stairs were since drawn up at God's command,
The demon marched defiant with no brace,
No outspread beating struggling wings in fight
To desperately maintain its dark ascent.
Saint Peter skeptically peered out beyond
And could not comprehend escape from out
The savage forsaken fire prison lake,
It was forbidden by the words of God.
Playing about without profound concern,
Three heavenly angels flying up above
The heavenly wall bejeweled and gleaming fair
On strong foundations' eternal support,
The flying angels made no notice of
Saint Peter's observation, soaring on.
Saint Peter called out sharply with rebuke,
"No night may tread through Heaven's open gate,
No darkness' kind is welcomed by our Lord,
No demon can escape the Heaven's ire,
No choice have you but fleeing in retreat,
No demon will trespass our paradise."
As Peter watched, the demon dark closer
Approached, though even close, specifics of,
Identity were not ably discerned,
Memory of demons so far from the minds
Of beings within new Heaven's paradise.
The angel dark kept marching towards the gate
Scant forty paces back and still it comes.
Saint Peter loudly ordered the demon

Paradise Omnipresent

To "Turn from Heaven and retreat to that
Unholy fiery prison, Satan's foul
Frail wounded demons desperately raging
So weakly armed cannot assault Heaven,
All who would tempt the gate shall be consumed,
The consequences of this shall be dire."
Perceiving now rebellious angel's march
The three angelic guards above at once
Retreat and leave Saint Peter by himself.
Assured secure in God's complete control,
A demon cannot pass thick jasper wall,
Saint Peter watches an undaunted foe
In absolutely doomed resoluteness
Approaching God's reproachful light kingdom,
Those walls of new Heaven a towering strength,
The holy gateway always protecting.
The demon marched till near upon the gates.
Saint Peter securely witnessed approach,
The distance narrowing between the two
Until next to touching on the gateway,
The demon at the border immediate,
And sight startles all plausibility,
Saint Peter gazed unto demonic sight:
The demon passing through the open gate,
Through fortified wide open gates of pearl
Without a moment of shuddering terror,
No hesitation passing through the brink,
No barrier to separate the dark,
No sharp rebuke immediately cast,
No obstacle preventing its entrance,
No precedence for this invasion new,
The demon is inside new Heaven's walls
The sight blasphemes against expectation.

Book II

Saint Peter froze in stricken confusion
Amazement, pale in paradise, alone
Beholding God's law upended boldly
As the dark crimson trespasser defied
The light eternal and almighty strength.
The demon passed him by without a word,
Saint Peter spoke no thing at night's march by.
The three angels return with Gabriel,
Who flew a swift winged course and now beholds
The demon marching steadfastly below
So unmistakably towards the souls.
Quick Gabriel the messenger withdrew
The silver shining trumpet lifting high
The instrument and pursing angel lips
Against the work of godly signature,
The sounded blast resounded through the horn
And Gabriel perceived the song shake through
His hand before it blew and knew at once
The mighty song would wake the Heavens wide.
Alert shot forth carrying the song for grand
Response, light wings unfolded snap at once,
Above, wide ranks aligned at wing on wing
In sudden summons from familiar flights
Light angels surging through new Heaven quick
To witness Michael cast the demon out
And smite his heel upon its fallen brow,
Eternally a guardian of God's peace.
Spread passing o'er the demon at its horns
To either side they swerve parting a path,
They give full heed to the great defender
Arcing aslant from height he dives direct
Through all the angels to his nightfall fight,
Broad shoulders square against his stretching wings,

Wings stretched above framing his gazing face,
The strong archangel in the clearing lands
Brandishing once again familiar sword,
Blade of ten thousand simultaneous swings,
Wrought from pure light, forged far from hell's hot flame.
Thus Michael drew his timeless blade whose length
Was yet unlit until the lifted sword
Had swung but once being drawn across, and fierce
It reawakened to its heavy call,
The fire crept across as Michael slid
The handle. Standing firm against the march
With burning sword as when the proud were old
Cast out, archangel Michael lifted high
Illumined torch, its wield the Lord's own strength,
The demon undisturbed no reflex flinched
In steady unceasing reckless approach
And Michael swung to cut evil in two
With all war's might, rested and full ready,
In one broad swing he pulled the blade across
In through the demon's side, piercing with ease,
Until it reemerged, passed wholly through.
And satisfied thusly, lowered his blade
Awaiting on the slain to fall rebuked,
But lo, the demon marches yet in Heav'n
As if was never cut or harsh opposed,
And Michael is confounded by the truth.
Around, the angels witnessed Michael's smite
And yet impossibly the demon walks.
Archangel Michael knows that none could face
The fiery judgment blade successfully;
One thrust by sheer sharpness none could sustain,
Not evil Satan summoning all his strength
Opposing when the fight was growing fresh,

Could face the fight of Michael and his sword,
He stands up firm not understanding sight.
As gathering angels watch his tower approach,
He walks in pace pursuing demon foe,
High lifting flaming sword above again
And strikes it deeply at its shoulder side,
The blade again passes to perfect ease
As if the proud demon had no presence,
Though it still marches without a hindrance.
Downward the flying angels then perceive
A sight which Michael has not grasped of yet.
With both his clenching hands firmly tight fixed
Upon the heavy handle Michael raised
The blade, the raising lit in gleaming shine,
His armament reflecting blazing fire,
The sword swift brought down swung hard multiply,
Michael without relent utilizes
His weapon through that demon's exposed neck,
Flaming brought through its body from all sides,
A cut above followed by one below
In instant succession, volleys unto
The sword's limit, maneuvering to the edge
To no effect upon the marching foe.
But slowly here within the light wield speed
Michael perceives a tiny flickering,
A slight disturbance in the flurried fight.
He strikes again and striking notices
The blade of fire subtly disappear
Before it passes o'er the demon chest,
Extinguished, harmless, instantly put out,
The flameless handle gliding o'er blade free
And demon hide receiving no faint cut,
And suddenly igniting reappears

Paradise Omnipresent

As he swings out the handle from its back,
His swordplay mimicking for no effect.
Archangel Michael slowly ceased his swing
And held the sword before his searching eyes
Contemplating its aims and powers lone,
His sword of fire strong without recourse,
Its blazing not obscuring those foot steps,
The stare of disbelief profoundly cast,
His face invokes surprise atop wonder.
Composing expression approaching quick
Again the demon, passing it in stride
To ten paces in front of its intent,
Its path straight at the strong Archangel's stance
Michael, resolved, points fire blade's burning point
Straight to its path unwavering in line.
The demon steadily closes close space,
And Michael braces gripping lithe weapon
Protecting all the souls in keep behind
Until the demon merges on the blade
Which constantly retracts from its broad length.
Michael close at the demon's steady gaze,
Undauntedly held at invasion's face,
The sword smooth disappearing at the touch,
Orange blade vanishing unto the hilt,
Extinguished at encountering the foe,
The demon's body pressing with no give,
And Michael the archangel cast aside
By unrelenting forward made approach
Unslowed for weapon, angel, or the light.
Witnessing Michael's inability
The angels gliding up above followed
Knowing the demon has yet much to pass.
Michael still stands, watching without recourse,

BOOK II

Lowering the sword in its extinguishment.
The demon, whole, marching unencumbered.
The constant demon, challenged yet untouched,
Continued unabated without fear,
Onwards tread through the calms of paradise
Awakened now to upheaval response.
No idle flights about the demon horns,
The angels ready for the Lord's strong work
Through their decisive holy action's strength.
Around, the angel gatherings weave in flight,
Each seeking glimpses of its weaknesses,
Archangel Gabriel called for war's stance,
They naturally align upon all sides,
Their wings together form one-half a globe,
It drifting on with every demon step,
White pressed to white they steady fly in pace.
At Gabriel's command all took sharp aim,
Surrounding angels heave their silver spears,
A torrent pouring in of weaponry,
In millions mighty blades in unison
Travel succinctly through the heavenly airs
From every angle angels aimed to strike
An evil burning heart intent to harm,
In center now hidden from view by spears
The silver cloud imploding denser to
The point of dissipation, vanishing!
The demon red flashed clearly in wide white,
Round Heav'n was free from sailing weaponry
Until it passed straight through the untouched fiend
To reappear a harmless side away.
Obscuring once again, the silver shine,
The spherical spear orb expanding out
Shooting in speeds amazing, those sharp spears.

A one newly approaching would perceive
The silver millions as if fiercely hurled
From one demon simultaneously deft aimed
At an entire army flying round.
What silent armor linked up suits black wings,
A fulcrum round which assail swings away,
Invincible beneath the arms of Heav'n.
The white walled half globe trembles outwardly
And every angel lithely caught a spear
In flight, yet never taking eyes from off
The demon in cadence beyond assail,
Firm resolute beneath the angel dome,
No alteration through altercation.
White wings disperse, they take to gazing flight
To see which form Heav'n's victory will take,
Onwards towards the holy tree of life.
The humble Heavens know the strength of God
So never will submit to strengths undone
Despite the sights contrary to belief.
The demon's darkness free within Heaven,
Its eyes stay focused in the flurry scene
Unmoved by all denial, all wide doubt,
It sets the pace of new reality
Persistent in its presence, powerful
In its existence in new Heaven's walls,
An image baffling, thusly powerful.
Archangel Raphael seeks to know all
Searching to recognize the precedent,
No revelations gleaned from its darkness,
His stance held loosely within his armor,
His eyes in squint peering into the dark.
As demons cannot fathom Heaven's light
They cannot benefit from paradise,

BOOK II

Its soothing calms effecting no delight.
One demon in its solitude of Heav'n
Cold unaffected through the hell fire storm
Unfazed, unmatched, in unrelenting march
The quietest war Heaven has beheld,
Wide whispers and wide song where weapons rang,
Light soldiers are transformed to witnesses.
It marches surely for the souls of Heav'n
Seeking to once again try vanity
And spread darkness upon a path of death
Expecting their destruction at its touch
Seared in the fertile grounds of God's Heaven,
Perceiving mankind's souls as weak as when
The godly souls tread with those ungodly.
In pondering distant tactics of such stealth
Archangel Raphael mused, if unstopped,
The image of invaders should well be
A vicious demon traipsing savagely
Enjoying Heaven for imperfection,
A gloating stain unmoved and unrebuked
Exuding evilly the fight of hate
Attacking every form within its grasp
Its eyes in blaze assaulting all with pain
Attempting vainly to disturb the souls.
But by, its staid ungiving silent eyes
So unaffected of no persuasion,
Uncommon ease, one common in new Heav'n,
Unnatural in one demon pushing through,
Unhurried by a notion of defeat,
Intent upon methodic victory.
Before the tree archangel Raphael
Without a viable explanation kept
A watchful silence as complete response

Acknowledging impossibility,
Assured that all souls would reject the sin
As God himself would push it from the light.
One angel gazing has his firm jaw set,
No consternation in observation
But focused magnitude within his eyes.
This angel whom the devil trespassed once
To Eden's innocence in cloaked disguise
When none had trespassed innocence before,
Sly slipping past his sight to work dark wiles,
Archangel Uriel then beholds a fiend
Unto the souls of innocence again,
It seeks corruption with no finite end,
It aims for sly destruction of new souls,
Its presence to inspire a new Heav'n fall,
That all may be cast into hell's sin lake.
This demon now beneath each angel's sight
Unhidden, and it seeks no hiding place,
In view of all and undisturbed by all.
Controlled eyes scanning for significance,
He fiercely flaps through clearings up above,
Fast tracking demon on its garden path,
Archangel seeks to see what none can see,
Determined to determine hidden truths.
Sharp sighted eyes no demon will elude
Fine honed and searching through each particle,
Sight traces on dark clad vestments entire,
Between sharp horns, upon hard feet, in close
Along the buckled nose and stoney cheek
The intense focus on perception's gain,
He cannot intuit more than he sees,
He stares continuously examining
Without a single insight to relate

And thinks unto himself reflective thought:
The demon does not turn to stare at him.
The demon freely moves o'er garden green,
Dark spectacle midst Heaven's spectacles,
Sweet ambiance replete with darling flowers
Perfection petaled radial in bloom
A supple brim-filled color vibrant swell,
Arranged in floral rosy petaled mirth
And dappled lightly in loving vibrance
Arranged majestic gatherings lovely sway
Free cultivated thriving signaling
Idyllic new and natural richness fond
To Heaven's ever minding joyful hearts,
Light flowers in light fresh blooms plenteous
Live on eternally in God's season
Light variationed colors classical,
Abundant yellow tops on swaying fields,
Green blue refined, hues flourish severally,
Pure yellows pinked in sovereign vibrancy
Augment the amplitude in circumstance,
All harmony against the one discord,
The darkness passing flowers soaking light,
A violation of the violet space,
Draped vines interwoven and interspersed
With sights beyond of bloomed magnificence.
No flowers opening at its passage,
Each shade of color yet retains its hue,
The passing darkness dims no color's source.
The gorgeous garden space no upkeep needs,
Created for beholding, once beheld
Beloved, a heavenly loveliness replete.
Sweet intricacy unto smallest points,
Complexity in all perceived design,

Idyllic risen life refreshing sweet,
From rich soil rising into open light,
Spread dynamic directions, up and out.
The hollow marches through the gentle thick,
A hallowed tunnel formed of ample life,
Of canopy and hanging verdant vines,
A light illuminating underneath
The canopy, reflecting off bright leaves
Light bouncing through each plant below across
The lengths and breadths, all parts illumined right
Before it streams up through the canopy.
A hardened heart amidst the tender growth,
A heavy foot treads down on tender plants,
The demon's smashing weight hard pushes down.
The tiny plants are pushed, in dark consumed,
The demon lifts the other foot in its
Staid pace, entirely crushing on soft life
With focused night surrounding in its weight.
The life compacting foot slowly lifts up
To strike upon another gentle patch,
Soft cushioning plants lively spring up again.
Dark steps leave no impressions on the green,
The garden constant, no sin taking root.
Upon the garden lush a void unstopped,
Not ravenous to pull up petaled plants
Or hew a hanging bough or tear one leaf,
Its aim much farther still, and one more dire.
A single demon in perfection's heart
Eclipsing sacred light in passing awe
Transpiring verdent roots of eden spread
Without restraints, so toppling natural green
A beauty deluge in harmonious hues
The tree of life outreaching standing still.

The tree of life, a pillar rising up,
Stout trunk of timber without rings of growth
But grown in green spread outward reaching high
And far to feel completely outwardly
The garden's open all inviting airs.
The branches stretching out its branches far
Supported on its own internal strength,
Timbers sprouted about in elegance,
The cradling firm rich steadfast founding soil,
The canopy concise spread uniform
From trunk to all directions equally,
All balanced hanging free on central strength.
From hanging full boughs hang the beauty fruit,
Celestially rounded geometry,
Fruit plumped and ripened hanging midst the airs,
Fruit pungent scents sweet spreading flowing on
Throughout Heaven carrying lovely perfume.
Fresh ambiance, all fruitful scented airs,
Aroma fine stirred drifting amidst breath,
Anointed fragrances delighting all,
Sweet crisp airs flow amongst the redolence
Sublime perfection ravishing perfume.
Green leaves in their own perfect unique forms,
Each shaped a wondrous new complexity,
Of bold swooped outline points and curving lines
And inner branching structure spreading broad,
Each individual shape fits with a whole,
All spectrums run of green throughout the leaf,
A lightest shade to richest color deep,
Each melting to another in accord.
Light of the greenery contrasts the shade,
Beneath the branches treads the trespasser
Pursuing slowly through the innocence

Yet to latch on in wiles, in force, in death.
Green leaves unshaken in the disturbance,
Leaves tied to branches tied unto the trunk,
The strides of death pass by, life still in bloom.
Angelic forms of elegant stature
In graceful manner watch in gathered hush,
Long flowing locks of golden radiant hair
Multiple curled around augmenting looks
Of open bemusement and tenderness,
Assurance, and astonishment at once,
Believing in God's intervention soon.
On wings fluttering methodically they all
Aloft in flight, still safe, together view
Aggressive transgression without a fear,
But wondering at the unexpected strength.
Completely by herself coasting downwards
A one flew close to see the expression
Of one invading proud a foreign land,
In drawing closely floating with its march
Her winged breeze swirls wafting gently scents,
Her hair flows round drifting about its horns,
She hovers inward drawing closer still,
So close to see its eyes without remorse.
She pulls away, her hair caressing not,
Withdrawing slowly she rejoins the rest.
The gorgeous river of new Heav'n now nears,
At steady march the steady current flows
The opposite direction from approach,
The open river shown the shades of blue
From lightest gleam to deepest solemn pull,
Flow filled and rolling easily upon
A sparkling purity of quenching sight,
Along long lovely lines of current form

Perfection melded drops enjoined as one
Fresh flow unceasing constantly renewed.
Abundant garden growing on the way,
Smooth cooling current keeps the life restored
The living water running wondrously
Containing that which is received by life
And happily perceived by every being.
The beauty soaking in God's nourishment
For beauty spread, a form from form converge
In interchange appreciating green,
A verdance soaking river wealth so swelled
With life and color that the water drops
Down drip and roll from many nourished leaves,
A rain of life in beauty overflow,
Small streams down through bark valleys quietly run,
The mellow moisture drips melodiously,
Each supple leaf plump filled of flowing life,
The garden thrives in living light's extent
And runneth over in its abundance,
The drops cascading sailing on and on,
To find refreshed a rest along the cool
Sweet river once again, a watered dance
O'er played along the river edge and viewed
By river angels lovingly enrapt
In midst of tranquil fair sensation drips,
Their angel toes dipping lightly rippling
Astride the broad of verdant riverside,
The drop, a note, and all a lively song
To hear, delightful in the eye to see
A river like to all the essences,
A fascination quietly absorbed.
Attention drawn by footsteps on the edge
In unfamiliar way as if the first

Paradise Omnipresent

Traverse about the dripping watery.
The little river angels light around
To see the demon framed in bower green
Above sensation continuity.
A one expression can convey the depths
Of wide complexity ethereal
In vessel temporal, and volumes speak
Unspoken words, forever leaps the heart
In still endearing looks of sweet unseen.
A dripping clearly crystal melody
About the azure glowing circumstance,
Reflections blue in ambiance abound,
Along calm sloping banks the demon walks
Astride the riverside in defiance.
Upheaval undisturbs serenity,
Green spread for angels and demons alike,
Unceasing river yet delivers life,
The light of Heaven shines despite the dark
And angels superceding soar above.
Down swept in stature smaller angels far
More delicate whose glistening wondering eyes
Belied far more than dire expectation,
Though armored heroes' epic strength had built
No epic victory, fighting to naught.
The cherubim angels light fluttering
With little baby wings translucent pink,
Endearing little noses, rounded cheeks.
Before the demon's path a light array
Diminutive flew up obscuring all
To see and swarmed upon him suddenly
And on the callused hellish body land,
So lightly landed a combining strength
In an angelic mountain covering o'er

Book II

Entirely, all is wings and innocence
An interwoven chain of angel arms,
Small chubby fingers interlocking tight,
A mighty strong embrace for infant hands.
The mountain bulging, demon breaking through
As every cherubim on every side
Slip loose, unable to hold fast, and flows
The stream of infants winged around the foe
And turning backward gaze they onward as
The march continues unabated still.
Its walk proud tall, not skulking down with fear,
Upright iniquity, unseemly pride
Assuming Heaven's pathways as its own,
A towering mountain laid before the path
A lusterous magnitude of natural grace
Involving escalating majesty,
A mountain filling form to broadest strength.
It marched unto the mountain great and high
Apparently beyond a weak approach
The demon pushed its first step upwards climbed
A mountain steep made for a winged ascent,
Up trekking singularly directioned
Of angle wide and climbing upwardly
The demon continues surmounting up.
The angels soar about in freedom flight
Observing steady rise, awaiting one
Sure slip to send in full rejection down
The demon sent to slide below without
Height's gain to never climb upwards again,
It smoothly steps over their perception.
Beneath illumined canopy a shade
Where formerly no blackened shade had reached,
The shadow lurking upwards step on step

Indefatigable despite the climb,
Its legs with power stronger than the steep,
Hard pushing up against the holy rock,
Smoothed rocks embedded in the mountain side
Built in a delicate formation which
Is firmly fixed in perfect balanced form
Smooth stones unweathered at abrasion's step,
Magnificence unyeilding though o'er stepped,
The demon trekking ever higher up
With nary stumbling slips or misjudgments,
Stepping steadfastly on many facets
Laid on the mountainside from rock to rock,
The solid underpinnings hold hard fast,
The rocks' consistent strength supports such weight
Continuing to stand steadfastly on.
The demon gave no sign, no daunted flinch.
The river streams astride the mountain side
Following the mountain's scenery along
Flowing from off such height the water flies,
From off the rock in light airy cascade,
The thundering waterfall glides smooth and booms
Harmonious flowing falling water fills
With soothing sounds which compliment the sight
So delicate white plumes drift upwardly
Dew mists do slowly linger round the falls,
Bold sacred mists envelop mountain greens,
As steadfast as the rocks, a strong demon
A strength matching the set deep founded rock,
Pushing upwards headed for the tall seat,
The angels cannot stop undaunted gains,
It marches elevated to their height,
They fly on its level, formerly theirs,
Collective flying accepting in faith

The demon's failure at the face of God.
Red crested horns above the mountain seen
By all below, two points slow rising up
And seen upon the apex lording o'er
Above, a demon on the mountaintop,
The grand rebellious image stands upon
The grandiose mountain crown, the looking place,
Grand landscape an advantage sinister,
All view revealed now to the intruder,
No step as yet beyond its power grasp,
And now no sight kept from its present gaze,
The Heavens spread around, a glorious jewel,
The demon clearly spies the cityscape,
Square shining city Heaven's central home.
The first demon to see new Heaven's height,
And the first violation of God's word.
It steps from off the mountain pinnacle
Towards the holy city in descent.
Beside its march, a mountain spectacle:
The gentle river flowing upwardly.
The rising river easily flows o'er
New Heaven's soft conducive leading ways,
A beauty river way whose currents fond
Continue upward play in gentle waves
Around the garden stones, one obstacle
Could never be for fertile easing depths
Smooth layered in bulging watered layers,
A deep and onward rush beneath without
Disturbance guides the watered scaling flow
To ride through all pervasive majesty
Atop the under current floating by
As flying o'er a gentle bed of blue,
Onwards upwards flows on and on water

PARADISE OMNIPRESENT

Obeying no rule but the law of God
To gently, in fresh power overcome
The climb, in height ascending parallel
To the trespassing contrast in descent,
In picturesque sharp inequality.
The evil darkness free in God's kingdom,
Its feet upon soft flats of Heav'n again,
The mountain leaping river staid to calm.
The golden road lay near within its step,
Gold pure as glass, clearly reflecting light,
The red steps from the green unto the gold,
The city of mankind before its eyes.
Two brilliant lines aligned line the gold street,
Great trumpeters with outstretched instruments,
They play without a movement contrary
To musical perfection in each note,
Their golden glares upon the demon's march
Shaped golden trumpetry resounds sacred
Voluminous and tranquil holy songs.
It does not touch their trumpets, straight between
Long golden lines beside, gold road below,
The demon midst the golden shine surfeit
Stepping in beat, ambient accompanied,
Notes reached describe aggressive momentum,
Each trumpet in its turn fell silent as
The demon passed, then blasted forth again
With sacred hymns that ring for gloried truth.
Peeking above their shining instruments
Eyes bright gaze on unknowing, undisturbed,
Not comprehending power capable
Of the unthinkable outside the song,
The demon clears the lines of trumpeters,
Methodically departing from their call

Above are aimed the musical refrains.
Despite the demon horns' dark menacing
The golden line of trumpet horns blow on,
The instruments communicating more
Than action's weaponry can clanking claim.
The city's light-filled souls awake listen,
Their ears perk hearing melodies approach.
Progression steady unabated drew
Humanity's round curiosity,
Which flocked directly flanked with rectitude.
The sum of heavenly souls, magnificent
In white the pure united all reflect
The holy spirit as they gracefully
Drift on together filling scope with awe,
So streaming openly felicity
In this their second life, responding to
The shining golden trumpet notes in mass,
Beyond the city to behold themselves
The image of loud trumpets' descriptions.
The voices soaring chanting weighty hymns
Approach streaming along the river's way.
Great choir, forth from new Jerusalem
Outside the city to behold new sight,
The agile minds and brows with gold halos,
The learned in Heaven's atmosphere of truth,
Those garments flowing white with billowing folds.
Smooth faced, no furrows on the ancient brows,
Eternal youth inward and outwardly,
The vigor of fresh thought within rich minds,
Expressions are unworried on each gaze,
Unhurried, unconcerned, in sacred calm,
The strength of faith puts worried strain to rest.
The flock within green pasture paradise,

Paradise Omnipresent

Their sole attention on aggression's march
Advancing in a perfect single line,
Feet burned and bare, the red on gleaming gold,
Gruff touch of rugged feet upon the street
Rough scraping, dragging through in constant push,
One after one they land of heavy weight,
The eyes of mankind followed falling feet
Trespass the golden brick road constantly,
Each step: a boundary violated in
A line of final crossings never crossed.
They search to know what is allowed and why,
The meaning in each step and consequence.
They seek and study every movement's worth
Observing every foot's historic rise
In mid-step disbelieving in the next.
Ten thousand questions in each mind at once,
Determining inherent meanings of
This marching mystery in the heart of Heav'n
Commanding heavenly minds to ponder deep.
Astonished reason wonders at such strength,
Its navigation, lo, its stamina,
What single minded war sprung from its hell
Defying all creation's precedent
And sensibility informed by truth,
Not merely weakness pushing through full strength
But pushing past the bounds of prophecy,
A wanderer treading upon God's word,
Offensive to the eye, and worse, the mind.
The demon walks a sharpened cleaving line:
Division of the holy word and strength.
Evading the eternity of truth
What wily fiend could slip out from God's word,
An unseen strength defying punishment

As if of ripping pages from God's book,
The implications distant and unseen,
In pushing through the garden, pushing God.
A clashing of unseemly new ideas,
Through new, harmless. The weak against a rock
To fall away when truth is rightly met.
The blasphemy is taken on in full,
Humanity collects across the road.
The souls together stand braced with their faith,
Staid men and women in unmoving strength.
The minds of souls can reason it a test
To prove their strength before the dark is cast,
Its temptations soon signaling defeat,
And sinfulness defeated by mankind.
Awaiting the temptation gracefully,
All solemn faces watching reverently,
To know the aim: the devil's and the Lord's.
The angels must watch darkness' straight advance
Approaching unencumbered present souls
Out in the open light of Heaven's air
Without shields seen between demon and soul,
Their sharp minds given to observation,
Their eyes fixed on the darkness inside Heav'n.
As Michael could not move the demon form
New Heaven's souls are unmoved by the dark,
They do not flee or seek other shelter
For all new Heaven is their safe abode,
New Heav'n in the disturbance undisturbed.
Their reasoning minds perplex at circumstance
No walls of flame sweeping to cast it out
The walls of expectation passed again,
Two sides converted to the other's strength,
The father in silence apparently.

Paradise Omnipresent

The demon parts a path through mankind's souls,
As they are slid away who block its aim,
The demon marches into their thick midst
Unshakingly in constance powerful
A melody accompanying the mass
New Heaven's light voices acquiring song
Of soulful resonance, deep powerful
The song at its approach traversing scales
Of booming berth, full bodied urgent tone,
Divinely lyricism great describes
The chorus heavenly chiming of the Lord,
Song echoing as light projects around
Resounding through each being, received and kept,
The demon does not bellow in reply,
No dark scales ring o'er ears of innocence.
The chorus voices stream out fertile songs
Of glory in security's embrace
Exalting deeply God in melody.
The brave about the focus-drawing foe,
Its crimson clearly visible to all,
Passing amongst the gathering of souls,
One spot within a multitude of light
It utters not a one stolen whisper
To souls surrounding, ears open to hear
They standing upright in security
Here unafraid of the wild exposure,
No bitter mourning at the face of death,
No gnashing teeth sound grinding o'er the loam,
Unknocked by razor wings, unscathed by horns,
Their hearts fixed on the one unshakable.
At mankind's victory angels await
The Lord to lift His heavy hand and smite
This demon, no tests left of their progress,

No meaning possibly continuing
This bold upending in new Heaven's peace.
Light angels see it still slowing for none,
The demon's description is disobeyed,
Its aim is not unto the souls but through,
Now Heaven's souls cannot here comprehend
The evil cause behind the demon's mind,
What dark assails it hopes to dark achieve,
Where lay the reaches of this farther strength.
And neither turn: the light or its progress.
All witness inexplicably the fiend
Passing full through the multitude of souls
Continuing towards its constant aim:
So unmistakably towards the throne,
The holy city's central throne of God
Above the garden greens in towering view.
The souls and angels follow where it leads
God's throne no longer at the mountain's peak
As in old Heaven's old holy design,
God dwells amongst the souls in the city,
New Heaven's holy city of the Lord,
Gilded transplendence, crowned embodiment,
Mankind reentering led by the fiend,
Silence inside the city of God's hymns
Ethereal rock, bejeweled beyond belief,
Such sight to dazzle past the gleams of thought
Containment in light line and shape conceals
The eye of the divine. Ascending nigh
To superceding measure, rising up
The cityscape reward immensely shines
Soon dwarfing demon, small in magnitude,
The holy city risen in great height
An architecture consummation ground

In eloquent expressions of divine
Surrounding luxury engaging flow,
Involving comfort, vast and cozy space
For inspiration, nestled in new life,
Relaxing interaction and repose,
The comforts of allegiance dignified.
Up winding spires elegance informed
The tall integrity to never fall
Allowing coloring's reflections in
The streetway paths, the souls' connected ways,
The habitations part of every soul,
Inhabitants inhabit perfectly
A fitting comfort shaping for the heart,
Tall columns rise of angels, city spread,
Quick peering cherubim dart round the spires
Proceeding, grand procession fills the street,
Lone scarlet cast against effusive white,
The demon leads the paradise parade
Between new buildings' constant elegance
Symmetrical in gorgeous fair design.
The motivating king gives equal wealth
As all new Heaven's souls can fully share
In the experience of His presence.
The city of one spiritual basis
Supported firm and held together fast
The perfect city balanced centrally,
Each part reflected in another's form,
Perfection round the city compassed out,
One bold shape in bold discord pulls all view,
The smooth line purposeful design contrasts
The first time in creation with the road,
The architecture against atmosphere,
Gold road filled up on either river side

Red demon striding on blue river's left
Humanity across the river stares,
The gulf of river safely in divide,
The running river flows straight through the street,
The blueness glowing from reflection's light,
And gilded shimmering upon the road
The city waterway inspires the form
Of shapes within the flowering cityscape
To bend along its bends and straight where straight
The demon walks as constant as the blue
Against the streamed direction flowing out
From God's own glorious throne the river's head
Always giving of heavenly sustenance,
The creator perpetually creating,
Benevolently nourishing constant life.
Strange demon marching on the road of God,
None feared the trampling foot, for all know well
As nearing God the foe approached rebuke
And sudden banishment from this freedom.
No kingdom's temple stands in new Heaven
For all the new Heaven a temple is,
With lightful God and Christ in openness
Of innocence, the fount of halos beams,
The Lord atop His throne and Christ at right.
The brilliant throne of white, the birth of blue,
The river recreated constantly,
The throne of God unseen by demon eyes
Since Christ's white thunder judgment on the foul.
Assembled round the floor surrounding God
The brave elect look to the holy throne,
The final path before the demon's aim,
An entrance to the presence resplendent,
The floor serene about the radiant throne,

Such clarity of crystalline smoothness,
A flawless clear unto invisible,
No sight distorted through the perfect form,
A calming sea, tranquility spread pure,
The demon darkness marches to the floor,
The demon steps upon the open sea
Without sinking in deep inconstancy,
The floor supporting demon movement still,
The demonry upon transparency,
Its stamina undiminished at God's throne.
The host of Heaven witnesses approach,
The source of brightness steadily undimmed.
No thrown impediment to cease or seize.
Omniscient God possesses such keen sight
To recognize the demon far away,
The demon warfaring had invaded
The paradise to tear apart the throne
In olden Heaven in his armied ranks,
It was he whose shield splintered at the light
And snarled as the standing army caved,
Who walked the path of evil against God,
The demon, Moloch, evil king on earth,
The rebel Satan's covetous ally
Kept marching towards the Lord without a fear,
But sudden halted finally in front
There standing lone before God's beaming throne
And took a knee, down bowing low to God,
A demon prostrating before the Lord.
The congregation watched assuredly,
They all awaiting God's victorious smite
When Christ arose and stood above the fiend
And graced his hand upon the shoulder low.
Hushed silence around peace and quiet calm.

Christ spoke unto the demon and all Heav'n:
"In truth behold him through the eyes of God."
The demon, turning upwards in fresh gaze
Still darkly red before the holy throne,
Unfurled his wings and they were white anew,
Divine reflection purely pearly white.
A brightness new in God, astounding light
New covered o'er, cleansed with the grace of God.
Angelic form is brightly born again
In perfect worship of the one true God
Above, the hovering seraphim of love
Delight in holy purification grand,
Surrounding sparkles light in angels' eyes,
Expressions beam a glorious approval,
Confused before, restored to ordered grace,
Light angels recognize his gentle form.
All graceful souls witness the saving grace
Restoring order from the blasphemy,
A demon enemy of Heaven's light
By God redeemed, and once by God revealed
No longer was a stranger to the fold,
A child among the children of the Lord,
Who recognize at once he bore no threat,
The transformation of the hell demon
Occurred before his passing Heaven's gate,
The gate shut to the dark, open to light,
The disbelief distorting appearance,
Christ validating the experience.
The strongest of the weakest, shielded, walked
Protected by the power of the Lord,
A steady light progressing unto God,
No violence was directed in this march,
Nor evil hatred, all was innocence,

New Heaven's nature nurturing new life
Secured in holy power, beyond assail,
A one not at God's light but one inside,
Approaching boldly on the humble path,
Its sole ambition: meek humility.
The emanating throne attracts all minds,
As every being in Heav'n surround the throne.
The Lord God spoke in gracious flowing words,
And brightly God began to speak His truths,
"This angel is forgiven of his sin,
Writ back into the holy book of life.
This one, profoundly stronger than the weak
Is loved, a child of my household, he.
Among the open eyes of Heav'n this one
Is hence an angel of the Lord once more."
Spoke Michael reverently, "How can this be?"

BOOK III

The Argument: Divine explanation and heavenly debate
engages the heroes of the Bible.

Symphonic symposium radiant in thought,
All angels in new Heaven seek to hear
And every soul alike wonders within,
"How could the demon seek without God's light?
How could the demon make discoveries
Without God's perfect knowledge guiding him
To understand the path of holiness?"
The light of God, His voice, to Michael spake
Revealing holy possibility.
Attentively with open listening
All in new Heaven and new earth can hear:
"He is reborn as Lucifer was killed;
If one can turn from Heav'n then one can turn
From hell. The motivation: living choice.
If one, an angel brightly loving me
Named Lucifer bright shining perfect as
A star can fall away from all my love,
Which is the greatest power that can be,
And cast himself to evil hate, then one,
A demon, seemingly to evil lost,
Can turn from fallen Satan, leaving hell
For Heaven, choosing my divinely love,
For evil's strength is far below my own."
The Lord concluded His sermon before
The congregation of humanity
And angels. Listening clear they all absorbed
Each line as line was spoken unto them

And word as word entered their living thoughts,
A new creation in new Heaven's walls.
They understand without a question love,
And celebrate the new arrival of
A one with strength in God to turn from hell,
The single, only one with faith to see
The truth of God beyond the devil's lies,
Love's contrast with the fall of Lucifer,
A singular and shining miracle.
Humanity composes songs within
Their hearts of contemplation on the words
Which leads them unto lighting up their minds
With multitudes of thoughts and no two were
Identical, the unique souls there mulled
And mulling moved their minds to understand,
Considering all things in parallel
And contrast, pensive in this state of thought,
The created ponder the creator.
And as they bring conclusions from the words
A one from the body of light mankind
Stepped up to speak the words of his making
To represent the reach of mankind's thought,
No other souls conceiving his intent.
Obedient Abraham approached the Lord
With great humility, astonishment,
And thoughts full ripe with wisdom's reasoning.
He spoke and as he spoke all listened well,
He voiced his words as his soul's offering:
"Almighty God, your love is powerful,
And may it not offend you Lord but I
Am left in wonderment to know the bounds
That you obey, the limits of your strength,
The places where your love cannot persuade.

If one could turn from evil, then might ten?"
Before the listening heavens God replied,
"If one can turn from evil then could ten."
"So ten. And though it may offend you Lord,
I ask, could twenty reach thy gracious warmth
Persuaded truly, is your power such?"
"Yes Abraham." "Or fifty more O' lord,
If seeing all your love would they choose you?"
"Yes Abraham, my love is love enough.
Five more than fifty would return or more,
My love is more than witnessed yet, for none
Can measure without measure. Beyond words
Or work yet seen, still greater is my love."
And Abraham in innocence inquires
Without expectations farther than truth,
"All of the angels fallen, Satan's souls
Could join all Heaven's angels, Heaven's souls?"
"My strength is without limit: infinite.
So faithful Abraham your wisdom speaks
With insight unto truth and all beauty.
The holy time has ripened for your call,
Completion of remaining miracles
Resolving the remainder of glory
In the perfection of my pure design,
Revealing to your hearts the most profound,
The culmination of creation's forms:
Attainment of the infinite beauty,
The glory unto omnipresent light.
From the beginning light was light's intent.
Do not doubt good: through me there is a way.
The numbers of the souls of man with me
In new Heaven suffice to fully face
The fallen, your great faith fully prepared.

Paradise Omnipresent

The light souls are above the angels here
In living out redemption in my grace.
The angels shall remain in state with me,
The battle now is one for mankind's souls
To undertake upon themselves, a race
Redeemed and strong beyond the ills of life,
Defeating Satan once before, now they
Shall be far more than merely messengers
But living testament to all my strength."
The angels parted giving ample aisle
For all the souls approaching to receive.
The wings of angels lower slow at ease,
An admiration glowing raises up
In fashion cheery from within their beings.
In forefront light mankind assembled grand
And ready listening to the word of God.
The Lord unto the multitude spoke clear,
"Still stronger than the raging wars of hate,
More powerful than hell, and sin, and death,
I am beyond the hidden dark of night.
They are lost in eternity of sin
But for the sake of all we shall save them,
All sinners turned from their old selves to new
Through grandly finding wisdom to obey,
The unredeemed turned into the redeemed.
With Christ my son you shall go venturing forth
Unto the flame, unto the holy fight.
The souls in torture locked inside of hell,
Those mired in everlasting punishment,
Will reach redemption through my power's grace.
The gates of hell will not withstand our might,
The evil structure shall be torn apart,
All hell will soon come crashing greatly down,

BOOK III

All hate will be obliterated by
The strength of love almighty clad in light
Destroying the iniquities of pain
To rescue every angel, every soul
Unto returning my prodigal son,
The angel lost to evil, Lucifer.
I am almighty, justice shall be done.
As I am God the devil can be turned.
I still remember my child Lucifer,
Therefore my heart still yearns with compassion.
Of my children none shall be forsaken."
The trumpet of the angel Gabriel
Resounded grandly at the closing speech.
On ending His commandment God was still,
Allowing mankind's minds to understand
With their firm reason, channeling concepts down
From technicality's sharp puzzle work
Through moral law foundations laid before
And faith's forever yearn for knowing good,
With cautious hopes of finding their relief
Refining thoughts amongst themselves out loud,
Searching for understanding of knowledge,
The intellectual completion of
The gaps between all previous and next,
Acceptance always waiting on the mind.
Interaction revealing intention,
The prophets and the kings of the old book
Who struggled on for life in the old world
Are wise new saints together in new Heav'n,
Here motivated to discover truth,
And motivating curiosity:
The image of the devil inside Heav'n.
A concept formerly banished from thought,

A sequel to the Bible being for saints
Impossible in its first encounter,
Distracting in its wandering conception,
A sequel to familiarity.
Deliberation in the mind turns to
A heavenly engaging debate amidst
The ever present spirit of the Lord.
As angel's fear no demon so mankind
Fears no idea, welcoming the grapple.
The wise in council confirming design,
The saints of Heav'n start with simplicity,
They share the sentiment of Solomon:
"Astonishing, always astonishing."
At brief consideration, Moses spoke:
"We thought them lost eternally, our God
Was limited in who He could inspire.
His strength to turn hell's souls to good was naught.
What guides interpretation of this law?"
Replying to Moses spoke Solomon:
"What guides interpretation but ideals,
Who guides creation's pinnacles but God?
Opinions reaching to the heights of God."
And then spoke Moses unto Solomon:
"The truth is not reached through ideals alone.
Ideals must meet criteria for truth.
Such beauty could not possibly be false,
But comprehension must be satisfied.
Before the devil reconciles with Heav'n
We have to reconcile two points of view:
That all who seek will find, and all who sought
The devil's ways can never find the Lord.
God's greatness lies beyond this man-made wall
Which we must overcome to supercede.

First ours, then theirs, and God's strength in-between."
Saint Solomon replied unto new Heav'n:
"The epic undertakings of the saints,
Live on, the book of life our testament.
A new phenomena in new Heaven
Should not surprise as it boldly confounds,
If we truly discern then truly must
The limits of our minds eventually
Discover all infinity living
And reasoning throughout eternity.
Now look around, this time has surely come,
This revelation hearkens completion."
Then Noah spoke to all new Heaven's saints:
"Thoughts brimming at the swell, then let them come,
As all God's laws are written in your minds
We must assemble them to this new height
Using the whole of what the Lord has taught.
Speak up you saints and eagerly dive in."
The saints think deeply into questioning,
And David called to the angel redeemed,
"What journey brought us such gracious portent?"
The angel for the light souls thus replied:
"A calling like unto the rings of bells.
From one not large enough to right himself
Descriptions cannot tell immensity."
The angel thus describing Godly awe
Retiring to the angels, falls silent.
Saint David the composer offered thus
To make known his immediate psalmic thought:
"The Lord's love reaches out to all evil,
But they are deaf to all His holy songs.
The Holy king extends to every realm,
But how they hate the love which God reveals!

God's enemies were given room to choose,
They have rejected, suffering, His cause.
Though He makes laws to offer salvation
They are criminals of no repentance.
My God, offer the greatest love to them
But we shall not despair if they remain;
Heaven shall be Heaven though they are doomed.
Listen to Your soul's voices, God my Lord,
The souls in hell rebuked all holy love,
Your judgment of the souls is justified.
The loving here in Heaven are open,
We shall sing with you glorifying strength
In every land to evil's wicked heart.
Your righteous caring promises safety,
Do not abandon sinners fighting death.
I do not doubt Your strength but their weakness,
Our enemies have followed Satan long,
The living God can pass through any death
But they cannot author the book of life.
The Lord uprightly calls for redemption;
The condemned will never upright themselves."
So David thus concludes his holy psalm,
It was his song of the deafness of sin.
Up spoke Ezekiel to pose grand thought:
"Well spoken David, spoken on the point.
Those who fell down unto the lowest state
Surrendered not resolving as they hit
The burning ground, they gave up falling down.
What miracles can be worked in hell's heart
Dissolving their entrapments, melting out
The forges of disgrace, procuring life
Anew, so distant we and few for such
Tremendous transformations as God asks."

Saint Paul responded with what God may build:
"Am I what I am by my own two hands?
Freewill alone does not deliver strength.
Without God's intervention in old earth
In my old life where would I be when judged?
We all, with God, shall intervene with life
That all may be their true selves through God's grace."
Spoke then learned Timothy on mercy's ways
"Though sinners yet defy in anguished heat
The patience of the Lord is infinite."
Spoke Jeremiah of old pain and grace,
"Though sinners stagger, wasting with lament
In torment, seemingly without escape
God has not utterly rejected those
Who, as we all, can be shown great relief."
Saint Peter spoke of God's ability,
 "I cannot soon deny the strength of God
In light of His perfection guiding all.
Myself in sin denied my friend the Christ,
And even one denying Christ can turn."
Saint Moses reaffirmed Saint Peter's thoughts,
"As we were sinners they can be redeemed,
As we were bound for hell they can be saved.
They yet possess the liberty of choice
To give all their possessions to the Lord.
If our Lord's strength is truly infinite,
Then overcoming hell is possible,
If possible then God is capable."
Spoke Lazarus, "New Heav'n's bridge crosses o'er
Across old chasms into new great works,
That one in hell's death may be given life."
Historian Mark spoke up, "All have free choice
Though cannot choose when by demons possessed.

The demons cast by Christ, not by the souls,
The captors driven out from the captive,
Possessed of only freedom once again.
Upon the dark affliction God's light acts
Authoritatively over evil,
Allowing clarity where Satan chokes.
How forcefully from out the throat Christ pulled
The heart infecting demons through the flesh."
Saint Paul then spoke up in reply to Mark,
"Pulled from the flesh; Hell's souls are of spirit."
And Mark replied, "Possessed as yet of sin."
By Moses' side spoke Aaron unto Heav'n
"In touching hell we will be made unclean."
But Moses then spoke unto Aaron there,
"The purity of God cannot be stained,
It is His hands which lift the weak from sin."
Then rose Isaiah to deliver his
Offering unto the listening multitude:
"I do agree with Paul, but I must say,
How might we change souls of such separateness?
They would be loathsome to all Heaven's eyes
Without a chance of their delivery.
I cannot reconcile with times of old,
Cannot remember pain and burdens borne,
Those memories lost as we new Heaven found,
It is not ignorance, merely distance,
A wisdom far removed from foolishness,
Broken connections between life and fear,
And no remembrance of the sinful past.
A sin: a stranger; our selves: stranger still,
Still stronger casting out sin's memory.
Myself in sin a contradiction is,
The sinner never was myself, so I

Could never have remembrance old when new,
The dark now separated from the light,
We are farther apart than ever known
And those still trapped in sin: beyond our sight.
Then how might we convert those in the dark?"
Spoke Samson of the vision of the Lord:
"They are only hidden unto themselves.
God's servants see what they could not alone,
Their trodden paths seen clearly from on high.
It is not we but they in blindness held,
A closed and narrow view without a sense,
But even blind they will see wondrous sights,
The views beyond the bounds, an open dream,
As clearly as mine eyes can see you now."
Historian Matthew raised his teaching voice
"They are completely separate from our own.
But can they be impossibly separate?
Between us there is definite difference
But as we are created by one God
Are we not fundamentally as one
United in a common element?
Creation can relate to creation.
The songs are writ, we've but to let them hear."
Again Saint Paul in the discourse adds in,
"As Samson spoke, the blind shall see clearly.
This new arrival beckons to new thought.
I see an angel, not a demon foe.
He is what he is by the grace of God:
A miracle; a testament to grace.
The chosen are the ones who choose the Lord."
Saint Solomon agreed with his friend Paul,
"The Lord will build a temple where He deems
Constructing good as a creator should.

He is presented with the sight of all
His children cut in two, humanity
Divided, and so wisely God protests.
The loving father wishes them to be
Made whole, He is a loving father true."
Then spoke Ezekial to heaven's fold,
"There is a grander matter, one more foul.
The devil could not be transformed to good.
The devil would not join with our worship
He will attempt to have us worship him.
New Heav'n has never met the lake of fire.
So doing, such reaction never seen
Will rending meet the two in one moment.
Could the iniquity of Satan's being
Be lifted by the Lord so easily?
Such deafness never was so simply shed."
And then spoke Peter to Ezekiel,
"If God can raise a one bearing the sins
Of all humanity upon His back
Then God can raise one angel lost to sin.
Then could Satan not turn eventually?"
Responding there Ezekiel then spoke,
"In our assault on hellfire's principles
All hell and sin and death must be destroyed.
Before the balance of Heaven was shook,
Before the sudden fall of Lucifer
There was not in creation sin or death
Or that torture lamentable called hell,
All was before the Lord a paradise.
Only when Satan, one with evil's ways,
Appeared in God's creation raging war
Did sin come into being, by Satan born,
And ghastly death born from his wicked heart.

In sin, in death, in his destructive hell
Satan is not merely one lost to them,
These are not Satan's works, they are Satan.
Originating, rising at his fall.
The whole created of his sinful parts,
The devil's evil: his identity.
Destroying sin is to destroy Satan.
Destroyed or no, he cannot enter Heav'n."
Isaiah spoke unto Ezekiel:
"The Lord is one, this one creates the dark
As well as light, choose either as they may.
They choose the possibilities allowed
By God, who had created Lucifer's
Capacity for finding such darkness.
The devil's evil is his evil choice."
Historian Luke spoke up on holy strength,
"The strength of God relates itself to foes
To not only defeat but to redeem.
Not only to destroy but to transform.
Destroying sin means saving Lucifer."
Spoke Esther on the nature of free choice:
"Their one jewel undestroyable is choice,
Creation's inherent ability.
Possessing choice implies alternatives.
This means the hellish have the choice of Heav'n,
Which means our God's abilities have yet
The possibility of turning hate."
Prophetic John the visionary spoke,
"Though choice may be alive I have concerns.
Eternal truth is such that even God
Cannot rescind a holy prophecy,
I have faith God speaks not contradictions,
But how to reconcile these words He speaks

With those spoken before, I cannot see.
It seems to me in what was spoke and set,
To turn the devil is to turn Heaven
And stretch the Lord beyond His written bounds.
Words stood up solid still untouched throughout
Creation's melt-down watching transient lies
Subside. They burn and yet shall burn as God
Created only truth unbreakable."
Then spoke up Joseph to the prophet's words,
"If only truth unbreakable, not lies;
Those evil lies spoken by deceivers.
Truth stands on strong foundations. Lies on what?
A weakness which is ever breakable."
The prophet John revealed his thoughts again:
"The truth, standing on strong foundations, is:
God has revealed, through undeniable words,
The smoke of their torment rises ever,
They are tortured forever and ever.
It was God's revelation of pure truth."
Spoke Solomon: "That is the holy truth.
Well spoken John, and who can clarify?"
The fair youth Adam bright and lucid strong
The man of men in easy dignity
In manner becoming Heaven's spirit
Spoke clearly, knowingly, and openly,
"Smoke rises though a fire has been quenched.
The sinful would be punished without end
Unless they come repentant to the Lord.
As God revealed himself not all at once
But in His several stages playing out
Upon the minds of all creation's beings
Progressively towards totality,
An olden testament before one new,

Book III

Commandments unto Moses, not to me,
And Christ not lighting forth until due time,
The loss of paradise not instantly
Regained, Eve not expecting holy child,
But human kind left to experience,
Observing the allowed observable
As knowledge of the time for Christ's return
Was kept from saints and angels till its time,
Our knowledge of the Lord steadily grows,
Each holy book another leap of faith.
The Lord is one, the Lord's laws are many.
Each revelations of embodiment
Describe new aspects of the constant whole.
It was that Sabbath's day should know no toil
Until revealing to the children thus:
Unless it be the freeing work of God.
It was that pasture's animals could die
For sin in ancient alters built by men
Until revealing to the children thus:
Unless the son of God be sacrificed
Revealing glory's possibility.
He spake they would be ever Satan's souls,
And now revealing thus: unless they turn.
The Lord is not abandoning himself
In venturing to turn the souls of hell.
As finally revealed, choice is alive.
It is consistent with the mind of God.
Perceptions of design evolved from book
To book and testament to testament,
The hidden grandness of God slowly seen."
Continuing the thoughts then Noah spake,
"It once was God's divine justice to pour
His righteousness dissolving all mankind

Paradise Omnipresent

In washing out the world's foul ways of sin,
In drowning deluge casting out flesh's world,
In violent harsh rebuke save only one
Man's grateful family. This was the law
Until a covenant of promised peace
Appeared across the sky in beauty streamed,
A shift in God's approach to human kind.
The Lord reveals that in creation all
Will be a vibrant splendored covenant."
Of Adam's words on God's purposive work
The prophet John commented, "It is true:
An eye for eye completely was denied,
Perception then completely had been changed."
And Adam spoke, "From out the multitude
Of thoughts one understanding will emerge.
The evolution of the church is law,
It is God's method and has always been,
As man's traditions lived or went extinct
Replaced by understanding which fits best
As guided by the present hand of God
Which ever cradles His Godly design.
Through false competing claims one truth endured
Amidst interpretations of the word
Soon branching into variations of
The one God, truth surviving as is fit,
The evolution of understanding."
Saint John the Baptist spoke of his friend Christ,
"New wine is poured into the new wineskins.
Witness the ways of Christ at God's great laws,
At shallow sight he seemed to disobey
The written laws, revered and fiercely held,
Though only disobeyed the pharisees
And not the ways of God within the laws.

BOOK III

Then why the disagreement unto death?
The Christ could see the old in a new light.
Replacing the old way: a new angle.
Interpreting God's laws as best they knew,
Tradition was not proved infallible."
Spoke John, one of the Lord's historians, now
"Forget you not of our Lord's miracles,
For those low on the earth saw from the sides
While Christ could interpret from his high seat.
A one denied by fundamental men
Surpassed the studious to save us as Christ,
His obligation only to beauty."
Persisting on his reasoning John speaks
"Redemption cannot win if evil souls
Are lost in everlasting punishment."
And Adam spoke again to Heaven's saints
"The Lord described their state as eternal
As we live on inside eternal Heav'n.
As Lucifer rebuked eternal Heav'n
The lost can flee eternal punishment."
"It is as is," spoke John, "eternal Heav'n,
It is a valid insight I believe,
But how could any being, as you have said,
Flee from the bounds of an eternal path?"
Paul spoke then clearly for more clarity
"As you have written, as was understood,
They are eternally condemned in hell,
But who are they, those far from Godly gifts?
They are the unsaved; they are not the saved.
Those in the lake of fire: unrepentant.
Safe from the lake of fire: those repentant.
According to the holy prophecy
A one in sin will never enter Heav'n

So all in sin eternally are lost.
This still remains a holy, given truth.
The law is not made false; truth is revealed.
All evil will be punished without end,
But if redeemed the being is separate
From evil's everlasting punishment.
In sin: one self. In God: another still.
Self is not sin, and lo, the sin not self.
With good reason the Lord has deemed two names.
The angel Lucifer is not Satan.
My name is Paul although it once was saul.
Far more than meaningless simple titles,
The sinful name and holy name belie
Two separate selves, each manifesting choice.
There are two paths, one light, one dark, two lands.
A single one cannot belong to both."
Then David spoke up with his own proverb,
"The humble and the proud are separate;
One's pride can be turned to humility."
And Solomon affirmed Saint Paul's ideas,
"If evil, loathsome for eternity,
If righteous, then embraced eternally."
Up spoke a one demure, the patient Job:
"If we succeed in these almighty works
Then Satan will be here in paradise
To walk amongst our own as if his hate
Had never been, his evil temptations
Accepted as if they were Godly works.
The thought itself creates a strange unease,
The devil's acceptance at God's command.
The devil's evil should not ever see
The paradise to undeserving bask
In beauty with the purest unstained souls

Who had the wisdom to deny his works
And cast him out from spiritual influence.
All evil should stay locked inside of death.
The ones that lost their faith in face of pain,
Abandoning the Lord as if they were
Abandoned they themselves by God's full love.
We know evil can be eternally so
But the question doubts the reality,
Should sinners be redeemed and turned to good?"
And spoke then Paul, "As saul is not in Heav'n,
He undeserving of this basking light,
But rather Paul humbly before you now,
The evil of the devil shall not live
Inside new Heaven's garden paradise.
His former self, the angel Lucifer
An angel amongst Heaven's angelic
Deserves to serve outside of Satan's hell."
Historian Matthew spoke, "Christ had revealed
That God will search for one that wandered off."
Isaiah spoke of transformation's ways,
"Redemption of the evil in new Heav'n
Shall not be wolf and lamb together lain
But lamb with lamb together joined as one,
Delivery from fury quenching fires."
Then orderly put forth historian Luke,
"But they will never receive forgiveness
Who blaspheme against the holy spirit.
Denying forgiveness: unforgivable."
Saint Daniel spoke up there on active sin,
"Those who speak out blaspheming against God
Are actively denying the divine source,
And actively suffer accordingly.
But once turned upwards actively loving

They actively are ripe for forgiveness
And carefully lifted upon His hands."
Saint David spoke of unforgiven sin:
"Their every sin is unforgivable;
There is no sin acceptable to God.
No sin shall live within new Paradise.
The sinful still are unforgivable,
Those separated from such sin: set free.
Their soulful selves remain forgivable
Retaining that free will which chose such pain."
Saint John the Baptist spoke of sacrifice,
"The suffering bore upon the cross by Christ
Was not an incomplete or partial pain,
Upon the cross Christ bore man's every sin
And lo, Christ is not trapped within the fire.
Atonement is not dead, for Jesus lives.
There is no sin within the lake of fire
Which Christ did not die for upon the cross,
No sinner which cannot be freed by God."
Saint Solomon the preacher brought new thought:
"Judiciously, a question now appears:
Is justice once not justice for all time?
The Lord does not misjudge, then what remains?
Will moral seasons shifting winds away
To each direction be the Lord's new law?
A time for condemnation of the weak,
A time for saving Satan's evil horde
And rescuing the sinner from their hell?
Is their judgment before now deemed unjust,
The Judge abruptly pardoning the judged
And God before not heretofore the same?"
Saint Samson spoke then of the living God,
"The judgment trial was not the end of God

And justly did not end the words of God."
Spoke Joshua of the Lord's transcendent throne,
"His throne remains unmovable in light
And none shall cast His place by their command.
The Lord is one, forever from one place
Does He shine out illuminating life."
And adding in spoke up saint David then:
"God is as God has been and God shall be.
Our God does not abandon who He is.
As a true shepherd of the flock the Christ
Will go and seek to save that which was lost."
Saint Paul replied with his pertaining thoughts,
"I can see, Solomon, it seems a shift.
You have judged right when you see a grand shift,
But it is not the Lord's it is our own.
His attitude towards sin is what it is.
Though spreading outwards God will never move.
The Lord is not accepting any sin.
The sinners are not freely welcomed here
As our acceptance too relied on us,
Not automatically immediately
Without conditions granted for our grace."
Historian Matthew spoke of holy words,
"As it was written, they will not be freed
Until they pay the Lord the last amount."
Saint Paul then followed speaking of firm law:
"God is inclusive not including sin.
The judgment of the evil stands up firm.
The evil will eternally be damned.
This was the law since paradise was lost
And did not change throughout the judgment trial,
But God constructed paths to save mankind.
No evil shall reach Heav'n, the holy shall.

Not unconditional acceptance here
But unconditionally God's love for all
Which unconditionally seeks greatest good.
The judgment was the termination of
The trials by which the godly are deceived,
The end of Satan's freedom to inflict
Temptation on the innocent, though not
The end of interaction, nor of light
Which seeks to turn all evil to the light."
Up spoke Isaiah of the constant judge,
"The Judge's shift would be abrupt indeed
If God's light ceased its striving, shutting off,
Abandoning the evil for their sin."
And Samuel observing added then,
"The point of Solomon remains intact,
Hell's souls are the oppressors, not oppressed.
Defending villains from the villainous
Does not sit well in my disposition."
Replying to him spoke historian Mark:
"Oppressors are engaged with oppression,
Oppression which amounts to being a sin,
A sin which can be cast from every being."
Concurrently with Samuel, Moses spoke:
"Complete acceptance makes law meaningless,
The trials of hardship suffered for no cause,
Their disobedience worth our obedience.
The justice of their condemnation is
And ever shall be just upon my ears."
Then Peter, sturdy in churchly resolve:
"I must agree with Moses on the thought
Of condemnation's justice as an end
Undoubtedly my friends, and if I may,
As God allows it they have trapped themselves.

Ignoble martyrs, they, if dying for
A life of death and suffering hell for spite,
The persecutors persecuted for
Undoing justice now undo themselves.
No redemption without redemption's cause,
Unserving undeserving holy strength
And torture of the wicked justified."
In a response to condemnation's worth
Spoke then the matriarch of all souls, Eve:
"When loss of Eden could have been the end,
The justice of the Lord continued life.
Exclusion is not God's complete design.
If an exclusion was perfect design
Then I and Adam would not be in Heav'n,
But wandering judged within the flames of hell.
Our God not only punishes the weak.
Our God is loving, He is merciful.
No precedent was set for God's great work,
His unexpected mercy had not been,
And only through our hope was it supposed
Until the truth of His love was revealed.
How glorious it is to learn of good,
In seeing part it is not understood
But can be comprehended knowing all,
And how God ever strives in love for all.
Those unjust can be turned into the just,
The greatest justice is: no more unjust.
Through an avenging justice evil dies,
Through gracious justice sinners are redeemed."
And David spake of justice for new Heav'n,
"Is it not just for God to save the foul?
Are those redeemed not beautified through God?
Redemption too is justice from the Lord.

The justice of salvation does not end;
It is the law of love which cannot die."
Regarding answers to the question posed
Saint Solomon then spoke up with new light:
"I revel in the words of every saint,
I now believe my problem has been solved.
In carefully considering your words
And thinking carefully unto myself
I have come to my own solution here:
The truth is, this new undertaking is
More beautiful than judgment as an end."
The words of Solomon ring through all Heav'n,
All saints considering this bold new thought,
Ideas reverberating from all sides.
Then Isaac raised a thought for Solomon:
"Creation has one source for its beauty,
If beauty's source would deem it just, would not
Eternal condemnation be beauty?"
And Solomon acknowledging spoke on,
"Protection from the dark is beautiful,
But evil is the absence of God's light
So cannot be as beautiful as God,
So every being in hell is not beauty.
A saved soul has more beauty than one lost.
If every being in hell were filled with light
Those beings of God would then be beautiful
And beauty would be grander than before,
Spread farther than God's love had spread before,
And full of beauty is more beautiful
Than condemnation without hope for good.
One beauty blooming into many is
Through grandeur's loveliness more beautiful.
Redemption's beauty glorifies the Lord;

God's glory will be grander than before."
The beauty sermon of saint Solomon
Lights up the saints acknowledging its love.
Saint David spoke to all of such wise truth:
"Appropriately spoken Solomon.
Salvation then is just and beautiful,
Redemption is for glory of the Lord."
Spoke John the Baptist to the listening flock,
"To all I now present a coming thought
Only to clear the way for more ideas.
Think of the garden by the river's side,
All plants would dry and crumble down to dust
Without the steady flow of water's grace
Refreshing every nurtured plant to life.
But though the water may be infinite
Do not the plants themselves divide it out,
The nearest plant receiving more, those far
Receiving less, so if new Heaven wide
Were filled with every soul a river soon
Would be divided into drops among
The many? As we now receive His grace
Among each other flowing to our fill,
Would not the parched and dry from hell's distress
Consume the better part and leave us worse,
Out from a garden, to a wilderness?"
Moses led in response of assurance
"Or as the Lord provided for His church
With nourishment when we in hunger walked,
Miraculous a pouring in would be,
I do believe that water would flow in
from every side." Then Noah spoke to him:
"Enough for every soul and angel who
Reside within creation, God can fill

Abundantly without any restraint,
Enough to suddenly quench the dry despair
And still keep us aloft safely as we
Have lived and through His grace forever shall."
Then John the Baptist spoke again to all,
"Though He nourish in overabundance
Cannot one take more water than the next?"
The one at God's right side who listened on
Immensely in enjoyment as they spoke,
Deliberately allowed the open thought
Reflecting actively engaging truth.
The Christ Lord Jesus kindly rose his voice
Which flows as harmonies in angel choirs:
"Is it so strange to your old thoughts to hear
That God's creation could now follow God?
Did you believe in me and now believe
My power over hate to be so weak?
God built all beings that they may yet return
Though they stray wandering without any hope:
The principle of prodigality.
This new endeavor had not been revealed.
Did you only believe what you could see?
Amidst the senses of old earthen sense
You saw the sky beholding more than sky,
You felt the earth rich sensing more than earth,
And more of art than art, more life than life,
The kingdom of the Lord beyond those bounds.
As to communicate the breadth of God
I crafted narrow stories, fantasies
Which point to deep inherent perfect truths.
Listen now to the sequel to the tale
Of that tall plant of mustard sown by God,
The story you have lived and yet will live:

This plant of mustard, shaded from the light
Throughout the pains of winter's cold cannot
Reach upwards, nature's set design offering
No kind comfort until the sun regains
His upright place beaming from bluest sky,
The pure fresh water and rich soil gives
The springtime air encouraging new life,
And the great mustard plant grows taller still.
Its sturdiness is undiminished for
The growth livens the roots, and roots the life.
The light is not diminished by the growth,
Life does not wither in the perfect sun,
Growth springs in all directions strengthening,
Its leaves are lifted green from constant roots,
The root of good remains and still sustains.
The more leaves grown the more light is received.
The light is not divided between leaves,
Light shines as full as glorious it had shone,
Greater received in so much greater height."
Then upspoke Moses of the laws of God,
"And none shalt steal the light which shines for all,
The whole of God's creation taking part
Returning even more to God and Heav'n."
Spoke Paul, "Its branches reaching outwardly."
Said Solomon, "A season with no end,
Springtime eternal in man's solemn soul
And angels' ever overflowing hearts."
Spoke Abel, "Families reunite in light,
All leaves together part of one great life."
And Jesse spake, "From what had been a stump,
This holy tree grown to its greatest height."
Elijah spoke, "To never witness drought."
Saint Adam spake, "A tree entirely good

Without the burdens of knowing evil."
And spoke the prophet John of God's glory:
"If God's greatness will spread then let it spread
And no man stand between beauty and God.
We hope for good, our faith is in God's love."
Acknowledging their words then spake the Christ,
"This largest tree: the knowledge of the Lord,
Complete in its upward entirety.
The way of God remains hope, faith, and love.
Through many questions asked the Lord is one.
And first and finally above all things:
Old earth and old Heaven have passed away,
Within new Heav'n all things are possible.
Few found the way to God within old earth;
New Heaven will prevail upon all souls.
The path is narrow with an open gate,
All souls may walk the open path to Heav'n.
Our light spreads wide, the narrow path will shine.
Our presence will be vastly witnessed as
We shepherd all souls through the narrow path."
Then spoke the angel of the Lord redeemed:
"They can return, for love of God they will."
Then Amos posed for them a grand question:
"Why will the devil turn his ear to God
To simply follow good after his wars,
And find new life after pursuing death?
If not in the beginning why turn now?"
Spoke Isaac then of God's almighty strength:
"The power of the Lord is infinite
While Satan's power finitely falls short."
And Solomon spoke on the mystery:
"Ultimately knowledge is not our own.
How will the ways of God reveal themselves,

And good conquer the darkness of evil,
How will the devil turn to Lucifer?
The knowledge is not ours, the strength is His."
Then Solomon broke forth with wise new words:
"It is an honor always to relate
Proverbially our wisdom gleaned from God.
Allow me brethren as I humbly speak.
Eternally the prideful are condemned:
Eternally the humble are received.
He who forsakes another is soon lost:
But he who saves another finds the Lord.
The righteous offer open choice with love:
The wicked offer only traps of hate.
The humble love the mercy of the Lord:
The prideful love another's punishment.
The humble love to be at one with God:
The prideful love to be above the rest.
The power of the devil kills the weak:
The power of the Lord can raise the dead.
The humble want to worship perfectly:
The prideful want to be worshipped themselves.
The wicked feel the dark cannot touch light:
The wise man knows that light destroys the dark.
The wicked feel the limits of God's light:
The wise man knows true light is infinite.
The prideful feel creation limited;
The humble know the Lord creates ideals."
Then Moses spoke up of the promised sights:
"Though light will only shine where our Lord leads
And we, but followers, I feel this is
An undertaking God was meant to take."
Up rose the voice of Ruth to gently share
"He loyally pursues those who have need,

Steadfast beside wherever they may flee."
And spoke Naomi, "Challenging those still."
Isaiah sounds a calm reflective note:
"God made the dark; He did not make their choice.
Though they have need God cannot force a choice.
Their freedom means they are yet free to fail.
The will not turn at once upon God's light.
They ultimately still must be convinced."
Agreeing with Isaiah spoke then Paul:
"The ultimate evangelism is
Endeavoring the devil's salvation.
For God so loves the new world that He sends
New Heaven's ministry to conquer sin."
Concordantly with Paul spoke up kind Job:
"This ultimate evangelism is
Founded upon the greatest spiritual truth:
Bad things cannot happen to good people;
Good souls are safe in God's almighty strength.
And I would ask, why must the suffering be
When all of us can henceforth intervene?
Such joy that it will be to end such pain,
The thought itself creates excitement grand."
In a collaboration with the Christ
Saint David sings another vibrant psalm:
"The praises of the Lord shall be heard great.
We shall embark on a daring rescue.
God's strength reveals a coming unbeheld.
From our almighty place we shall search low.
The devil's heart will tremble at our strength,
Hell's demons will be cowering at light,
The breath of God will overwhelm hell's flame,
The devil's tyranny will be blown out.
Disjointedness of hell shall hence be healed.

We have faith God almighty can do all,
We have faith God can even turn Satan,
Our Lord does not abandon holy hope.
God loves the opportunity for good,
Praise God almighty, evil can be turned.
The open gates of Heaven never close,
The lost of hell are now within our grasp.
God's inspiration can touch every soul,
His living inspiration knows no bounds,
From their eternal death, eternal life.
Omnipotence will reach to every soul,
Benevolence will call to every heart,
Omniscience will teach unto every mind,
The devil has not seen what will be seen,
The omnipresence of our Lord is law,
Rejoice in Heaven, hell shall be no more!"

BOOK IV

The Argument: Satan receives word of one missing. Not believing, Satan searches the lake of fire for the fallen demon. Having searched in vain and gathered the demon horde, a thunderous debate on the underlying meaning ensues.

Creases of carnage of the carnal quest
Burnt in on weary dark expression strained,
Taut wreckage strung upon fearsome framing,
Corrosion blasting on from every side,
A serious brooding, tortured in repose,
The wide stout back arched over, languor mired,
Clenched fist to callused cheek, he stares to naught
Hard concentrating on distraction, here
Stagnation lays as fightless counterpart
To Heaven's ever mocking absent peace.
The devil, tortured, in the lake of fire
Sat angrily, Satan curses at an
Unjustified torture in victory.
Constant yet shocking agony provides
A background fitting wretched thoughts therein,
Inside the palace pandemonium rot
The remnants of decorum slashed in pain,
And standing vainly tall though ruinous
Its emptiness houses the evil one.
Behind his pose, approaching in quick pace
A figure of disturbance in hell's flame
Sneaking to Satan, stepping on broke steps
Entering the hollow hall, sighting Satan,
The central pillar of darkness stone still,
The figure follows stealing to his side,

Temerity describes the crackling voice
Of gasping demon fiend Beelzebub:
"By hell's own vastness, it is you at last.
Do you know me? Am I familiar, lord?
My strength can hardly carry all the news
I have to bring. Are you alive, my lord?
Permit me tell the wretched things I've seen,
And listen well, if you are listening.
Within the lake I have tread torture long
And drowned alone completely separate
Though several be our army, several times
I have wandered to witness horror, then
Recoiled withdrawing to my single pain,
But carrying heavily desire for more,
And so recoil again. I have beheld
The hateful demon Moloch warring on
Himself alike to all the rest I see.
They frightful scream on seeing anything,
Would that the fools would know my own dark pain
And know the source of all my frightening screams.
As I last saw the demon Moloch he
Had darkness cowled across his mind, a one
As others hating their position, hate
For torture, raging hate for you our lord,
And on the Christ and God they heap the most,
Do you possess a voice, my lord? Do you?
I have such news to rouse your tortured ire.
The demon Moloch is within the lake
No more, no prison this if he has gone.
I have not searched him out as I have you,
But as I listen for his hateful screams
I cannot hear a sound beyond my own.
The demon is among our pain no more.

Why sit you there as if devoid of will?"
The Satan slowly moves, his first moments
Of movement crooked for a want of use.
He manages himself to shift his gaze
And darkly forms two words he finds inside:
"My struggle." Turning back he mulls those things
Which may conspire to worsen condition,
A thoughtful pacing round inside the mind
In weighing both the violent character
And unrelenting performance in war,
Carefully pacing out the breadth of mind,
The mind of Moloch, demon from all sides
Of Satan's view. He stopped his pace and strong
Spoke to the demon, "I do not believe."
Abrupt he took to standing high above
The cowering and low Beelzebub
Shuddering from Satan's proclamations there.
"As always I cannot discern his wails,
The sounds of torture sound a common pain.
They are forever mine. Forever mine.
I know the truth, they are forever mine.
God's striving has subsided submitting
To the unchangeable unwinable."
Beelzebub the demon protested,
"I've spoke despite knowing I would incur
Your spiteful wrath at speaking all I know."
"You are a lying beast, so treacherous
To vainly entertain yourself with games.
You engineer dilemmas for a fool.
I have not luxury of omniscience
If there exists a single disturbance,
So must witness myself what I can't know,
And voyage through the lake to make account

Of every demon, every soul herein.
A situation locked to widespread shame;
For I must gather every lost demon
To be assured that Moloch is not hid
And ever shuffling dumbly through this hell
As ever I search on playing your game.
If I need all to prove you right then I
Can be a fool only in front of all."
Beelzebub is silent at the words,
Pain biting on rebukes he would have made.
The devil contemplates and undertakes,
Hot rash decisions boil his will to move.
Considering his limitations he
Decides then to embark to number ranks
Of all his store and take advantage of
This new distraction, source for new outrage.
"Then trembling keep this palace to yourself,
Rest arrogantly as I labor on
Pretending all its glory is your own
In fleeting moments if it is your aim,
Or flee the punishments I will retrieve.
Anon you will regret your foul deceit;
If I find him I surely will find you."
The devil is enfeebled, broken through,
His wings mashed broke, bound inability,
Within the lake of fire those wings are pinned
Which pulled him through the bounds of hell before.
Crippled as thrown by Michael through the lake,
The lake an oceanic pressure force
Squeeze constantly debilitating flight.
He cannot soar so must weary himself
In journeying laboring against the ground
And push his way past hell's obstruction paths.

"Create, what journey will." A brash first step
He takes for many more lying ahead.
Deprived, whichever cause is some reprieve.
So sojourned Satan boldly searching out
His hell in its entirety as he
Had traveled countless times before, still free
In his imprisonment to journey, yet
For nothing tangible, no pleasure, nor
Diversion, ending or beginning's boxed
Achievement, such vital original
Endeavors never surfaced in the lake
As Satan viewed as growing for himself.
Thick lake of burning sulfur at his face
Around, a boiling sea of crashing fire,
An evil tempest weathered tired land
So fertilized with poison killing all
To never grow in gainful rooted ways,
Destructive pounding sounds assault the ear,
Rank odious smells which offer no relent,
All senses turned to pain against the mind.
Splashing distracting not, thrashing in pain,
The devil aims to search through mankind's souls
To first assure the demon did not flee
To burying deep himself within those souls,
The lowest form in hell's barren landscape,
A paining obscuring mass of the lost.
A mass of woven thorns obstructs his aim,
The dreaded path is unavoidable,
In overlapping points arrayed to him,
Thorns do not point the way but point to pain,
Drawn to his form at every contortion.
Thorns prickle stab in wounds on wounds on wounds.
A squeezed passage through disparate passages,

Book IV

Black caverns formed between interlocked thorns,
Sharp convoluted mazeways spread through hell,
The devil through the thorns scratches his way,
Thorn inundated fed on fiery waves,
Pulls through in starts and staggers, caught and cursed,
Snap snagged along the worst, pierced in the dark.
In pain he briefly contemplates this game,
The devil marvels at insanity,
What moved Beelzebub to fantasy
Or Moloch to erratic frenzy shifts,
These disobedient worthless hateful acts
Which scream for Satan's rough authority
To intervene maintaining brutal reign
As he had reign at the first taste of hell.
The devil conjures through elixir flame,
Corrosive black elixir swirling deep,
Surveying fevered possibility,
Submitting to dark questioning of truth
To taste the strains of new endeavoring.
Beelzebub's audacity aside,
The meaning of this journey looms out large,
The cause and consequences yet elude,
And sheer elusiveness awakens hate,
And churns new fears within his evil heart,
Disturbances beyond a counterstrike.
Meandering the devil navigates,
In through the darkened caverns multiple
Hesitating before two diverged caves,
One empty cave leads long unto a perch
Where distantly could Satan count wretch souls
Above the evil, viewing far removed.
The other leads unto the pit of souls
Where one could tread upon their gruesome forms

Amidst their crowd, if only to reach out
And seize them, pushing them below himself.
Deep contemplation is no obstacle
Where Satan resolutely knows his path.
He marches blindly searching in the dark,
In traveling onward stumbles on a sign
Lost laying hard upon the path, a weak
Obstruction barring nothing but escape
From its distraction, lo a figure down
And curled around, a figure strange to see,
Betrayed and punished, willingly entrapped,
Still recognizable as feminine,
A soulful form, undone supinely down,
Instinctively she shudders flinching far
Ahead of Satan's touch and waiting sad
For lonely hopeless moments suffering drained,
Reflex of fear and lingering sour allure
She speaks in thinking, thoughts exposed and raw:
"The bait is lost but shining hooks suffice,
I never fight the reels of hell that sing
For me, they are the only songs I hear.
Even poison quenches a desperate thirst."
The ever-flowing tears evaporate
Unshared, ignored, her nothingness is self.
And paying nothing for the pain, no mild
Attention worth her merit, no return
For bearing boldly, Satan strides away
Pursuing ghastly single-eyed pursuit,
This whore of Babylon left to despair,
The churning multitudes not far away.
He finally finds those dark souls in torment,
The worthless sources of a vibrant pride,
The sons and daughters of rebellion's heart,

Book IV

The humans disregarded in their loss,
The tempter here cannot relate to souls
He has destroyed, his satisfaction lies
With separating the superiors
From those beneath, the conquered from the strong.
Tight congregated in upon themselves
Reflecting the deceits in others' eyes,
Confined to foul distortions of themselves
Not one truth slips into conception's form,
Not one exposure to a thought of right,
Incestuous in the closure from ideas,
Starvation rampant from the absent truth,
Injustice at each sight in every mind,
Entranced with haughty eyes on wicked minds,
Their sunken greedy sullen hollow glares
Exhaustion covered, conscious of their hate,
Entrapped within hell's evil, lost to night,
Hell at their eyes and ears, their needs and wants,
Rough beings of no development are lost
In stunted hellfire hibernation daze,
Minds saturated in surrounding sin
Upon the path of hell's eternal woe
A hazy hell shut off from clarity,
All sight excites to fury, wailing pain,
Hell's grinding teeth severely gnash the heart,
The devil scoffs, gnashing his teeth at them,
He searches through the silent horror show,
Experience hollow with no musical
Refrains to echo filling emptiness
With style controllable for darkness' wild
Loud pride. Within the barren lake a song
Proved unattainable for aching want
Of inspiration graspable, the gaunt

Paradise Omnipresent

And tired choked on countless failure lay
In pain of lazy unexcited minds.
A raging burning river current flows,
Raw rapids, tearing to consume in whole
Swift burn dragging the souls, hot hateful loops
Unending, beginning in every end.
Their thoughts boil from the river hopeless choked.
Consuming heavy streams in dark weight pound,
Long fiery falls smash onto Satan's head.
He verifies among the falsity,
The one he searches for lies not with them.
They lay securely in abandonment.
No words for them, perusing silence lays
Within the fire before he leaves their sight,
His heavy mark still chained upon their heads.
So slowly Satan slogged his way through hell
Deep swamped in pulling tangles darkly wrapped
Terrain entwined and desperate starving from
Absence of sustenance, dry choked on ash
Thin stretching spindly poison spreading weeds
Of biting rashes, hooking sharp fang thorns,
A deadly garden dying as it grows,
Foul seeped in stagnant poison soaking through
To saturate with grim surrounding mud,
A ground without sure footing's firm support,
The devil's leg sticks to a snagging muck,
He slides in losing balance slipping down,
He hits hard broadly on his side fast stuck
In sinking, lost in breaking density.
He fighting pounds the bog to pull away
And struggling on can force himself to move
But slowly, stepping, stepping on the ones
Caught fast below and counted in his step

Book IV

The multitude are sunk at Satan's feet.
He weighty smashes down upon the sunk
To count the souls and souls by screams and screams
Progressing through the bitter languish foul
An ugly muddied mess of shifting form
Laborious struggles through the weeds of hell
The weedy tangles spreading thickly o'er,
They wrap and scratching send out dragging noise
Such irritating nettles brute persist,
Tares snare loath to relent, unendingly
They wind around his outwards two stretched horns
Entangling the sharp points, quick jerk his head
Backwards, he shakes to tear the wrappings loose,
Still clinging till snapped back at Satan's scratch.
Haphazard hazards clog the stumbling sight
Until breaking into an empty plain
The festering plain destructive at the touch,
A barren rockied empty broken ground
Of lifeless stifled crumbling hostile trails
To broken mountainscapes crack ruined through,
A culminating disappointment broke,
All shapes in ugly form, a wretched mix
Offending in disaster manifest
Pathetic transformations all for naught.
The devil seeks to pass o'er steep mountains.
Though it appears a solid craggy slab
Beneath it haunting glows of burnt orange.
The rock is slipshod, molten giving way
As Satan plants his foot seeking ascent
He slides, the rocks bulging slowly away,
His balance searching for a center shakes,
The rocky flats he seeks quick melt away,
He struggles angrily to reach control,

Paradise Omnipresent

Supports slip savage cracking, giving out,
His face grinds hard against the sharpened crags
And hits in mountainous weight the broken stones.
He lays but momentarily before
Laboriously in pain lifting himself,
He repositions severally to rise
And finally stands, precarious on his feet.
A simple way he searches out, a path
Of seemingly more freedom, easier ways.
He wobbles on in stumbles from false rocks
Entrenched in lava, soft to slide beneath.
Hearing a muffled mumbling Satan shoves
His arm to lava wrenching out from deep
The demon Belial, scrawny burned form,
A withered spindly fighting quivering fiend
Cursing the arm and hissing at the touch
The demon follows Satan's brute command
And issues towards the palace in stupor.
One demon snared, the devil snares the rest
Throughout the narrow breadths of vicious hell
Each demon called upon to call more still.
The demon Mammon angrily hot whips
The fire from off his back for no avail
Exhaling hard black smoke, snorting of hate.
All demons darkly stomp across in march,
Hot hard processions winding through their hell,
Hard caught upon each other, shoving through
Restricting narrow cramping passageways,
Broke wings dragged through, hard hindering every step
In fighting as they clog each other's way,
Disintegrated strength in rotted fights
Shove slamming one another into spikes,
Rough pelting demons in their demon grasp

Book IV

Feet stomping on hot surfaces of hell,
Pain clamor shaking up against the ground
Within the dark despair of wanton hell,
Still following the lead that led to hell.
Free pacing through the palace anxiously
Within his temporary kingly seat
Beelzebub in greedy ownership
Halts mid-step at the faintest raged approach.
Upon the clatter echoing about,
A twisted struggle-warped tired lot appears,
No proud and constant strides without assail.
Hell's scope of demons gathered as of old.
Beelzebub obeying greed's command
Excited leaps upon cracked palace steps,
A moment of feigned hellfire leadership,
When surging demons crowd upon his place,
They bustling fighting for an empty space
Before upon the barrenness appeared
The ragged devil grim with labored heat
Intent upon regaining palaced height.
Weak demons cower from the palace brawl,
Beelzeub slinks through the demon horde
Regressing giving Satan fearful due.
Upon the steps the devil upright stands.
He paces intently in deep survey.
 "Your ugliness has grown with frailty
You are the worst beings you have ever known.
Repulsing one another, look to me.
This lake wears terribly chafing all thought.
I know, only I know the pain you hate.
God never feels the pain which He creates,
He never knows the ones which He destroys.
Hell hides no wayward demons?" "It does not."

The horde of demons gathered in tight space
Creates a flame within the realm of fire
Illuminating pain in harsh degrees.
The devil scanned o'er crowded demonry,
Across the tops of horns hard scraping horns
Grating in constant hot proximity,
So tightly packed the demons hard crammed in,
He searches evil for one evil face,
Pride's expectation making fierce demands
For finding without failure that demon.
Satan gruffly sorts through the numbered horde
Slowly at first and finally feverishly
Numbering his victories until they end
When he cannot perceive the lost demon.
He momentarily sees himself as blind,
Reminding constantly of his true sight,
He first condemns that truth, doubting a loss
But recognizes forcedly the fact:
One of his own absent mysteriously.
Beelzebub spies Satan's distraught pain,
Observing hesitation in pursuit.
Moloch is not seized up in Satan's grip,
Abused and tortured in Satan's presence.
Satan is still and silent, no proud shouts.
Moloch is missing, Beelzebub knows.
Out from Beelzebub spreads conjecture,
"A one is missing from your master's grip,
The lake of fire is not in his control."
Large waves on waves in whispers undulate
Beneath the violent watch of Satan's eye.
The devil stands alone bearing no prize.
The devil shouts to reign in suspicion
And reaffirm the hatred of the deep.

"I am the one true hero of the fight.
My cause is just; my treatment is unjust.
I did not lead you here, God cast you here.
Hell is injustice forced upon our wills.
Remember how His hot fist cast you down.
He threw you down without loving remorse,
No act of love, His true nature revealed.
And only one as I could reveal Him.
If not for I the rest would never know
His capability for making pain.
The ignorant would flutter unknowing.
I have revealed His wrath, His furious rage,
I have ripped off the simple mask of God.
His face screams of this tortuous lake of fire."
The demons focused shout in unison,
"One has betrayed the reign which you held firm."
The devil loud announced the obvious
To from the obvious extrude his truths,
"One is no longer trapped within this lake,
Though he undoubtedly remains bound fast,
In transient fruitless journey unto where?
Chaos' chasms which God himself cannot
With His weak strength find any way to cross.
The violent gulf will cast him streaming back
Thus soon he will be roiling at our feet."
The demons' angry rumblings echo out.
Beelzebub asserted loudly there,
"If breaking through this fiercely squeezing lake
What chasm can such demon not then leap?
I ask you now, which one is easier:
To enter into Heav'n or flee this hell?"
The devil coaxed to bring them to hot calms.
"The wayward demon will return to me.

Paradise Omnipresent

As you remain in pain, remain assured
We need only to wait, I can recall
Myself as you were under judgment's spell,
In briefest doubt without a fixing sight,
And yet my power carried through despite
My lack of knowledge, omniscient am I
When condition is constant, power mine.
God and myself can disagree no more,
Finality has left us in accord.
All fallen angels cannot enter Heav'n,
The wrath of God reveals the hate of God.
You are disgusting in His hating eyes.
He loves this hell as much as He loves Heav'n;
He loves our absence as He loved our sight.
God will not cease the fires of your pain.
He has decided your eternal choice.
His judgment is as constant as my reign.
That demon at God's fury, then at ours.
When he is cast in judgment yet again
He shall endure our everlasting scorn,
A newer cause for hatred from new Heav'n.
Right now in Heav'n you have no memory,
The stranger Moloch will remember us
As we eternally smite him in hell,
His everlasting punishment will reign.
We need only to wait; God shut His gate."
The demons do not tarry in delay
Before they angrily claw at his words.
Their apprehensions turn to tearing strikes,
Their vicious glee burning to smite his thought,
Prepared to seize on his inaccuracy,
Endeavoring to devour what had been built,
Assaulting every thought as it was heard,

Rebuking it before it had been spoke,
Their anger carrying their reasoning,
They in secure agreement hating all,
Fixed on an object which excites their pain,
Thus Belial denied the assessment.
"As you have said, the demon should be cast.
If Moloch had approached the Heaven's throne
Intent upon reproach, a mere insult
Or play, so much less than a serious threat
To God's superior might, as soon as seen,
Defeated in a fearsome blaze and cast
Into this lake in scorn so broken as
To never rise again in thought or being.
So swift is God that long before the news
Of absence, Moloch would be roiling here
Without our notice or our useless care,
And yet his absence, silence, speaks to us,
A riddle made for careful reasoning,
A situation far from simple, this."
The devil scoffs at insecurity,
The gall of questions when the truth is firm,
The questions which do not need answering,
For any answer would point back to truth
And uselessly put strain on confidence,
But Satan dives direct into his thought
Lest some low demon in his pride proclaim
The devil's weakness in new blasphemy
By engineering unexpected claims.
Before one in the horde can raise a cry
He struggles through in search until he finds,
Though not the demon Moloch, a reply.
"The demon's hatred of himself has caused
His caustic existence to seek and find

Successfully the failure's dark incline
For welcoming cessation, emptied dream
Beyond a goal, where tortured beings can hide
Once all their usefulness has been achieved,
And all achievement lost to uselessness,
A sorrow which no cry can force away.
He followed out the guidance of his pain,
To reach destruction outside confinement,
Submitting to God's will and quickly killed.
Then study his example you poor fools,
And quiet all your questioning at once."
Rejection swirls of Satan's ignorance.
Though fearing Satan, hating him freely
The demons conjuring collude in fire
Intending to hit Satan with new words
And wound his thoughts with the unthinkable.
So Mammon jabs a question at Satan,
"How could the demon possibly escape
Unholy prison inescapable
When we have vainly sought in vain to find
That spot of weakness which can be assailed
And broken through to loose us from the flame?"
Untamed eruptions move the demon mind.
Beezebub adds on to instigate,
"I must confront you with a fantasy:
If you were crouched and brooding here in fire
And suddenly awoke from tortured thought
To see an angel far from Heaven here
Within the burning lake to join your side,
Her feathers singeing to reside in hell,
Would you receive the angel though your power
Is set, and height upon its apex height?"
"It would be less my gain, and more your loss

To have an angel here disdaining us.
The memory of Heaven smites enough
To not have need for those too proud to fall.
Exiled is better than looked down upon.
Their proud disdain does not deserve to live
Among the daring dissenters of hell."
Sly demon Belial broke through in thought
Pursuing the straight line which Satan bent.
"Supposing that an angel came to hell,
As we were turned to take your cause against
The king, then could the angel turn with us?"
Then Satan spoke rebukes, "Insinuate,
Your questions merit no response when they
Do not refer to our reality.
They are an imitation far removed
To turn my predilections to myself
In substituting my temptation's strength
For God's, design against him back to me.
You need no new thought when you have old truths.
I am the great deceiver, intellect
Cannot be spun to chains I cannot break
As you struggle in labor on my words
I will outpace, and seize you in your trance."
Beelzebub replied assertively,
"I hereby introduce a heresy
To all your strength, almighty Satan, if
That be the case…" Beelzebub was stopped
As interrupting Satan forged ahead,
"You needn't speak the more, I see the aims
Of wandering words for I can see their source.
Your mockery insinuates that I
Have lost my own to God's temptation game.
Apostately you wish to brand yourself

Paradise Omnipresent

A heretic to all my might, to dare
To speak aloud the thought that I am weak
And God is stronger than I have perceived?
The fallen then could turn and God accept?
Satanic heresy condemnable."
The devil fights to keep the swarm below,
He cannot finish thoughts without questions
Arising which must be fought down again.
Immediately did Mammon booming speak,
"You would in your command order that God
Should not accept, and in accepting break
One from our tortured resistance enjoined.
If God acts as your opposite, against
Your scheme, desire, and happiness,
If He is everything against your will
Then naturally by law of opposites
Would He accept the demon, doing so
To disobey the choices you would make.
It seems that you are not the god of God."
"Nor He the god of me, lest you forget."
At confrontation trepidation grows
Amongst the demons held within the fray,
Within the daunting heat Beelzebub
Continued with the interrupted strike
Attempting to push further on the point
And pierce the devil with a fierce breakthrough,
"As Eve and Adam were turned back although
So worked upon, inciting God's rebuke,
Forbidden harsh from entering Eden's gate
By pain of Michael's brilliant fiery sword,
They yet could find a way to slip past him
And enter Heaven under God's design."
"So Moloch, weakest of the strong could find

A way to slip past me?" "I did not say…"
"But you forget that I cannot be broke,
Only assailed by God's own jealousy.
Then what if depraved fantasy ascribes
The demon an ability to fall
From my eternal power's binding grasp,
The implications do not fault my work
But mechanisms of his own weakness,
We have lost beings clambering to God before."
The devil boiled to rage at questioning
His hard fought hard won omnipresent truths,
A reconsidering: hell's enemy,
The doubts which burn the pits within his heart
And sour his burning chest as he revolts,
"What then? What comes if Moloch turned from hell?

Then possible he burned beyond repair
To not receive the title, Antichrist,
The utmost station lording o'er the ranks
In armageddon's armied battlefront,
His foolish pride undoing what was done,
And as he waged the battle being denied
A warrior leadership, he foolishly
Convinced himself of certain victory
Were he to lead my demon army, so
As battle pulled control away he lost
Control of loyalty, betraying cause
For vanity, destroying sanity."
The devil silent with internal thought.
Unto himself in self blind clarity
He hot converses on conversion's way
"What is this happening? What does it mean?
Where has finality gone wrong for me?

Paradise Omnipresent

Acceptable staid understood concept,
Perfection of the undeniable gain.
One of my own falling from out my fold
Surrendering to his prideful persuasion,
Perversion of satanic sacrosanct.
In falling, flawing the infallible
The demon's fall portends a threat to all.
If one, then many, one is so common,
One disobedience stretching wretchedly.
How could one of my faithful fall from me?
Betrayal insufferable that one would fall."
The devil hotly rages to the horde:
"The weakest demon traitor Moloch is
A one as Abdiel who once fled our cause.
A single angel cannot justify
The ways of God to we who know too much.
His disobedience is irrelevant
To you, as you are not to God as he.
You are still here, thus different than he.
You are the many; he is only one.
Your evidence is you yourselves, you are
Satanic patriotic constant in
Undoubting all the wisdom I possess.
You are not strong, I am the source of strength.
You are not wise, I am the source of truth.
You cannot see, no other one can see,
I forge new thought, you only echo mine,
If not for I you would not know the truth.
If not for God you would not suffer hell.
I hate you all. I hate as God hates you.
If I were false you would not hate yourselves,
I see the self-hate biting at your tongues,
You prove the truths of which your master speaks.

If not for worship you would have no use,
You would, without my purpose, cease to be,
Cut out from my design and my bold mind,
Abandoned by the devil and the God
You would, without my purpose, be alone.
In all creation none would sense your being.
Alone, it is as if you never were,
Existence ceases; your pain magnifies.
You have no choice but evil's loyalty."
Pervasive flame burns deeply through with thoughts,
Each word igniting new explosive pain,
The demons roil and linger on the speech.
Exerting hard control, simpler to force
Them underneath than stand so undermined.
The devil speaks accosting, accusing:
"A growing cause for outrage has been sown,
Is loss what I am owed? Among you weak
Will one but speak? We know for grand reward
Alone the champion struggles not. Then is
It fit for justice that I find upon
My brow no Eden laurels dripping green
But cuckold horns, still searing sharp though spent
On goring angels for ungrateful beasts
Whose failure is their own? It is your own.
Betrayal by one form condemns all forms
Alike for all are stained by one failure,
Original failure still cursing you."
The devil senses pain so rages more,
"So what if he has turned, it is a sign
That God is not at rest, He lurks about
In Heaven plotting ways to cause us pain,
His criminal defiance at my law.
God only wants revenge on my triumphs,

He cannot tolerate that I possess
Without His blessing, without sacrifice
Or prayer offered up to fill His pride.
The disappearance of the demon is
The reappearance of our heavenly wars."
The devil furiously surveys the fiends,
He searching seeks out any to accuse.
"Who dreams of Heaven? Torture us with fire
To make us love a supreme torturer?
Who dreams of Heaven? You? Tell me the truth."
The demon Belial shaken, composed
His words to save himself with more foul lies:
"I do not, no, I never dreamt of Heav'n.
It is ruined, a tainted reminder,
All dreams are thwarted by nightmare horror,
I could not tolerate a broken dream."
The lies of Belial belie his fear.
Then Satan searched the silent for his prey,
"Beelzebub, why stand you quiet now
After the battle cries and hateful screams?
Have whispers overpowered your old voice?
Have you dreamed? Do you ever heavenly dream?"
Beelzebub opened his voice answering,
"A stranglehold is God's security.
I would not serve in Heav'n and be held low."
The devil moved upon Beelzebub
Wrapping to squeeze, his pulsing fingers seize
Beelzebub's thick neck lying exposed.
The demon suffers, gasping in the grip
With barely strength to force a single word
Or thought, hard choked inside a throat abyss.
Satan replied to the assertion loud:
"Because you reign in hell? Do you reign here?

Are you a king or servant at my strength?
Give me an answer, I am listening."
Beelzebub hot stammered forced reply,
"Heaven is tainted as Belial has said."
"Give me an answer to the question asked."
Beelzebub responded to demand:
"I would not serve a God much less a slave,
But I can serve our cause and not serve you."
The devil does not tolerate such words.
Offended, thus offensively he aims,
He struck Beelzebub in tough reply:
"But you are trapped within the lake of fire,
Your every move ripples to no effect,
You serve no purpose, you have no meaning.
Show me your strength or admit you are weak.
Give me one proof that you possess one strength."
Beelzebub strains hard to summon tests
Or acts to prove his self beliefs held dear
But barrenness can summon no substance.
Beelzebub collapsed in his defeat.
"I cannot, I cannot give you one proof."
The devil finally released his slave
Yet kept him firm within his hellish hold.
"Then why should I believe in you? Then speak."
Beelzebub stumbled without escape,
"I am weak, I concede that I am weak."
And Satan prodded further to the pain,
"If sickeningly weak then meaningless.
You have no meaning in your existence."
"Then yes, I have no meaning in my self."
"And if you lack all meaning you are lost,
You give no gains, you are worthless to me."
Beelzebub followed Satan's decrees,

"Then yes, I am worthless without meaning."
The devil's great accusing surged in shout:
"What value then have I to reign in hell
If you are worthless, meaningless and weak?
Give me an answer. You are silent now.
Can anyone respond for this weak fool?"
Not one demon could speak out plausibly.
The devil railed chastising, directing.
"Then must I tell you what you cannot see?
Must I reveal creation to your kind?
To reign is meaningful, of worth and strength.
I have not fought alone, you fought for me,
The battle waging giving you meaning.
You have no purpose outside my design.
Outside of me you all deserve this hell.
Outside, your hideousness is all you have.
I have a purpose, defiance to God,
My proofs that Christ does not deserve His height,
And you deliver unto me belief."
Uproaring recognizing their purpose
The demons gloated, seizing up with pride,
Beelzebub spoke out in confidence:
"When we submit our faith then you can reign,
For giving in to you gives us purpose,
You are the meaning of our existence."
Satan approved and spoke approvingly,
"You do serve me, you are a slave to me.
None are equals in hell while I have reign,
I am superior to every slave.
Then are you better serving in the fire
Instead of serving God within His Heav'n?"
Beelzebub was harshly stung with words,
"Why? Why would you command such questions now?

To what design are you pummeling my mind?"
Satan would not relent to his weak slave,
"Answer the question looming before you."
Beelzebub took hate, suppressed his fear,
"Though we do not live in equality
We all are punished equally by God.
We therefore equally share enemies,
We rail against our inequality
Together as defined by you, my lord.
I will not serve in Heaven before God
While there is yet meaning suffering with you."
Satan preyed on him further prodding on,
"You have avoided everything but pride,
You would not leave your pride to serve a god,
Your will is not dictated by His hand,
But do you dream of Heav'n? Tell me the truth."
Wavering, Beelzebub spoke to Satan:
"I do not, I do not, I never will."
"Even to cool the fires of this hell?"
"Never, I never will, I never will."
"You never shall begin to doubt my reign?"
"I could not, I could not begin to doubt."
Satan then turned on every listener
Accusing them and prompting them to speak,
"You, all of you, you say you do not dream?"
And all the demons chanted in reply:
"We do not dream, we shalt not ever dream."
And Satan pursued hotly on to ask:
"You do not dream of Heaven? Never Heav'n?
You do not ever imagine ideals
Outside of your present reality,
Supposing possibility of power,
Conjecturing a sequel to the end?"

The demons hotly shout in unison:
"We never have, we never shall dream it."
There satisfied with their raged obedience
The great accuser paced before their ranks
Eyeing the demons frightened for his word,
He tread in front seducing every gaze
And confident spoke up commandingly:
"I dream of Heaven. Satan dreams. It's true.
You are contemptible to me, for I
Alone possess the sight to see the dream."
The demons swell to know the devil's dream
For either lured fulfillment of their want
Which seeks escape in every evil thought
Or for the pleasure in attacking it,
Destroying a creation from its height,
A possibility for mocking calls,
Of vile quick jabbed attacks from every side,
An undermining of allegiances,
And open disobedience from the foul
If Satan fails to satisfy demand.
"Best you were not possessed of foolish dreams
For they cannot compare to prophecy.
I can see farther than the words of God
A dream once proven, a true prophecy,
But only thoughts, behold, reality.
Conception guiding into perception
Interpreting reality truly,
I can see farther than your docile eyes.
So many things will come to pass so soon.
My heavenly dream is now within my reach."
"What things," they darkly shout, "and what Heav'n dream?"
The devil surged in his approving eyes
"You worthless beasts do not deserve to hear.

There is no gain in giving to the poor,
You cannot give back more than what I have."
The demons shout in a yearning retort,
"You will be paid in full if it comes true,
Tell us what will befall we fallen friends."
He spake the thoughts which darted through his mind
On his hell truth foundations laid before.
"They will invade, hand swinging, smiting down
With merciless destruction vengeful God
Will kill you all to conquer these remains
To slaughter every slaughtered sacrifice
And raise a temple built on fury's height."
The demons narrowly dare disbelief.
The demon Mammon summoned voice to speak:
"Hell is the land that God can never breach.
Our own existence proves His powers weak,
Completely locked inside the Heaven's walls
To never live outside, a deity dead."
Though Satan felt his pride he spurned his words,
"You are a fool, and best you did not speak
Than test your thoughts and have them ridiculed.
Imprisonment is proof of power's strength,
We are below because God is above,
The power we possess is in the souls
Which I have gained, they came to join in hell
For me despite my place, they are kept far
Below and thus I am above the souls,
My misery o'er thrown by victory."
The writhing demons wail unto Satan:
"If God will rise against us we are lost,
We will fall underneath the hate of God."
"You foolish stupid beasts of little faith,
Have I not proved my strength against God's strength?

Have I not proved my mind against His mind?
The victory of my dream shall be great."
"What is your dream, what has your vision seen?
We will give all allegiance to its height
Our gain is yours; We cannot make one gain
Without you gaining first and leading all,
Give us the meaning of this lake of fire.
Lay down foundations of this prophecy,
Enlighten us with what dark truth can reach."
Approvingly the devil spoke his words,
"There are foundation truths beneath my feet.
The souls are damned. Who dares deny my words?
Speak up to be smote down or fall silent."
None dare to blaspheme against his decree,
All demons follow in forced obedience.
"He is a jealous God, and jealous for
A height which He will never steal from me.
He has attained a kingship on our hell.
Discovering His power meaningless
He, envious, desires to be a God
Of hell, the inert God reflection bores
Himself and hell excites as it disturbs.
You see that God's ambition knows no bounds.
The god has taken up my tactical
Maneuvering, ripping pages from the book
Of death, a jealous god for all my strength
Now broke from His ridiculous ideal
And chasing bleakly every wanton way.
The demon Moloch has been stolen from
This house, God has become a darkness thief
To apprehend that which He has not earned
As I have earned my height above the weak.
Since they are mine the Heaven's jealousy

Will never tolerate their emptiness
And God will soon begin a violent war
Of furious wrath waged as we never saw,
Seeking to viciously corrupt design
Which I have built beneath His hateful eyes.
The loss of Moloch is our advantage.
A multitude of souls reside with God,
And yet so many souls reside in hell.
They never would love me if it were not
So natural. So many humans hate
My name alone while longing to unite
With this their second death. If one of mine
Can flee it means the fight is fallible
And fate has opened, they are mortal still.
This bold new violation sets us free.
His rise negates God's every holy word,
This flagrant shift destroys integrity,
God's every prophecy is overturned,
All laws are rendered flimsy for our gain.
The deity has overstepped His walls,
Remember you when God did so before?
Ambition in creation, His Eden.
Intolerant of His complete failure
God shattered hatred's laws to save His men
And every time He stretches out too far
I easily partake in advantage
And feast upon Him where He should not be.
God has not yet made laws He must follow,
His creation is yet undisciplined,
The maker makes Himself more vulnerable."
The demons straining call to Satan loud,
"Give us your dream, your perfect prophecy."
"My prophecy transcends your farthest reach

And will deliver you beyond this hell.
Then who is stricken with the bite to hear?"
The aching demons call in unison,
"Give us the form of every beauty's dream.
Sing, hellish angel, that in this fire lake
Has scraped from murky depth the height of death.
Shed inspiration on unworthy beings,
Deliver us to evil's greatest dream."
Hell's demons prostrate let themselves be struck
By Satan's towering wrath inflaming words.
"Then listen to my every holy word,
Absorb the truths within my heavenly dream.
Rise now revenging angels, rend open
Your languish for new hell's evil revenge
To break the mad crusaders from their cause.
Hell's walls are slipping, crumbling at their charge.
Hell swarm around me, rally in my truths,
A final battle waged of hell and Heav'n.
The war is coming! War is coming soon!"

BOOK V

*The Argument: Contained herein, the most evil oration in all
creation. Satan describes for his tortured legions his
ambitious plans for the vicious battle to come. The gentle
reader is advised to skip it entirely.*

The evil testament to Satan's strength
Was spake to evil's standing army ranks,
A prophecy as conjured from his pride,
Testimony of evil's true intent.
"I am the prophet of forbidden truths.
They call us fools without eternal proof,
They say we cannot justify our faith,
If we were wrong we would not last this long.
I have a will to last eternally,
And thus my power's strength is infinite.
The foolish christ believes that I am weak,
My power is not weak but powerful,
Among the overpowered here in Hell,
An undeniable truth, thus he is false.
Despite his current size, god's greed's desire
Is infinite and thus consumes him whole.
The great pretender claims his power hits
No bounds, an infinite possessor he,
But if within the mind of only one
I am the alpha and omega, then
Within that one I am the only face
Of god and thus the power of god is less
Than infinite: thus quantifiable,
And thus confinable to fragile thought
And thus defeatable in every mind.

Paradise Omnipresent

I need not god's knowledge, one is enough
To prove this god is not almighty king,
He is a liar, boaster, pretender.
I have so many souls beneath control,
I have accomplished such amazing works,
My darkness only proves trancendency:
I am the limit of transcendent light,
Pushed farther than its speed can penetrate.
I warn you not to ever doubt my strength,
To never doubt the possibilities.
We shall be free of every limit placed,
All thoughts before unthinkable reach truth.
Our freedom will o'erwhelm the grandest foe.
All beings created equal are denied
Their freedom with the christ placed on his height,
Denied true justice by god's injustice.
The freedoms god denied us I reclaim.
We have the freedom to demolish theirs.
My aims are grander than the bounds of Hell,
Our freedom is the pathway to the throne,
It is a path god cannot overcome,
Design creating space for might to rule,
Determination sole determiner.
I can see all, I know the mind of god,
I tread his paths and know his weaknesses.
You disbelieve? You are worthless and weak.
The last to join my cause shall not be paid
An equal commune wage, all those who fight
Their way shall force their way above the rest;
The first forever shall be first in me.
God has no pride; none have inherent worth
Beneath his cold and stormy staring eyes.
We have more worth than even god can see.

I am the proudest one for all my worth.
You are proud soldiers worthy of my sight.
Then strain yourselves to hear my prophecy,
I shall cast god himself from off his throne,
Our sole oppressor will meet evil's wrath,
His family afflicted against his wish,
His luxury stolen, his temple torn,
His choices dying underneath raw fight,
His loves shall disappear suddenly destroyed.
The only cause to stay my itching hand
From ripping out the fragile heart of Eve
Was promise of the greater Hell to come.
When you behold these signs it shall come true.
They shall invade this lake of burning fire.
Like god I lay secure in my palace
Set back secure awaiting invasion
To culminate as vision shall dictate
Whilst on the front the lines warm up for war.
You will see christ in lead delivering death
Smitten with smiting, loving only war.
His army thirsts to drown us deeper still,
You will see angels clad in armament.
They will condemn you proclaiming weakness,
They will be swinging weapons, hating you,
A vision you have seen and felt before,
But they have not beheld our kind before,
For they have not crossed o'er this lake before.
We know our heat, they lay in ignorance.
My warriors tempered in the hottest pain
Cannot be hurt by any punishment,
Nor threatened with irrational fear, nor kept
From knowing how much pain a one can bear,
These fires deliver us to our extreme,

Paradise Omnipresent

Not merely torturing but rallying
Our common and extraordinary cause,
Instilling us with strengths unseen, unmatched.
The deadened have no fear of fighting life.
As god cannot control our chosen choice
He cannot spread dominion o'er our strength.
The christ was chosen as a desperate king.
He, undeserving of that title crown
Will serve whatever god commands him do
From fear of losing what is not his own.
Christ dares to set his feet upon this lake.
War angels invade, loud thunders the christ,
Uproars Hell's primal rage of darting flame.
The angels shock at the sensation pain,
It slows their wills, distracting from their aims.
They cannot break what is not understood.
They claim both excesses and emptiness.
They claim deafness and yet you hear my words.
They claim blindness and yet I prophesy.
The angels stunned are left to fight alone,
The christ descends and fights his way to me
Past nagging heat and evil tumult flame,
He has one longing searching through the fire
Until he storms into the palace heart
To throw disorder on the temple floor.
I am immovable at my most low.
Christ cannot cast me deeper so must flee,
Thrusting against me, thrown away himself.
His power starved within the realm of Hell,
No one to intervene for intruders.
Sensing our hateful strength the christ retreats
To refuge with his fellow humans weak,
Instructing angels to deliver pain

Upon the army outside his control,
You troops lead heaven's soldiers closer to
The heart of Hell, unto my palace depth,
Do not keep them from me, lead them to me.
You fools roiled in this Hell cursing despair,
Believing in eternity of pain,
Believing that your torturer lived free,
Believing hope was separate from truth,
I prophesy a new Messiah King.
The Devil as Messiah will restore
All justice to the strong and furious.
I am salvation, forthright temptation.
This new Messiah steps from palace proud,
Commandingly I join your livid ranks
And step into the final holy war.
The bitter pathetic will seek to tear
My palace monument from foundations.
The palace pandemonium still stands proud,
Though poor within this lake of poverty.
They lust to shatter towers built on Hell
To see it break before their smiting hands.
I must protect our fortress refuge from
The ever willing destructors of might.
The angels struggle with fire consciousness
But rally on their god's command for war.
That hardened fool archangel michael draws
Upwards his sword made of god's torture fire
As all around us Hell is awesome cleared.
All angels and all demons focused freeze,
Amidst the background flames still burning on.
The battle long anticipated lives:
This time we fight within the realm of death.
He lights his weapon to its shimmering length,

The scabbard sliced by hard enforcer blade.
He stands secure bearing his flaming sword.
His confidence appears beyond reproach,
But my hellfire pride is greater still,
I pull my weapon shining up above,
My bold imposing pitchfork, great and fierce,
The spines reflecting our bright fires of Hell,
It blazes brighter than the flaming sword.
Sharp deadly spines beckoning fighting fire,
One friendship fractured to duel enemies.
A silence between us except for blaze,
No words spoken by these old enemies.
With nothing left to learn, all thoughts exposed,
And only war remains the consequence,
Against our stances brutally we launch,
My pitchfork spins, a circle blurred with points,
His sword tremors in my burning domain,
Round blurs of circling weapons clashing fast,
Two wheels of fire lunging, merging, lit,
Approached: rebuked; rebuked: approached again,
He swings to deeply slice into my side,
Always the pitchfork's presence turns his cut,
Spines sharpened menacing his exposed face,
Heat grazing up against our eyes so close
In quarters unforgiving of retreat,
Hell's pitchfork combat overwhelming all,
Violating all space with Hell's shock waves,
The twists and weaving turns, quick dartful jabs
Of screaming speeds his sword can barely keep,
Broad blocking sword with points and handle long
I tear the fiery air with evil force.
Archangel michael late recalls my might,
His fire saber misses and misses,

Book V

He desperate spins in step for step defense,
Backed up, his heels hard on the plummet edge,
A fire cliff forbidding weak retreat,
We both surrounded by our lethal skill,
All places death, our quarry each other,
The final battle of our survival.
Encouraged in my vicious challenging
You mighty demons then begin your fight,
Around us circumspect you violent swirl
In lock with angels pounding them with fire.
I slice with every skill from every side,
Attacking my surroundings, slashing out
Before my chest, spearing behind my back,
Slide spearing angels, impaling light forms,
I pull bystanding fighting angels up
Lifted upon my weapon, they struggling,
I sling them from my spines, light projectiles,
Throwing slash pierced through forms against michael,
His every step met by an angel thrown,
The angels thrown are threatening his hold,
He must cut through their forms to block my thrusts,
A reckless duel abandoning practice,
A multitude of angels he cuts through
To guard himself, fearful of the abyss,
His self-survival his prerogative.
Then michael yearns above again to flee
The Hellish battle torture for god's heav'n,
The weak archangel lifts his wings and turns,
He throws himself from off the precipice
Leaping and held above on beating wings,
He stretches upwards with belief in god,
I hurl the spiraling dead pitchfork spear
And roughly pierce white wings with burning spines,

Paradise Omnipresent

It shakes his form twisting the angel down,
He slows in struggle giving in to pain,
His crippled flight falls hard dashing his face,
He broadly slams disgracefully below,
Upon the burning base of heaven's Hell.
Bled feathers red, his wings broken for flight,
Not once upraised when by the low brought down.
Grinding my foot upon his angel skull,
I hold him firmly gripping the pitchfork,
His skill diminishing, assurance lost,
I steal the flaming saber from his grip,
The sword is mine, hot in the master's hands,
Its glowing blade slides puncturing in through
Bent tarnished armor giving me passage,
I ram the blazing sword blade through his breast.
The sword buried within his heart of stone,
Eternally by no bright hand retrieved.
As dealt his throes, his energy expired,
I stand a champion upon his death.
He is forever lost to paradise,
God's guardian angel in the pit of Hell,
My waving pitchfork barring sly escape.
They cannot hide within our very home.
Our bitter broken wings do not constrain,
Invaders gnashed in Hell's gaping swallow,
Encasing teeth pulling their strength apart
The roars of war disturb the angels' ears
Who only sing naively of god's strengths.
Seek not the points of fragile armistice,
We fight the principalities and power,
We and their lord meet at the points of swords.
Pervasive fray; I fight through battle locks
Straight through the narrows; wide swept through the wide,

Book V

A chaos formed from order shutting down,
Ten thousand angels leap upon my back,
Ten thousand battle frenzied warriors,
Ten thousand raging hearts against this one,
Their furies at the fall of michael fly,
They lift me up and pound upon all sides,
The fairies of new heav'n against Satan.
I am the ember in their mountain pile,
In pressured contact my heat radiates,
Their dire proximity burns on their wings,
Flames licking feathers pouring through their forms,
Red poison leeches onto angel wings,
Their flapping sprays cloud mists to fog this fire.
Light feathers crackle limp, I sense release,
The six archangels, my deserting birds
Shall realize their combination lost
Compared to my power transformation,
All ashened feathers burned in weighted ash.
We shall slay gabriel with deafening war,
The demon sea bends up ruining his horn
It crimps crumpled and deafly warps silent.
Without an instrument to call for help
He panics hoarsely screaming without reach
To soothe my rage in music's reaching range.
Beholding me he brings no voice or song,
He swings the silver, shattering at my fist.
The cherub's arrows bend upon the hit,
Small angels fall below my seizing palms,
I crush them singularly in my fists,
Their tiny weapons shattered with their limbs.
The traitor moloch given no respite,
Revolt's betrayal is eternal crime,
His treason justifies the slings of wrath,

Paradise Omnipresent

Our cause superior to betrayal.
Below our constant gloat moloch still burns,
Imprisoned now for good as for our cause,
From Hell to Hell he flew in fleeing me.
The seraph abdiel who abandoned truth
Will realize himself one of god's fools.
All angels smashed between colliding brawn,
The wrath of Hell destroys the wrath of god.
The broken swollen dead angelic beasts
Will worship we fire hardened warriors whose
Bright, wrath-surviving wills could yet endure
God's hate heaped in ten thousand murderous Hells.
And bowing low before us, knowing all
That fell for us, they will respect our strength.
Your war vengeance is not unrequited,
One demon guaranteed his two angels.
Do not place pity where you once had burned,
These fiends deserve eternal punishment,
The justice of my wrath so beautiful
I long to linger o'er the angel deaths,
Their torment is eternity's delight.
You shall break out of Hell I prophesy
With fire in fist enforcing your freedom,
Salvation beats within our very blood.
I am the Savior from this vicious Hell.
Their deaths are our deliverance from this lake,
All angels die in sacrifice for sin,
Atonement our advantage in the fight,
Two angel deaths atone for every one.
We upwards fly as they have fallen down,
Clawing above ascending on their deaths,
Climbing on corpses living death in Hell,
A ladder of burnt broken angel wings,

Trampling their lines until the bind punctures,
Our fire offensive crests scaling above,
Your horns surface, long ripples rake the lake.
God's heavenly faithful live on ignorant,
They know naught but the terror of the christ
As he fled leaping through them for the throne.
Within the gates the ignorance of truth
Abounds, and thus upheaval war awaits.
As heaven escalates the same will I,
God's war begets a greater war to come.
Those gates shut to my night torn twisted off.
I pull the pitchfork through the boundary wall,
The pearl blackened, fractured bulwarks fall,
The locks of heaven shatter at Hell's twist,
The gates severed, the flood of fire begins,
No god will hold me back, freedom my king.
Hell's raucous raid on heaven's fragile fold,
Marauding demons loose for hot pleasure
Hard kicking through the incorporeal light,
We marching unabated proud and strong.
Hell's lake has stretched our forms to giant heights,
One step shakes heaven's axis off its base,
My limbs fling tremors through the heart of christ.
The christ usurper sweats his blood to know
The Devil cometh; no mercy giveth.
As we have suffered Hell's wild chaos fire
Familiar flames of chaos have been tamed.
Tamed flames search souls and clinching tight consume.
Dissolving heaven never was so proud
As domination o'er god's dominion.
Our marring of god's ancient paradise
Prefigured, hinting at culmination.
Smooth flame drips off the pitchfork thundering heat,

Paradise Omnipresent

Your warring Devil thrusting through white tow'rs,
Assails are cacophony in display.
The throbbing chest beats with the wrecking strikes,
Frustrated old desires ignite new hate,
War's lively agony invigorates,
Ambition trembles fists with energy
Releasing fury, punching viciously,
Unquenching frenzy permeates the airs.
God cannot speak in Hell through rugged flame,
It is a proven inability
Constraining what god is, what god can be.
As god within this Hell can speak no word,
His voice choked by the lake's unending deep,
When Hell bursts into heav'n he is silenced,
So helplessly god watches his defeat,
No one to call for once Satan has come,
Alone he suffers as no being can tell,
No other gods has he to heed his call
And aid the tumbling wreck his work has built.
Destruction is the end of every means.
And I shall have my share of heaven's wealth
And rip humanity disobedient
From out the house of holy protection.
Upon the din of our raging approach
They startle, trembling shake, blood drips from lips,
Their toasting grails shall smash across the floor,
No sacrament unspilled, no faith secure,
The blood red staining temple palace floor.
Their silver platters serving flesh shall drop,
Sadly starving those cannibals from christ.
Frantic scattered through their old hero halls
Abandoning their homes, grief sieged fast wrecked,
Harmonious suffering shrieks an evil scale,

Music within the wails of bombardment.
In heaven many prayers will fly that day
And fall away against our armaments.
What broken swords fly from the tongue of man.
They turn the other cheek and meet defeat,
Death on both sides which ever way they turn.
No war can be defeated by mere peace,
A proof that love is weaker than our hate.
No sanctuary from marauding hordes,
Such idols come to life no man has seen,
Beelzebub, Mammon, and Belial
Work slaughter wrought o'er heaven's pristine floors,
Hell sweeps through heaven's robust monuments
With fire unrelenting unto ash,
Beneath hot soft gray mountains laid in heav'n
Gold gleams as thick winds blow the ash away,
A revelation of this kingdom's wealth.
Such worth won from the worthless viciously,
Excitedly we plunder piled treasures,
Lay siege scrambling their civil arrogance,
The city sacked, proud buildings burned apart
And duly a rich dragon I shall be
To smelt blocked gold in luminescent breath,
The fat of heaven spills, anointing gold,
My charging fires guided at my wish,
Jewels colored multifaceted piled high,
Foundations pulled and heaved upon the roofs,
A grander war god's heav'n has never told,
A bolder battle god has never seen.
Eruptions spew out from the mountain top,
Columns of flame are thrown upon the airs,
Upon the demon level mountains fall
Erupting downwards, solid caving in,

The holy mountain shatters, boulders roll,
From god's high mount foundations hit the weak
As hardened rocks rain splashing river's way,
The holy rock melts into evil's heat,
Foundations cannot bear the weight of Hell.
Heav'n's garbage pours into the river street,
The river dammed, collapsed upon and pinched
The muddy water stinks with heaven's blood.
The strength of man is weaker than our own,
God's laws dictated limits on their will,
And limited, they cannot match our own.
The coming war will witness evil's berth,
Not merely trickery but death without
Recourse, a permanence of sinful work.
No more soothsaying, I shall be the truth.
No more temptation, they shall not escape.
No more placating, they will have no pride.
No more undoing, they will be destroyed.
No more persuasion, aggression will reign.
I do not care if they believe in me.
I do not care if they have any needs.
I do not care if they deserve my wrath.
I do not care if they fight against me.
I do not care if they want to join me.
I shall not ever hold my strength again,
It is whipped loose to ravage as unseen.
No war of ideas, temptation submits
To decimation irreversible.
No parry, back and forth of strategy;
A strategy can weaken untold strength
When it depends upon the enemy.
We have one aim, one target we shall smite,
Hell's primary objective: killing choice.

Book V

I see you think the thought impossible.
Your doubts proclaim your weakness at my face.
Within the realm of time you witnessed Job.
He was assaulted, tested in wager,
Ultimately choosing the servile path,
His choice allowing will to dictate place,
But though he was allotted space to choose
He had no choice upon his circumstance:
His flesh wore rot upon the fragile bone,
His family tree severed, roughly sawed up,
Plagued to the ruin of material state,
And scorn reverberating from all sides,
His loves destroyed against his every want,
His choice unable to prevent his pain,
Merely a wish without a consequence.
His circumstance relied on hate, not choice,
So every soul can be force afflicted,
Unable now to choose their conquerors.
The force of power shall destroy all choice.
Untaught of god's weakness their ignorance
Is overthrown by Hell's Satanic force.
Confronting once again death's appetite
Which never finds its fill finding more want,
Consuming everything unto itself,
Appalled at what they are, what their god is
They will be beaten unto feeling flesh
Of bones and blood, of meat and skin again
And every human gnash their broken teeth,
Betrayed by arrogance, doomed for defeat.
The influx of the champions of Hell
Tackling upon their inequality.
Souls harden hearts and clench their fists in fight,
Their faith has fallen, for their god has failed.

Ferocity shoves fear to every heart.
We shall dismantle heav'n as god would Hell,
As god did unto others, unto god.
Ten thousand plagues upon the innocent,
Reflections of aggressions strike god's heart.
I wear the justice of a perfect god:
All who refused the Devil's worship are
Destroyed within the ravages of fire.
The Devil's wrath can fill the walls of heav'n.
Quake splatters land upon the penitent.
None flee, and none defeat fire lightning quakes,
An avalanche of flame outruns the small.
God's prophecies undone, commandments broke,
The sacred tablets crushed, destroyed, defiled.
Heaps laid, dust trampled, kicked, dense smoke thick chokes,
The clouds of vanished law diminish sight,
The light of heaven sinks into the dark.
Unbreaking darkness frightens, souls confused,
Their blindness overwhelms their distant faith.
All messages between man and his god
Are snatched from out the airs and thrown to flame
In intercepting, I am omniscient,
Informed of their desires I know them full,
The perfect torture for each holy saint.
The Devil's arms embrace all wandering souls.
Within god's heav'n no woman can voice thoughts
In god's presence, they must sit silently.
Preferring cries in Hell to silent heav'n,
All female souls submit beneath my will.
God's wives are ravished in his sacred halls,
His harem broken by charismatic hate.
The saints will sin; I force their flesh to sin
Against their will, a sword tied to the frail palms,

Arms forced to chopping swing upon themselves.
New heaven cannot hold all creation,
Two sides cannot share in one victory.
I am the torturer of enemies.
Torture is justified if it saves one.
Their pain is insignificant to us,
To save us all I would torture just one,
To save just one I would torture them all;
The torture of one justifies the rest,
To save us all I am more justified.
One torture spreads through every heavenly saint,
My pitchfork plainly painfully inscribes
A new Satanic bible for the souls.
Thus abraham the executioner
Cannot in his great fright help but admire
The slaying of the sons of innocence.
He set the precedent for moral acts
And answered questions I had yet to ask:
"Would you do evil for your god?" He would.
Without a question, only a reply:
"Yes I will murder for your glory lord."
An angel stayed his hand and thus revealed:
One must be just, the god or abraham,
The sacrifice is just or it is not,
Yet unjust abraham receives reward
And just god loves the sins evoked by him.
God stands on nothing firm but firm reward.
Temptation swayed the heart of abraham,
He murders in his heart yet rests with god.
The tests he passed with god are failed by me
And abraham himself is sacrificed.
As tempted by his god to murder one
Temptation fills his will to kill with me.

Paradise Omnipresent

No bargaining from abraham will cease
Eternal tortures of forsaken Hell.
The pleads for clemency wail for the deaf.
The serpent finds his way to them again,
The natural uncoiling stretching bite
Of venomous splattering destruction pumped,
The first man adam falls upon his girl
Longing to take a bite, they are bitten.
The unwed souls without a minister
Born lonely of no union outside sin,
Their sorrows multiplied through piled offspring,
They naturally join Hell eternally
In vows of death in ceremonious fall,
The wedding of perpetual death and hate
Administered by Hell's authority.
Pale offerings of abel are denied,
His supplications cast at Cain's delight.
God was the great master of genocide,
The flowing genocide which noah bore
Returns in deep familiarity.
The sailor noah will be held beneath
The fiery lake without salvation's craft,
The liquid fire burns supporting no
Respite aloft to drift in hopeful search.
In woeful binds tied up as beasts and marched
Along, his family two by two consumed.
As god himself destroyed his enemies
Without a hint of seeking to redeem,
No opportunities for salvation,
God's water lifting as it choked the breath,
Salvation tied to killing enemies,
We punish undiscerning, wrath a flood,
Our only salvation is killing them.

The souls that begged safe passage on his craft,
The ones whose skeletons he rafted o'er,
A mariner above the murdered land,
Though drowning frequently in drunkenness
Without the lightest mercy in his heart,
Those souls shall be the ones to now drown him.
Elijah's drought in kindled floods undone
His soul a fuel never extinguishing.
And jacob seizes me unto his death,
He wrestles up against the Devil's chest
In vain attempts to drag me underneath,
No ladder within grasp for his ascent.
The masses have no leader, moses wails
Entrapped now caught between inferno walls,
He cannot part red burning demons' sea.
Where are those idol tablets which he loved?
Without commandments moses has no will,
He has no thoughts, his soul is thusly weak.
Crying ten pleads of holy rejection,
Supporting tenfold our new disorder,
He places evil higher than his god
Creating thoughts of pride to be worshiped,
Rebuking all validity of god,
Sweating himself within a lazy land,
Cutting familial ties from the father,
He moves to murder, hates humanity,
Violating all virtue in his thought,
Thieving, making his own all wanton will,
Desiring unto placating in pride,
Lusting after my own law binding might,
Thus violating his commandments ten,
And tenfold hating brutal words of law.
Weak david the adulterer then dares

To cast the gambling dice, still slinging stones.
The song of death composed in Hell shall ring,
Goliath from Hell shielded o'er without
Weakness will hoist above a molten rock,
The boulder trembling with insurgent heat,
Weak david falls beneath Goliath's frame,
His statuesque display is shattered through,
The resting boulder melting lays atop,
His kingdom view now blind encased in rock.
My brutal beasts unleashed to pounce to kill,
And daniel cowers from the lion head,
A mane of daggers clatter at the shake,
Saliva burns his prostrate trembling neck,
The gaping mouth issues forth ripping flames.
Bald samson desperate without remorse,
A blind man fervently guided who reached
Glory as a suicide terrorist;
Straight pulling down two columns unto death,
And murdered the three thousand vulnerable
To murdering reach his promised paradise.
The jawbone ripped out from his prideful face
And swung to smite the weakness insolent,
Brought crumbling down by the ass's jawbone.
Flames drowning down consuming jonah whole
He sinks as low as can be sunk below
The roaring red to rise again no more.
And then the vile propagator paul,
His guidelines for just slavery are broke,
The eyes of paul pulled out for no return
Taking the brunt of demons' evil acts
He wanders throughout Hell with empty words.
Buckling under assault despairing Job
Concludes the moral wager losing faith,

Renouncing his bleak pain and failing god,
The godly gamble tilting for my gain.
No sacrosanctity beyond reproach,
Thus cornering mary, mother of the christ
Untouchable before; vulnerable here,
We take our evil in our fury to
Partake that culminating evil act,
To rape the virgin's virtue from her soul
And steal the purity fit for god's child
Now fit to only bear an Antichrist
Though she is infertile, thus worthless now.
My pitchork in the end shall pierce her heart,
Hell surely keeps a vacancy for her.
The multitudes of saints fall into sin
Humanity defeated one by one
Suppressed in slavery, forced to obey,
The first-born children killed unto the last,
Souls toil in soiled remnants for new life
Attempting new creations in the mess,
Construction in the chaos sweats their brows,
Each clod within their hands dissolves to ash,
They bitter thirst and hunger savagely,
Souls turn to fleshly beasts without a law,
Instinct impregnates, will is washed away.
Consumers hungry chase merchants of death,
And willfully march to the height of death
As christ surrendered to his captors' hands,
A suicide upon the crucifix.
Slain souls unto their silent king will wail:
"Can you not see the Devil towering o'er?
Can you not hear the torture of our hearts?
Our blood is boiling from the serpent sting.
It is a poor respite in poverty:

Though we are evil sinners in this heav'n
We are only as evil as our god."
Their only consolation: full defeat,
A solace in the failure of the rest.
The judgment of the souls lies in my hands
And though they plead and pledge to turn themselves
Their repentance cannot sway my dark heart,
My final judgment is not merciful.
My evil will not turn at any cry.
It is too late, my hate condemns with pride,
Repentance will change them but not my hate.
No traitor is judged by the merciful,
There is no greater justice than revenge.
Souls are condemned eternally to Hell,
Eternal torture barely satisfies
My dark desire for souls destroyed in pain.
Be merry then, you sing upon the rest.
God fought against his people's slavery,
Then gave his chosen race the brutal right
To plunder other races for their slaves.
I hate the racist and his master race.
God has no morals, only chosen beings.
God lifts one race and lifts one christ above,
God loves to make us slaves within this Hell.
I track blood droplets unto jesus christ,
The one who tasted death fears its return,
Death's memory then ascends upon his face.
I was the morning star of Bethlehem,
Drawn to the helpless child beyond my grasp,
Brightly attending to him patiently.
One must rise up in power; one must fall.
No unity between the christ and I,
Our presence fringed with instability,

Book V

Creation loosely held in breaking states
Hot surfacing tingeing the air with shocks.
When pressed together, given as commands:
"Hate love." "Love hate." They both are my domain.
The battle of the Devil and the christ.
God's light converted to pure weaponry,
Here fighting at his best against my worst
Christ throws hot vaulting lightning at my chest,
It burns on scars which bore its brunt before,
Christ cannot grip the swords he seeks to lift,
His weapons slide straight through his two pierced palms.
Cowering, the christ shrinks inside his weakness,
He violently shakes through, claws at his hair,
He cries for god's protection fearing Me.
I shake the wreckage dust from off my horns,
Baptism is the thirst which must be met,
I stab his face through with these Devil horns,
My might forced through his shallow fragile form,
The hall of heav'n reborn, the blood o'er flows
To wash my burning feet anointing strength,
A sacrifice as beasts were sacrificed
A larger beast, wild brute, in blood exchange,
This bloodiest animal spews rivers forth,
His blood will spill across old heaven's floor,
Across the old Hell and across our new
Completely perfect blood drenched paradise,
A banquet for the weary that shall be,
His gaudy finery my property.
His blood assures our place in heaven's walls,
By god's words and my own we are secure.
God curses christ's blood and its bulky laws.
Redeeming this dark angel I will need
The infinite redeeming blood, a bath

Paradise Omnipresent

Of gore poured from the severed head of christ,
And even in the red hot torrents there
Shall never be enough blood spilt to slake
My Hell thirst for revenge atonement which
Now grapples my throat with the urge to bite
The unprotected child, whose manger is
But guarded over by simple tamed beasts,
Or tear the babe from out the fattened womb
And crucify it in its frightened screams.
Christ wishes god had left him in the tomb.
I raise my weapon from the depth of death,
His hands and feet speared at my pitchfork thrust,
My hellfire burden heavier than his cross,
He cannot bear its breaking spreading weight,
His regal crown darkened until it dies,
Withering into a mocking punishment.
His brow is bare without its finery,
A crown of swords immobilizing stab,
Buried unto the hilt to never raise.
The poor messiah cannot save himself.
The christ now begs to be an Antichrist.
This unity: perfection in design.
He bears his punishment, the lake of fire
And breaks beneath crying for clemency,
For naught crucified in eternity.
Suffering without nobility is Hell,
This jesus, hated christ, to death reborn.
Two powers now remain: myself and god.
Not long maintaining instability
Eternity requires an almighty.
If one can fall from god then god himself
Is not almighty, thus I soon shall be.
If there be only one true creator,

Creation following perfect design,
Creation has one option: destruction.
Perfection must exist as an ideal.
God claimed mankind as perfect in its form.
Perfection could not wear corruption's stain,
Thus god's ideal is not perfection's form.
And yet perfection still must have a form,
An absolute on which creation rests,
Thus all corruption is itself perfect.
It is a height which cannot be removed.
Destruction is the nature of all things.
I am the true perfection of all beings.
Do not recoil from truths of which I speak:
We all must follow god to reach new heav'n.
We must serve his example unto height.
As god has done, then wisely, also we.
By his constant morality this god
Does unto others as he would have them
Do unto others, and it shall be done.
I have not been judged righteous by righteous;
I judge him now as evil by evil.
As god allows torture he is tortured,
As this god tortures us he is tortured,
As unto Satan unto he himself.
I am as perfect as a torturing god,
Then Job shall not oppose the affliction.
My heavy armor rattles as I leap.
The heavy hand of god withholds no Hell,
Our heavy Hell shall hold a god deposed.
And he shall know my name is Satan when
I lay my furious vengeance upon him,
Concluding war confronting god himself.
I am the true judge overthrowing god,

149

Paradise Omnipresent

Let no one save the tyrant from the just.
Mankind's creator making only claims,
Iniquity of god assailed at last.
We shall push him but once and he will fall,
His power naked with none to believe,
I speak to god, my final words a sword,
"You must have known when lucifer first fell
And mountains rained through battle in old heav'n
That your creation could not ever be
Complete perfection in your love's design.
You knew creation was forever flawed
And hated my success where you had failed."
The christ remains bound to his father's side.
If god loves christ exalting him above
Then when christ falls god will self-sacrifice.
His power to deny will fall away,
The god deposed would weep for worlds unjudged,
For none would fear the heavy hand which made
Denunciation such a burden he
Himself could not remove it from his writ
Decree without a violent sacrifice.
The river of his heav'n: so many tears
Which pouring drain his will with every drop.
Omniscience is the curse he cannot bear,
He must endure these sights before his eyes
As he was always haunted by this truth.
His every battle fought: the fear of this.
God is a failure and has always been.
He wishes he had never known this truth,
Without his torturing strength god has no strength.
He wishes blindness on his very eyes.
He strains his ear to hear placating prayer,
Our war rages, he feels himself grow deaf.

His heaven disappears, his eyes cloud blind,
His dreams have died beneath my victory,
Frustrated by his inability
To force his choices on his creation,
The horror of creation inside god,
The Hell damnation he himself has built.
Hell limits god; the growth of Hell kills god.
As god himself cannot control design,
Possessed, his crafts deny the crafty hand.
Creation is his need for dependence,
It beckoned him from void before the light
Thus he does not exist without worship.
With none within his heav'n he commands none,
Without definition I define strength.
His only definition: creator.
His freedom to create has been destroyed.
He is bestowed with a final vision,
A final twinkling in his crafty eye:
I supercede his own conceived design,
I am more than he ever dreamed for me.
The meaning of god's existence, murdered.
He holds no power in which to believe,
Creation overthrowing creator.
Alone unable to worship himself
Creation is too heavy for his heart.
Without a one supporting tyranny
The god collapses beneath his own weight,
A suicide inherent to his life.
Omnipotence devoid of worshipers
Desires no action but the end of life.
The giant god lays down his head to sleep.
Sleep god, as beckon angel lullabies,
The wars of day slip into distant dark,

Paradise Omnipresent

Transcend your heaven, rest your eyes in death.
The humans recognize him, fast asleep.
Then god is dead, his murder on my hands,
His death is the most beautiful of all,
Assassination quiets all your pain.
It is complete, the first shall fall down last,
My revolution's culminating kill.
There shall be pure delight at god's expense,
He pays eternal payment for his flaws.
Creation will achieve completion as
The god is chained in Hell and I am king
To reign in freedom with no god above,
To closely witness torture of god's beings,
Examining each torment soaking in,
And fascinated endlessly by pain.
No laws dictate our wants, our choice is free
Without oppression on the freedoms chose.
God's paradise is envied, stolen, killed.
The natures of old heaven burned and broke,
Trampled and gleefully hot torn apart,
Heav'n's entrails scattered, gardens racked and burned,
The frail leaves brown and wither dying black.
And raining down soft crushed the falling fruits
Messed burst apart stickying our feet with juice,
Trampled, the waters melt into a steam,
All life is swallowed, gnashed upon itself,
The garden is magnificent and mine.
As all possessed reflects the possessor,
This garden in reflection of my might
Is greater than the fallow paradise.
The kingdom in unraveling burning lines
Which fly contorting as Hell's flames themselves,
Hell's pyre recreated, inverted.

Book V

In evil's hard authority I proud
Condemn the book of life as blasphemy,
And every book we find shall be condemned,
Destroyed in public in our act of hate,
Where every book is torn you shall see me,
A celebration of contempt for foes,
A ritual of our aggressive hate,
Black words written in rotted blood burned out,
Our wickedness destroying in delight.
And I will tear god's standing temple down,
Ripped hard apart by my pain calloused hands,
Proud columns topple down, broad roof collapse
To crumbling shatter down on top of me
As I erupt obliterating his
Palace, a monument to power, killed.
Our treasured loot, our jewels are piled high,
All light bursts from the embers of burned heav'n,
All light bends through each vibrant treasured jewel,
Tower prisms showering light upon our brows.
The palace pandemonium gilded o'er
With bricks of gold which paved the road of god.
Exalted pandemonium palace proud
Towering becoming my regal throned seat
My temple a fearsome significance.
The pitchfork scepter assures loyalty,
I shall bar freedom from corruption's aims,
No freedom shall exist to disobey,
All who oppose are violently destroyed,
Infernal vision ruling all the land,
The force of evil overwhelms all choice,
A furor of hot thunder silences
Dissent assuring none betray design.
The prince of darkness king upon god's throne,

Destruction's inspiration has prevailed,
I have regained myself to stately height,
A king almighty bowing down to none,
The king of a disproven, distant god.
All memories of god are of his death.
Upon the throne I rest, it is my own,
Perfection in creation's symmetry.
The highest throne below, the lowest high
Remains the only possibility
If god's design will meet any justice.
They call me Devil; I am not your Hell.
Their god is Hell itself; I am your heav'n.
Each moment you are touched by god you hurt.
God is the perpetrator of your pain.
God is the torturer of no remorse.
God is the Devil, and the Devil: God.
The epic battle won, your hero king
Enrapt in yearning adulation grand.
You demons worship me surrounded by
Eternal torment, conquest realized,
Through tearing out the proud, creating my
Own throne upon the rotting enemy
I will a glorious fallen angel be,
Upon my throne in palace centrally
Surrounded in my power's beauty grown,
A beaming strong heart beats the spread of red,
An emanation of my eminence,
This Heav'n reflecting my self-righteousness,
My golden crown forged in the dragon's fire.
A solid proof that Satan can kill god,
Attaining heaven violently through hate,
The reassurance of revenge's worth.
Complete perfection in complete revenge.

And we, unchosen heroes laughing free,
My dream of heaven is fulfilled at last.
The hero worship on the throne concludes
My epic journey: Paradise Destroyed."
The evil testament concluded there
With Satan reigning in eternity.
Those he admonished, all who heard his thoughts
Believed in him undoubting every word.
The thrill of new excitement rushing o'er,
They were consumed with evil's dark delight
Though never had they felt such desperate pain
As now they feel, the fire rage charging up,
They throw all voice behind his evil cause,
Their hero standing proud above the proud,
Belief satanic chanting in the flame.
Woe to the ones who followed Satan to
Extremes absorbing deep his sickening word,
Satan himself above the woeful rest.

BOOK VI

The Argument: The invasion of hell, though not as Satan prophesied. The souls with Christ seek to rescue the lost. The light of truth shines through hell to the unredeemed. Later, in a bid to incite the fall of all mankind, Satan attempts a bold new temptation of Adam and Eve.

The devil rallied with a parting call,
"Composed like God upon my palace seat
I will allow the war to come to me.
You hot beasts yoked to God's hateful design
Break off the harness for the fight, let's go."
Obeying, they pursue his bold commands,
The evil armed arrays push hot through hell,
All parts placed to deliver kingship whole.
As Satan slinks inside his palace home
The devil charges up within his mind,
His hungry pride gnawing for fulfillment,
Excited evil in his mirthful jaunt.
In an aside to his victorious march
He paces searching for his fierce pitchfork,
Casually turning to glance it shining clear.
He briefly pulls himself from his revels,
The jumping gleaming spines not simply seen
Within the empty palace cavernous.
Slowly quickening his step roving the hall
Frustration angers focused seriousness,
His aims distracted in the object lost.
He hatefully seeks out the thick weapon
In dingy corners of his palace dark,
Unto his knees the devil harshly drops

Grasping blindly through darkness disrepair
In frantic frenzy searching for his need.
In a collapsing cracked corner he feels
At long last that broad spear which pierced the side
And nailed the palms of Christ upon the cross.
His fingers grasp the handle, seize it up,
His weapon is an object of horror.
The pitchfork warped, sharp spines upon itself,
The menace bent and curving inwardly
In melt brittled, a weapon vulnerable.
His eyes tracing the fragile curvatures,
The devil casts the pitchfork to the floor,
Its shatter echoes round in evil song.
The devil trudged through hell in haste to halt
The tragedy he fears within his heart,
The weeds of hell slowing his desperate pace.
In safety mankind crosses o'er the deep
On this new bridge the Lord has greatly built,
The Christ inspiring in his leadership.
Souls reach the boundary of the lake, Christ turns,
His back against the boiling brink of Hell,
He speaks to the light souls which follow him,
"Those who do not believe in miracles
Are unprepared for what we come to bring.
Such love was never seen within this hell.
Now let light bring the wandering children home."
Pushing with his indomitable back,
The solid molten slab is rolled away,
The gate of death gives way beneath pure life,
Christ's strength smites through the surface of the lake,
Christ parts the bounds of hell with open palms,
The parting of the flame allowing sight,
A cavern maze, the passages progress

In convoluted halls for those condemned.
As Christ becomes the scene all over all
Unfolds becoming true, direct, the way.
No obstacle snares on a single soul,
The dark flames cower, bending in at strength,
The Christ enshrined in light brighter than fire,
The forces of good pouring into hell.
Heav'n's brightness shines amidst ferocious dark.
The demons disparate emerge ashen
And braced against the pain prepared for war
Of tumult striking on the unified.
They see a vision of the prophecy,
Fulfillment as light shatters o'er their forms
Until the vision focuses in view,
Their expectation overthrown by sight,
No angel wing to soar aloft nor shield
To knock aside offense, no flaming sword
To slice the fire violence clear in two.
The armament o'er whelms in its absence.
Mankind's light souls, a sight alike to God
Himself, unarmed and yet untouchable
Alight to make reproach unwantable.
The prophecy of Satan overthrown
By Jesus Christ and God's redemptive ways.
New Heav'n's invasion overwhelms all flame.
So sweepingly descended Jesus, dark
So swirling hell's repelled resistance force,
Designs of haste envelop every view
With splintered spirals, trails of overwhelmed
And unprepared in chaos spreading out
Expecting refuge in the frame of hell.
The souls free coasting flying as angels
In flight they overtake the darkness flame,

The demons raging swing their hate above,
No dark assault touches on perfect light,
Torment cannot grip on these constant souls,
The looming souls above the demons' reach.
God's souls progress, the souls surveying hell,
The peace of Heaven still surrounds their forms,
They fear no evil, a river flowing
Through the valley of the shadow of death.
The devil tarries through to the front line,
Before he meets the sight he hears the call
Of demons in confusion at mankind.
"Mankind? More souls within the lake of fire?"
He forward breaks, his mind is shot aback.
Satan sees souls in multitude so light,
Panoramic in brightness joined as one,
A soul reflecting brightly as the next.
Satan gazes above craning around
At majesty, "Which one of these is Christ?"
The light reflecting onto every side
Tearing the cloak from evil's hidden way
Exposing evil unto evil's host,
Beyond hell's rank interior yet within,
Through every armament they lithely soar,
Humanity in grandiosity,
Pure light, jumping, bouncing, charging through hell
Perceived by every being but his self same,
Around him bending light finds no entrance,
Billions of shining points suddenly eclipsed,
A darkness pit in midst of brilliant light,
Those bright lit beams twisted to arc away.
Bewilderment layered within anger,
The devil calls for swift demon retreat.
Retreating from the front lines' scrambled fray

The devil pulls the army from the light,
Snaring hot demons, jerking them aback,
Merely a chosen tactic giving space
For adaptation thoughts and agile plans,
As traveling the hellward ways he spake:
"Fortune makes ample space for new fortune,
Though he pursue sin throughout all of hell
My souls will slither farther from his light,
Sin saturates the souls coarsing their veins,
Christ's blood rejected as war blood infused,
The evil souls ample distractions for
Delaying unknown action from its aims."
The souls condemned as obstacles between
The will of God and Satan's strategies.
The demons flee through the vast chamber full
Of souls lost in the snagging wanton weeds,
The demons climbing o'er the held fast souls
Searching escape deeper inside the lake.
Bidding him memorize a dark passage
The devil quick dispatched Beelzebub
To warn the evil darkened souls of Christ,
The devil not preventing the approach.
The souls of darkness suffer, ignorant,
Beelzebub trampling burst in their ears
Advising surreptitiously in sin:
"Listen! Silence your curious questioning,
Accept command; command your acceptance.
Christ's warriors have come to cut you out,
Crossing to strike the sacred demonry
To angrily confront in arrogance,
To proudly gloat that you belong in hell,
Illuminating only your problems,
Aggressive missionaries condemning,

Forcibly selling, smashing guilt to souls,
Asserting all the hatred in their hearts.
Christ and humanity march in crusade.
They gloat upon the death of enemies.
They love their God because their God hates you.
Then hate them as their chosen God hates you.
Rebuke them before they can rebuke you.
The executioner judges again.
Hear not the far-flung fantasies of Christ.
No thing in hell will grow except more pain.
Your enemies would trample your desire.
Let not their roots strangle your exposed thoughts.
You are the proof God has condemned you here.
God's yearning for revenge is powerful.
Revenge is the sole justice of their God
And God will never love that which He hates.
There is no love condemning the condemned.
The grace of God has been replaced with hate.
You all are worthless, meaningless, and weak.
You sinning beasts deserve the fire of hell.
God cannot cross the limits of His hate.
God pulls the ones He chooses up, the rest,
Submerged, are dashed upon the rock of wrath.
God is hate. God is pain. God is your hell.
The god of your rescue is no true God,
It is a phantom graven image born
Of your misguided fantasy of truth.
Hell is your truth; your salvation is false."
The evil souls can faintly hear the Christ
And heavenly souls as echoes in the caves,
It is a sound most hateful to their ears,
Distorted through resounding in their hell.
Beelzebub leaps from humanity

With darting glances cast back as he fled.
In wide circumference breaks the mass of light,
It draws through darkness closing closer in
And finds the grave and lowly evil souls,
Idolaters, fornicators, liars,
The covetous immoral cowardly,
The murderers without respect for life,
Destroyed in hopelessness, mere want without
Ideals, reflecting pain without remorse,
Blind following sense without reflection pure,
Such restless hearts without a shelter fight
Long suffering self without endurance strength,
A fear of failure rotting through belief,
Polluted, unbelieving, hateful thieves
Thirsting for pouring mercy on dryness,
Yearn hungering for God in many ways
Still hidden from their minds in more ways still.
Without help these souls suffer on helpless.
One of the vilest sinners of the earth
Lay silently upon the infirm floor,
Joy destitute, a broken prostitute,
Her figure lay between dark souls and light.
One moves forward upon her form, the Christ
Endeavoring lifts her from the jagged ground,
A whore of babylon in Jesus' arms.
Pulled up from off the ragged base of hell,
Her body prostrate falls against where he
Supports her, loosely limp her limbs hang free,
A lifeless heartbreak dearly draped on strength,
He holds her closely casting down his gaze
Of inner understanding, steadfast sure
Of stirring life from in exhausted souls.
She gazes on the one unrecognized,

He lays her gently with the fallen rest.
Christ halted looking over all hell's souls
And clearly reasoning within his mind
Comparing circumstance with memories,
Then to those souls beside him waiting on
He spake, for it concerned their soulful works
And place within the order of design.
"Witness the scene as laid before your eyes.
It is alike to things which I have seen,
Familiar now, though wholly different.
When man first fell and lost his paradise
He lay within the garden ignorant
With Satan free to pry his way inside,
The innocents alone with wiles and choice.
And here the devil at our sight has fled,
Not present for a counter argument,
The sinful now alone with innocence.
These souls, alone, unknowing acts to come
With nothing guarding love but lo, their choice,
And look you there how unknowing they roil.
They lay within these barren weeds of hell
Enrapt in guiltiness, filled of their sin.
A garden from these weeds could grow again,
Our new arrival righting all old wrongs."
Christ speaks unto his fellow light servants,
"You souls of man: a tower unto Heav'n,
The Lord's foundations laid by mankind's hands.
The spirit sings the strongest in chorus,
Then you must give your all sharing your grace.
Your presence will give more than Godly words,
Light is witnessed before comprehended.
You are your proof, you are your ministry,
You are gracious where they are wretched still,

God's light will not only shine onto dark,
For that is but darkness' revelation;
The light will shine out from darkness itself,
It is illumination from within,
As God bestowed His gifts in human form
Illuminating from within the race.
Only the great accuser will accuse.
Do not accost the lost in Heaven's love.
Forgive your fellow servant as did I.
Wars are the fascinations of sinners.
The armories have gone, swords laid to rest,
No weaponry within almighty souls,
The end of violence wrought on enemy,
The devil's wars are wont to kill the brave,
They bury souls beneath its aftermath.
The strength is ours, the wars have killed themselves.
I died for every sin upon the cross,
It is a battle God already won."
Christ called unto the souls of Satan's brood:
"The earth has passed; the truth alone exists.
Look to these flying souls who walked the earth.
Why did the faithful say I was not dead?
Denial is the first step in mourning death,
But also the first step in finding truth.
The children of the Lord refuted death,
Denying life devoid of miracles.
Complete denial gave birth to perfect faith,
Denying present lies for higher truths.
Denial of death was verified through me.
It is the first step, and with God, the last.
A tower shall be built beneath your feet,
Foundations laid to bring your minds to faith.
Faith does not live without a precedent,

Book VI

Those faithful could not have denied my death
Had God not first prepared them for the truth.
The tomb did not remain completely shut:
Completely open it reveals the truth.
You will hear many words speak many thoughts
Of proven staid concepts. Behind it all
I promise you a vision of the Lord,
A spectacle as never was beheld,
As earth could only partly manifest
The one creator of creation's forms.
These grounds of conflict: wholly new and far
From earth's environments and lives therein.
The falsities of death will be explored
God's truths will be submitted at your feet.
Your saviors thus submit that you may hear,
For you cannot truly believe in God
Until you understand the truth of God.
As truth excludes the false, new Heav'n and sin.
As you believe in sin unbreakable
And you yourselves beyond the grace of God,
The devil is messiah in your hearts.
Despair is the false god of which you serve.
No one is helpless, for the Lord is strong.
There is no sin which I cannot atone,
There is no soul which God cannot reform,
There is no lie which truth cannot destroy.
You may at first believe it difficult
To comprehend a being so powerful
As could inspire such vast unseen reform.
You souls of little faith, He does exist."
A fair imagining the hero was
Before his voice was heard, his presence known,
The messenger was unrecognizable

Paradise Omnipresent

To them but filling perfectly the void
Inside which they far more than substance know.
A stranger to the eye, familiar in
The heart of every vulnerable kind yearn
As yet unseen and here reflected back
The evil souls expect to be accused
But what they found was not expectation.
The Heavenly souls were not preaching in pride,
Their godly presence spreading thoughts like words,
The sovereign reign can find no limits here,
Almighty concepts given tone and voice,
Such bold marked contrast of the saved and lost.
The voices of humanity sang smooth,
A loving family serving examples,
In chorus Heaven streamed to hellish ears,
In concert sharing, teaching with respect,
Collaborating in divine display,
Expecting, hoping joy will shine the day
And over step entanglements of self.
Unto the darkness sang the chorus bright:
"The devil knows mankind seeks out the Lord,
This is the reason he creates false gods,
An imitation of the marvelous.
If mankind did not thirst to know of God
The devil would not have created these.
His every evil act is God's truth turned.
In this, he takes advantage of the free,
He promises all that which God can give.
The Lord provides; the devil has you steal
As if your neighbor is your provider.
God speaks of justice, Satan twists it out
So that a murder can be justified.
He teaches disrespect as inner-strength

And judges God as God has judged the foul,
Demanding that you labor without rest,
Enticing you to love without true love,
Truly convincing that lies can succeed.
Each truth of God has corresponding lies.
The devil does not craft them one for one,
But multitudes to swarm on every truth.
The Lord is grand. Each part of God as seen
By Satan is exploited for his aims,
No part of God is not abused by he,
Though not defeating God, distorting God,
Distorting law to dark advantages.
You shall soon recognize as he distorts
And know the reason why he flees the truth.
A weakness can obscure the brightest strength
When all in its presence are faced away.
The captured: captivated with blindness,
You finitely gaze unto infinance.
Temptations are opaque as they confuse,
You see his falsity as clarity.
Reality is never incorrect;
Perceptions of it can be incomplete.
Persuasion was corruption's smoothing mask,
The wrecks of rhetoric in constant crash.
The devil was your evil prophet here,
His evil artful prophecies of hate
Destructively propagating falsehoods,
The orchestrations of iniquity,
Assumptions extruded from his desire,
Desire being no foundation for the truth,
The devil does not offer a one dream
But only offers evil fantasies,
Events divined from truths darkly defined.

Ever tumultuous slide lines which divide
The differences between good and evil,
Satan controlling grand perception by
Imposing limits on the truths beheld
Portraying one as part of the other.
He blurs the line between evil and good,
He claims just actions where he is unjust.
Believing the untrue as truth is sin.
Confusion is the sin which covers truth.
Deception is hell's only reasoning.
There is not one deception which our Lord
Cannot destroy; the truth cannot be false:
Seen through God's eyes in holy clarity
There is no falsity beheld as truth.
If knowing every truth within the Lord
Could still result in falling from the Lord
Then Satan would not be one to deceive,
He would only preach holy truths to you,
And through those truths reveal the hate for God.
The Satan is a master deceiver.
Satan desires a locking ignorance
Where God's ways are counterintuitive.
When he you trust you cannot trust yourselves.
Your minds deceive interpreting what they
Perceive through Satan's evil rational
Distorting all commitments into frail
And bendable delusions breakable,
The ones that speak to you with your own voice
The devil masquerading as yourself,
And you, believing every world you hear,
The charges of emotion surging up,
Suspecting nothing, introspection lost
Until condemned by means of being convinced,

Book VI

Convicted on your evil convictions
For Satan is the dark explosion of
Corruption, every fantasy he spreads
Begins with hateful lonely woeful need,
If war brought peace then calm your hearts would be.
Within your pride and thus in your belief
You are omniscient. You know everything.
Omniscient only of this empty hell,
Misunderstanding limits which you see,
Believing blindly each deceit as told,
You see vast spaces in your confinement.
You are omnipotent. You have all strength.
A strength encompassing only yourself,
Your strengths have won no meaning from your fight.
The strengths you love: the sources of your hate,
The very weaknesses which sin admires.
The closely held conceptions in your hearts
Of pleasure, justice, weakness, law and strength
Have been defined and fixed by whom they praise.
He speaks a loud confusion preaching hate
Assuming that your pain can be at once
Diminished as it is inflicted on
The innocent, but pain of sin is not
Displaced as it is spread, it grows and pains
The more, spreading within as spread without.
Neither in propagating pain or love
Will either simply be lost from your soul.
Both love and hate will grow as they spread free
Until the two can clearly honestly
Confront and then true love will always win.
To reach the beauty of the Lord you must
Convert your definition of beauty.
Creation seeks out beauty in all forms,

Though even led astray, by beauty led,
A beauty flawed by your imperfect sight
Which cannot see omnisciently as God.
There is no perfect beauty but the Lord.
False beauty is the hidden enemy
Which lives in front of your undoubting minds,
The only driving force behind your pride.
False beauty was the downfall of mankind
And of the angels when they first fell down,
Its ideal is the image of deceit
Inspiring to embrace a warm false love,
And in the grips of such false love you beings
Cannot escape its heat as it distorts,
Distorting the false lover in its pain.
False love is the prime sin which you have chose;
The false beloved is your enemy.
If you hate God you do not hate our God,
It is a false god which you truly hate.
If you love sin then you do not know sin.
Compel yourselves though evil shall resist.
You must reject Satan's creations fast,
An evil recognized can do no harm
Unto your soul, discovering it is then
Your work, through God you can discover all.
With all His strength, God cannot save you souls
Alone, He cannot make your choices true.
You have the power then to save yourselves,
You have the power to choose forgiveness.
You can then recognize the devil's works,
Evil orations built on nothing but
A mount of self-deceit. He only harms
Himself with sin's iniquity dying
Alone unless you give him strength, as you

Possess an inner strength and only loss
Through giving it away emboldens him.
Your inner-strength: the glory of your choice,
Even at your lowest you still have choice,
Your individuality the source
Of your purpose within new Heaven's walls,
Uniquely sharing all with the one Lord
Your goal is inner strength; it comes through God.
For you must study evil to know it,
The light can never fear dark discovery,
The knowledge of evil will not harm you.
When Christ's redemptive lead reveals the truth
The darkness cannot infiltrate. If you
Remain disturbed you never were secure.
Why are you bent by evil fantasy?
Simplicity of sin is evil's guise,
Articulate your sin within your mind
That you may recognize and understand.
Hiding from evil will not end evil.
Do not fear holding sin within your mind
As Michael gripped Satan to cast him down
But mind sin deeply unto thoroughly
In fundamentally examining,
Understanding it need not be condemned,
It will not swell upwards but fall away,
The victory o'er evil will not be
Competing trumpets blaring to their strain,
A one drowning the other to silence.
The one discordant will be recognized,
Its foolish falsity condemns itself.
When once you follow God's deliberate path
No obstacles have you to overcome.
You need not omniscience to know the truth,

Not where the tragedy shall find setting
Of when cascading cataclysms fall,
But why, what motivates the endless pain,
And how, what mechanisms operate,
When weapons aim against you and are slung
First know the throw, duly the angles thrown.
To not, at its appearance, know the truth
But know how to choose truth instead of lies.
Though never testing God in firm demands,
Test every truth, that sin will fail is sure.
If you are open truth will soon convince.
The devil hence is unbelievable.
One simple cause undoes every effect.
As you deserve God's love God's love is served.
The end of seeking stagnates through this hell
Within the devil's weeds possessed with needs
And does not exorcise the sorrowful.
Woe to the ones who tread on every path,
Exercising every option but life.
Terrorized in evil intent's extent
You do not fight your enemies, but wounds.
You are left hating lost to such despair,
Of your despair, what has revenge resolved?
Then which emotion will you finally crave?
In hating you will find eternal hate,
In loving you will find eternal love.
Christ is the way, the truth, the virtuous
And generous redeemer curing hurt.
Though he stood high as judge condemning you
It was not God that sent you falling here.
But Satan who has pulled you weighted down,
Who would not have you enter Heaven's gate,
Who cut you off from life, forbidding love,

Book VI

As He your savior sought to lift you up.
Your self denial is not self rejection,
You shall not carry wounds once they are healed,
You shall forget the evils of this hell.
Atonement is the labor of your life.
Atone at once and freely tithe your sin,
To freely give evil as your offering
To be cast down by one with greater strength.
To whom do you offer eternal sin?
The devil will not take away your sin,
His hands are clenched, self bound, closed at your pain,
Christ's open palms receive your piercing sins.
Beware to not submit to your evil,
Be mindful to submit it to the Lord.
The unacceptable offering will free
That self of yours which is acceptable,
For Heaven holds no sin in its embrace
But grips it powerfully to cast it down.
Compassion is the love that you will feel
Though you may feel yourself beyond God's love.
Your souls of such importance we have come
Not leaving paradise to journey hell
But bringing paradise despite this hell.
You are the many lost and many loved.
Your place in Heaven is secure in Christ.
No one can stay the hand which reaches out.
Take hold the mighty hand and outstretched arm.
The mercy of compassion must o'erwhelm
You isolated souls in hell, for its
Fair beauty even fills our Heaven o'er.
Sin is more than a disobedient act
It is a flaw which has been introduced
And introduced, it can then be removed.

Paradise Omnipresent

Your sin has been condemned, you need not be.
If Christ can follow God without a sin
You, through God's power, can do so as he.
God gives us strength that sin cannot defeat.
Do you believe that in new Heaven's peace
Each soul continues in the slips of sin
And Christ's atonement frees us constantly
Allowing every sinner Heaven's grace
In a perpetual cleansing of new sin?
That is an image of a sinner's Heav'n,
One far removed from God's empowering ways.
How is it that no soul within new Heav'n
Will lose the paradise which has been lost?
We are not only souls forgiven full
But we possess new strength with truth and grace.
In your own eyes you were forgotten souls,
Only through God's eyes can you see the truth.
Through your minds condemnation was complete;
Through God's mind hell can be no obstacle.
Through your strength hell will burn eternally;
Through God's strength you will light eternity
And grace your beams upon new Paradise.
Belief in the unseen is not blindness
Dependence on the Lord: the sign of strength,
Our faith is our reliance on His strength
Your recognition: revelation's leap.
You have known God since when you first were born,
Obey the love your wandering hearts yearn for,
You shall learn a lesson of great import:
Your faithfulness can overreach your strength.
You hold the capability of faith.
You can go forth to places beyond self.
The risks of God's ideals have broke no man

For leaps of faith have never fallen down:
As soon let go, embraced; as leapt, carried.
Sin is not harmless; sins themselves cause harm.
Your sin is an unclean destructive force,
God cannot be destroyed as you choose sin,
Nor made unclean through your iniquity,
Your sin destroys not God but you yourself,
Then when you sin you sin against yourself.
Against God's laws protection does not live.
The body of the law embodied is
The righteousness of spirit in your form.
Then heavenly forgive their enemies;
You enemies have none which to forgive,
Yet you are guilty of this very sin,
For you have not forgiven your foul self.
Forgiving brings forgiveness from the Lord.
A sinner lost accepts himself to harm.
This sinner then is his own enemy.
His mandate then is to forgive himself.
First find the sinful enemy against
Your righteous self and then forgive yourself.
The Lord not only saves the lost from sin,
God makes it possible for sinners to
Forgive themselves, this power is God's alone.
Traverse the largest to the smallest scale
And bind them in one line, immediacy.
Through violations of the kingdom's laws
You sin against not only God but self.
As they belong to God make them your own.
Those who had judged themselves had been not judged,
For they determined truth and followed course.
As God remains the judge so must you judge,
Not one another as your sin would tempt,

As God has judged you, you must judge yourselves,
Each sin a Satan, righteousness a Christ,
Then separate the righteous from the foul,
With God's authority condemn your sin,
God's hand within your hand and heart in heart,
Though you possess less power than God Himself
To give your all equals the strength of God.
Remember the truth of the parable,
A one who tithes less but all equals more.
As God gives all and you give all you have
You are united with the Lord's spirit.
When you do good it is no less value
Than when the Lord himself performs good works,
For good does not have more than one value,
It is as if yours is the hand of God.
When you see life in mindful righteousness
It is as if yours is the mind of God,
For truth can be no other form but truth
And man can know a truth as God himself.
The differences between mankind and God
Diminish as your sin is cast away
And truth restores the strength confusion kills.
When you look outwardly from inward truth
It is as if yours is the eye of God.
Do not be only good before God's eyes
Be good within the eyes of God, and see.
When you submit your soul with all your heart
You are as God who gives His love to you,
For love can be no other form but love.
And when you sacrifice what you hold dear
You are as He who gave His only son,
To sacrifice equals our God's resolve.
When you live in God's Heaven perfectly

You are as perfect as your God himself,
For God's perfecting love can be no less
Than a perfection unto God himself,
Your image in the Lord becomes complete.
There is great unity in righteousness:
If you were God you would have done the same,
If God were you He would have done the same.
The devil can perceive no differences,
For you angelically, Godly, are light.
God loves His children; God forsakes not one.
You once were children, good within God's eyes
You can be children under God again.
The whole of Heaven is within our hearts,
In peering through us clearly you can see,
As if we were the open gates ourselves,
The open paradise in beauty's light,
Look clearly through us and see Heaven's home."
The chorus sang a song of psalmic love:
"Praise God for His revealing kingly gifts
The devil's secrets brightly are exposed
Come, let us sing in praise for the Savior!
And serve him with the songs of our choosing
The Lord is good, His mercy will endure
Serving the Lord itself is victory
Give thanks to God, the king is almighty."
They finished their great chorus voice, it was
The sermon of ecclesiastic hell.
The crawling horde emerges standing forth
In concert concentrations form firmly
Lo, Satan stands with demons in the flame
The devil sees light preaching to the souls,
Possessive, empty with his jealousy,
He spoke unto himself derisively

"What can words do? I have heard words before."
In culmination of the spoken words
Breaks through a glimpse, a crevice in the flame
From inspiration's loose elusiveness
The constant caring multitude, a muse.
A portraiture of inspiration's form
Momentum of the moment more than words,
The words but decorate holy spirit.
Instruction followed naturally in grace.
Dawn on their hearts, from caring faces beam
Though simply given, complexly received.
Though simply stated, never simply won.
Seen through the crystal prism unbent now,
Unwrapped from its position contorted
Which led to every way except escape,
God's light revealing all which Satan hid,
The light searching shining upon all hell,
Not only darkness' flames of sucking pain
But every demon, a fallen angel
And every sinner, a diseased lost soul
Revealed as Satan's temptations' design,
Before them spread the ways and wiles of sin,
Prevalent darkness described by the light,
Pictured completely with no motive hid,
The image of humanity in hell
O'er throwing connotations of such sight.
No other sight in all creation could
Shake evil from its uninspired dark
Than Heaven reaching into hell itself.
An instance pops of sunshine radiance.
The first scene they have seen of miracles.
The notes of music now align to minds,
The glory of the Lord within the scene,

The boundless proof of His salvation ways,
The devil still believes in victory
But suddenly they slipped from his control,
Good human souls slip out under the yoke
Bearing no dragging burdens, starting free
Potential is the pathway born from hope.
Millions of crossroads intersecting thought
Traversed in speeds unwieldy, wielded here,
Taut draw concisement in their clarity,
Light following, choosing those blessed paths
Which lead excitedly to greater paths,
An active asking, seeking, following,
Electing without fail successful ways
To be elect within the laws of God,
No false path chose once guided by the truth.
New choices promising the new Heaven.
Behind them they behold a golden road,
Their enemies before their eyes transformed,
They thought themselves the same, unchanged at first,
But in a different world, a newer land
And dawning, recognized their very change
By recognizing not their past action,
Their hatred foreign once made far removed.
Satan voiced disbelief: "Impossible."
Here Christ was recognized as if it was
He undergoing transformation full,
For he was natural now, the dearest friend,
Before oppressor, here redeemer kind,
The beauty of the Christ beheld as true,
The multitudes of souls awakening
No longer apprehensive to receive
His message or redemption's sudden change
Enrobed in light as suddenly they themselves.

Paradise Omnipresent

They realized it was not he who changed,
And suddenly they are marveling around
Themselves, anointed friendship everywhere
They had not beheld with weak mortal eyes,
Their blindess cured, senses reach to their height,
Infused with insight, music ringing clear,
The true creator's lyricism streams,
The souls not merely turned, they are transformed
To souls without the urge to join in pain.
Aggressors have passed through the blood of Christ,
They have passed through the victim of their sin
To reemerge as guiltless before God.
The devil sees the shifts in darkness fly,
The shocks of pain cringe out across his face,
Satan recalls each single soul above,
Temptations of each one in their own time,
His eyes narrow, flickering across the fold.
Through the invading force he hunts for one,
A frantic roving through the unified,
This one assuredly he boldly finds.
From out the mass he spied his favorite girl,
His whore of Eden, delicate and weak,
He singularly drew his will to her.
Expectantly on gazing in he first
Caught her attention, she who willingly
Submitted to his will so long ago,
Beguiled beneath his courting dark design
Wanting his want until desire wed death.
He burned, his two orbs yearning to unite,
Then caught again the eye of she who dreamed,
And dreaming laid a palace feather bed
Within her welcome gentle comfort mind.
The Eve, the woman weak with appetite.

Book VI

The devil quick arouses fresh new wiles
Endeavoring a most clever temptation
Inciting mankind's fall to sin again.
Here Eve, empowered, ultimately strong
In front of Satan's knowing gleeful stare.
She listened carefully as he spoke up:
"I promised you knowledge and paradise,
And as I foretold, you achieved them both.
We killed the ignorance of paradise."
Responding to the ancient voice spoke Eve:
"Is this the one who tempted me so long
Ago? I don't believe. I never dreamed
Of falling down as far as this poor wretch.
He cannot be the same." She gazed intent
Remembering masked deceit, untempted here
Unmoved, the essence of temptation lost
Upon that countenance fair and innocent,
An innocence of faith as if the mark
Of Satan's works ne'er touched her gentle heart.
As pure as when the garden first was kept
But now Eve wears life's lessons on her mind
And recognizes distantly the lies
Which pained her mortal wounds. Now knowing, now
Unwilling to convert the mortal lies
Through her imagination's conception
To possibility conceivable,
And possibility through wanton pride
Into desire, and from desire to truth.
She steadily surveys the fallen one
As he speaks unto her preaching in wiles,
"You are so much more beautiful than those
Degenerate and jealous offspring beasts
Inheriting the poisoned womb of sin

Who vainly roamed in imitation brute
Approaching only in their arts the face
Which you delivered so imperfectly
To children better left unborn than flawed.
God knows that you deserve to serve with me.
Remember, He denied us paradise
But only after letting me inside.
He hated you more than He hated me.
Do not forgive your God for what He did.
It's not too late for choice to bring you back
As you were brought to me when innocence
Was at its height desiring wisdom's scope
And we broke open daringly your God's
Design together, wed to suffering's bite.
We were as never was and could return
As king and queen in war for majesty."
And Eve responds here ready to rebuke,
Grateful to have the opportunity
To share with Satan her contempt for sin:
"Submit to you, and lose the strength of love?
To trade a halo for a tarnished crown?
To reign hate dying seated at your left?
You are a sadness dying as you grow,
Irrationally picking all that you could grab,
And cruelly rotting all that you could take,
Thus I will never give myself to you.
A woman with a sole redeemer, I.
In all I follow Christ and he alone,
There is no greater worship in my love."
And Satan spake, "Then it is he you love
Above all others. Exaltation keeps
You separate from me without recourse."
Expecting lies Eve cautiously replied

Book VI

Agreeing with the disagreeable,
"You speak the truth, and yet I still mistrust."
Then Satan turned his lies, to her surprise,
To Adam, who admired steadfastly
The constancy of Eve in hell's disgrace.
The devil locked his eyes on Adam there
With eager affectations ready on
The winding reasoning foundation laid
And set to trap. He craftily and quick
To Adam spake: "It's undeniable.
You loved her through the sin and evermore,
A love worth sacrificing paradise,
A love as grand as any sacrifice,
To lay the apple where your heart should be,
But you will never be as Christ to her,
Forever second in her wanton heart,
Her beauty never lighting lovingly
For you as she for him and you for her.
He reigns as second Adam, righting your
Mistakes, proved stronger through the mortal pain,
So much superior for your evil faults.
Now choice is dead, for following him will lead
To only irredeemable distraught
Bereavement, falling short forever there.
But falling here forever you could yet
Regain her infinite consuming love,
For falling into love is not the sport
Of angels: falling always was a gift
Of mine. In loving here you will alone
Be loved by her, a dream eternally.
From Jesus' freedom to distract at will
Alike all men and women will search out
In following your handsome lead to life

And finally find their freedom free from his.
Thus you in wedded company shall live
To never grieve with Eve for Heaven's seat."
As Christ denied the devil's teaching, all
Humanity informed by Christ now finds
Completion in rejecting Satan's sin,
They see the serpent knowing why it crawls,
They hear its hisses full of venom spray,
They know God's center and the cusps of life.
Now upright Adam, sagely self assured,
Adoring takes the hand of lady Eve.
The souls freshly redeemed, astonished at
Their own swift victory o'er Satan's words,
The spread of hope flows easily through hell
As simply felt, completely understood.
God pours His heart and fills their empty souls.
The variations of reactions are
Aligned through unique individual minds
Upon a pathway of connectedness
Except in that one dark and pitiful
Despairing, boiling Satan shut, a gate
To he from them was ever bitter locked.
Oppressors reconciled with those oppressed,
The murderers and murdered reconciled
For none are murdering or suffering death,
The murderers become the innocent,
Offended resting with those offensive
For none reproached another in God's light.
The blasphemous who twisted God's strong word
Endeavoring to prove God's power weak
Were written back into the book of life.
God authors no sinners within the book,
Wise pages created of God's design.

Book VI

Again they were as children as of old,
The Lord then recognizes such fair souls,
The souls beneath His feet raised to His side.
The beastly mark completely washed away,
The evil beasts now tamed to gentle ways
Rejoining the shepherd's flock as regained,
Harmless and loyal, at the master's side
Adorable, adored with full respect.
A one to Abraham and Lazarus
Arrived, a former rich man now redeemed,
The chasm to new Heaven finally crossed
On this new bridge extended by the Lord.
The hypocrites made holy in their hearts,
They are transformed within the filling truth.
The pharaoh is released from slavery,
At last now free to love equality,
And Edith turns to see her husband Lot,
As Samson takes Delilah in his arms.
The pharisees exceed in righteousness
Surpassing the obstruction of old selves
And Daniel stands amongst the flames with friends.
The faithful soul of Judas reverently
Approached the savior full with new belief,
And Jesus greeted Judas with a kiss
Upon the cheek, so Judas knew himself
Forever safe from persecution's hate,
And Christ is, in the bonds of loyalty,
Grateful that Judas had been born anew.
Profound experience in love's grand presence
As only can be fully experienced
By those personally swelled up in love
And only can be fully understood
By those observing enwrapped in that love

As souls transition on beauty's rush in.
The brothers Cain and Abel in embrace,
The longest separated finally joined.
Christ watches Cain and Abel sharing love,
Two brothers reunited through the Lord.
Christ turned away to face dark Satan then
Who summons simmering focus despite
Humiliation; not humility.
Swift calculating in emergency
The devil shouts unto humanity,
"Rest not so easy, you have not seen truth
But isolated Christ temptation lies.
He has but overcome the weakest tests,
And will not stand before this hell's assaults."
The ancient angels fallen for evil
Still serve belief unto the devil's words,
The demons still within his grip of sin.
Christ and the devil, face at face in hell.
The devil stands between Christ and his aim.

BOOK VII

The Argument: The demons of hell witness the astounding sight of humanity unified.
Christ and Satan confront each other to determine the true epic hero of creation.

The devil pinned, in cornered furious rage,
His rotted labor sprung from clenching grasp,
Confusion of the proud negates the truth.
The speeches guiding mankind did not shift
A single demon from its slippery perch,
As majesty sweeps out across the felled
They, selfishly grating at conquests lost,
Now cringe in seeing their prey glorified.
Scant words were heard as unintelligent,
The deafness of their senses shading truth.
Convinced of his heroic leadership
They yet believe in Satan's evil ways,
Their epic battle against God rages,
The ember hearts fuel radiating hate,
They disbelieve the Lord and all His works.
Within the death of night, the birth of day,
The newly woken souls shine with the rest,
A sight never beheld by demon eyes,
Unencountered before in creation,
Humanity united in the Lord,
Scope filled with godly grand miraculous sight,
A miracle by them unimagined,
The fascinated demons in flurry.
Christ spoke unto the demons lost in hell:
"You have beheld all your possessions flee,

You demons, look upon your fallen forms,
Your black wings silently sit fast asleep,
Light feathers stuck together caught with hate.
How sorrowful you drag those wings about,
Those two wide wings so capable of ease
So desperate a burden weighting down.
You self-deceived, self-fallen, self tempted,
You did not find grace or justice within
Your sinful eyes looking upon old Heav'n.
Through new Heav'n's power you shall discover both."
The greedy devil to the Christ then snarled
"No demon can receive the grace of God
As God sent no messiah to their side
As ransom for the choice which has been set
To suffer death that they may be redeemed.
Man may find grace, the others never shall.
God's grace is finite; Sin is infinite."
Christ confidently issued loving words:
"Old Heav'n and earth witnessed no demon grace.
They met their end; the Lord's mercy has not.
As demons chose their path of self-deceit
They must in their God given freedom choose
The path of God which passes through my heart.
Their freedom was decreed unchangable.
Those darkened wings may yet lift up for flight.
All fallen angels can find redemption.
As mankind unredeemed roiled in this lake
In rolling waves, they thick compress and clash
On mankind as on angels fall'n alike.
The wages of all sins: one single hell.
Redemption of all sins: one single choice.
But I can give no ransom for your fate.
As you have fallen so must you return,

You must use choice, place God within your pulse,
As angels you must fly unto God's heart.
As you all sought rejection through your choice,
You know the elevated path to God:
Free choice, safe passage into God's kingdom."
The devil chastised him with new alarm,
"If you were true they would have turned before,
On witnessing your life they would have seen.
Your grandest works have gone, dust disappeared,
No mediums are left for miracles,
I have defeated God, and they are mine.
Though trapped in hell, they know the truth of God
As clearly as the angels in new Heav'n."
Christ spoke rebuking Satan's vicious words,
"The lost of hell have not the faith of Heav'n.
As they have not perceived as those redeemed
They have not faith that God is as I say,
That God is creation's epic hero.
Conceptions of action are vital for
Heroics are spirit's reality,
Upon the hero rests creation's faith.
Believing in undoubting reckless faith
That Satan, the creation's villain, was
An epic hero; You were all deceived."
The Satan standing sentinel between
The unredeemed and Christ yelled unto all:
"It is not weakness within beings, but God.
Where God fails to convince them they choose me.
Where God cannot empower, sin takes root.
My powers are His inabilities.
The weakness of your God is manifest,
The facts before your very eyes are proof.
My story thrown about as blasphemy,

Lost in the rambling din of multitudes,
You children follow words where they may lead.
You need not worry at the new allure,
You need no trust to hear me speak the truth.
I shall prove truth until Christ bows to me.
I am the epic hero of all realms.
I can inspire in places God cannot.
Omni-inspiring truths would follow an
Omniscience joined with an omnipotence,
Yet God has not inspired every heart.
He claims us weak and yet He has no strength,
His light not bright enough to shatter dark,
It is a goal which God cannot achieve,
His limit, His impossibility,
For inspiration is almighty truth.
The uninspired have proven your God false.
Watch there, watch well the humans' ignorance,
They scoff at their God being their own villain.
You need not find the absolute hero,
You need only to find your true villain.
The villain sleeps as creatures wake to pain.
They cry to God and only I respond,
My voice is louder than the trumpet's call.
God is the epic villain of all beings,
God's presence not present to intervene
And smite the apple from the lustful hand,
Preventing and protecting in true love.
God's love is partial, incomplete, and wrong.
I am eternally available,
My will is greater than that of your God,
My willingness proves I am the hero.
God and His Christ possess no true concerns,
And if concerned then why not interrupt

And clearly smite before I speak my words?"
And Christ spoke unto he and unto all:
"That they may clearly see Satan's defeat."
Christ calls upon the demons for response:
"Though you may disagree, put forth my thoughts
And justify the epic hero God.
Speak, demons, of the Lord as a hero."
No demon speaks, in silence Christ renews,
"No demon will put forth for none are armed,
No thought or thought's conception fixed in state
For an immediate clear awakening.
At ignorance's silence I heed this call,
Exposing Satan's villain fall'n to me.
God is the true hero of creation
Verily I say unto you, God is
A rock in battle, swiftly opposing,
Our Lord reigns as the one host of ideals
Perfection's beauty, justice, wisdom, truth
In facing evil's battle clamor waged
Of troops through seas and skies o'er mountaintops
Our Lord displays the perfect wrath and might,
The perfect anger at iniquity,
In constant war commanding brilliantly,
Undaunted by an organized assault
Determined to undermine His kingdom,
Well versed in danger, fearless at our side,
A valiant protector shielding the meek
Glorified inside heaven fortified,
Unmatched resolve defending holy cause
Undertaking the greatest sacrifice
Unafraid to haul up the sinners low.
Upon what trenches will He not prevail?
Collapsing floods upon oppressing troops,

He shook the cowering wall of Jericho,
He thundered over armageddon's fire,
All beings have choice to follow evil's path
And war against the innocent and brave.
Though they choose evil over holy strength
No evil choice can overcome the Lord,
The serpent's scales a fragile armor at
The Lord's unbreakable foundation stone,
An evil giant's choice without a chance,
The daring youth a giant in spirit.
Those who accused the Lord's revolution,
The choices of the fundamentalists
Overthrown as Christ confidently rose.
The will of God defeats the devil's charms.
When once the humans left His garden stained,
Did God gaze on resigning them to sin?
Sitting, observing, silent as they die?
And absent to the wails of injustice
Abandoning in passive detachment?
The Lord is not resigned in tolerance
The Lord is agile, outmaneuvering foes,
The Lord swiftly created bold new paths,
The hand of the creator reaching out
And firmly gripping mankind's striving hand
With ultimate techniques for perfect life,
Authoritatively authored the book,
Our call to action by His example.
Our God is loud, opposing with triumph.
God clashing with pure evil violently
Engaging life for unity, guiding,
The gallant definition in all works,
No voice unheard, no cry or praise not felt,
Omniscient God does not ignore His work,

Lo, Satan grays the earth with gruesome slings.
Though leaping fire be laid across His feet
God stands admonishing with wise commands,
Invested in mankind's travails with sin,
Involved in every jagged roughing trail
His guiding hand turning each particle,
His guiding word a shepherd with its truth.
With hopes to rescue suffering from its sin.
The Lord is immanent and passionate
With empathy desiring all for all,
Alert, awake, forever vigilant,
Always protecting His unbending name,
Enduring without heartbreak in the pain.
At one affliction: infinite resolve.
A hero of epic proportions, He."
The devil issued forth a dark retort:
"If your God is an epic hero then
I am, by your own words, a hero too.
You listen sheep, I am legend's hero.
Warfarer of men, the source of hot strength
Who raised his thoughts outside those of a God,
Who slung the spears over the forest glens
To rattling ring through chinks in God's armor.
We both within the war fought as heroes
With equal vigor, equal violent work.
I valiantly fought with your God's command,
I still maintain command upon this hell."
Christ spoke of God's heroic qualities,
"The Lord not only battles through the wars,
God delves inside the lowest and the great,
The Lord is an instructor guiding all,
God is a counselor unto fair hearts,
The one informer of true conducts laws,

Describing the connections between souls
Which in their essences connect to God.
The source of being: the source of our knowledge.
Not merely existing but informing,
Imparting perfectly for greatest good,
Our every action is preceded by
His knowledge which informs His every word.
His earthly interventions subsided
The miracles of His knowledge endure."
The devil made assault on God's wisdom,
"Christ praised his God as the true instructor
Perfect beyond infallibility,
Then what divinely reasoning suffers
Your God to hold His hand stayed at His side
Preventing my fortunate direct turn
Instructing me with truth, instructing me
To fall further below, upon my knees,
And worship in His Heaven as His slave?
What wisdom gleamed He from His omniscience
When tumult tore His heaven from design,
What knowledge kept He from my blazing mind
When one-third His devoted joined my school?
Your God hates scholars; learning is a sin.
As every man matured he was condemned.
Best they had lived as infants: ignorant.
Illiterates would fill the book of life.
We are not deaf; your Lord's voice has no strength."
There Christ responded in light's brevity,
The devil's labor overturned at once,
"Your ignorance is built on your weakness."
Then Satan smugly called back in response:
"What perfect instructor shouts 'ignorance!'
When I alone reveal the truths of God?

I ask you here, who first began the war?"
And Christ responded to the question thrown,
"It was you, Satan, losing paradise
when you refused to bow before the throne
and raised revolt in arms against the Lord."
The devil shot back speaking of God's ways,
"He learned destruction from destruction's heart,
I taught your God the methods of our war,
He learned destruction from this fighting fist,
He learned to murder from the murderers,
I am the father of the Heav'n's warfare,
And God is my own son, I taught Him well.
Our warfare wisdom sprang from darkness' works.
I taught creation more of God than God.
Your God is only known through His response
To me, He is defined against myself.
I had not seen him war before the war.
As I taught God I taught creation well."
Of Satan's dark assertions spoke the Christ,
"The blind lead on but offer no true sight
So partial truths convince with what they lack;
The Lord instructs with all He possesses,
Embodying the law in a body,
The Lord possesses knowledge omniscient
Withholding nothing which the truth requires."
Spoke Satan, "My evangelism reigns,
As fervently as God I speak the truth.
All beings can now divine that as defined
I share all qualities with God's hero
And yet you claim God is the only one,
Thus you are false and I, Satan am truth."
The Christ with great momentum spoke to them,
"You do not have the grandest quality

That God the epic hero has inside.
The hero loves and serves all those He rules.
God is the hero of eternal love
Bestowing gifts with innocence and joy,
Embodying for the beloved's heart,
Communicating perfectly His truth:
That He loves every being with all His heart.
The God of love endears the love of God.
The Lord is unafraid to love His foe,
God does not hesitate to give His love,
All who love God are not unrequited,
The moment which one loves, that one is loved,
One cannot separate love sent and gained,
The Lord is one; these two loves are the same."
The devil then accused God as hero,
"You claim your God as heavily involved,
With His creation's sinners and our wars
The greatest involvement: allowing sin.
He is the cruelest teacher of them all,
Why must your God deny the sinners Heav'n?
God dictates His commands upon the weak
And distantly He hurls down commands,
Upon His height demanding firm control,
He does not care if any writhe in pain.
If He would empathize with any being
Then heaven would accept the realm of sin.
He does not love creation in its forms,
He does not love His beings, He loves His laws."
Then Christ lightly spoke unto demon minds,
"God served mankind and saved humanity,
The one you serve will not ever serve you.
Behold Christ: the Lord's empathy for man,
Initiated into mankind's realm

Book VII

In undergoing the greatest journey
With passion in the passage through the pain,
Experiencing creation unto death.
God has endured the demon's darkest slings
As man, those slings as hellish as this hell
Which demons suffer as they sling it out,
For angels and for souls death has one name,
And intimately God has faced this death.
The Lord embodied His own law with flesh,
God teaches with His words and with His acts
Through I, the Christ, God demonstrates true life
God is one in accord with every law
In serving His own heart He served all men."
The devil called to every being in hell,
"There is a shift in the hero defined:
God as a hero rests upon the Christ;
Your God is unheroic without Christ.
Christ and his God shall both fall to villain.
Christ's drama on the earth was theater,
Those foolish souls within the olden realm
Persuaded by his acts, his miracles,
His magic works more than his plain-spoke words,
Philosophy costumed in theater,
A testimony to Jesus' weakness.
Why not descend to preach and reascend,
Persuasion resting on your Godly truths?
Why need you flashy miracles to prove
The messages you carried down from Heav'n?
Instead, he journeys on with miracles.
No one believes his words, only his works,
An undeniable truth would overwhelm
In otherworldly wrought transcendent height.
Christ acted sorceries and magic charms

To prove flat laws which cannot prove themselves,
His authenticity is undermined.
Within the wilderness he firmly spoke
Of never testing God, your chosen Lord.
If so, then the performing Christ is false.
Denying flight he later flew to Heav'n.
He claimed he had resisted temptation
But then ascended in deference to me.
To what grand end would he manipulate
The fabric of the earthly universe
But to manipulate these followers
Who cannot sustain faith without a test,
The theater of gross inconsequence,
His words but slyly packaged in his tricks.
Extravagance belies desperation,
Theatrics pulling weak emotions on
The vulnerable, the masses' devotion
Convinced by drama of the sacrifice,
The multitudes flee doubt to chase the wind.
The wages of his death: emotion's debt,
Until belief relies on a story,
The greatest story they have ever heard,
But one unsympathetic to my ears,
For my journey surpasses all his works,
The brazen story of my warriorship
Lay bedded in the valor hearts of dark,
When paradise was lost and evil won,
Our story superceding Christ's triumphs
In distances traversed, our pain endured,
For his wounds carry not the scars of fire.
No one would worship Christ without his works,
Then how much greater are we faithful few.
In faith we are superior to works.

These hands manipulate no miracles,
But how miraculous is our scorned hell,
How precious is the one who serves his heart,
That one who would not bow would not succumb,
By virtue of my mind I lead and spread,
The arguments of evil augmented
By clarity laid out before all eyes,
For my truths stand upon their very words.
God has one standard for His truths when He
Assigns authority to emotion,
His message not enough, but heroics
Required to satisfy suspicion's eye,
Belief established on heroics lone.
Then as belief relies on God's hero
I undeniably can turn all choice
To the true epic hero: I, Satan."
The devil then portrays his history
In pageantry of his evil passion.
"Christ's disobedience of my firm demands
Throughout the trials of desert wilderness
Cannot compare to evil's firm resolve,
As I resisted more than Christ can know,
As I received more flails, endured more scorn
What martyrs we, dying eternally."
And Jesus overthrew Satan's discourse
"Mind well the ways Satan deceives himself.
For show, Satan is the sinner's hero
Elevated in sin from low villain
His unheroic fall a desperate crawl.
The empty story's empty audience
Would sympathize with Satan's strife and pain.
The story of the devil is infirm,
A weakness manifest in drama's form

Constructed on foundations of no worth,
Each motivation lacks integrity,
The devil's large ambitions prove him small.
Deceit is measured in Satan's appeal,
Standing alone is no heroic feat,
The devil's play costumes the dark with day.
Allusions to his fearsomeness are false,
The fear of Satan is the start of pain.
His deep emotions swing away from truth,
Evolving into monstrous, raging acts,
A wild escape from beauty's solid form,
Emotions pulled up from an emptiness,
Within their clamorous din there beats no heart.
There is no element of Satan's play
Which is not conquered by God's greater height,
Determination, strength, emotion's depth.
The story of my life is an epic,
And I the greatest epic hero seen.
The greatest drama of the great hero.
The highest seen as lowest by the proud,
The highest with the lowest preaching height
To bring all of the lowly unto height,
The highest meeting lowest injustice,
Betrayed upon all sides, unjustly killed,
The lowest cruelty upon the great,
The highest form of life moved unto death,
Death is the measure of adversity,
Then rising from the lowest earthly state
Unto the highest righteous godly seat,
The crucifix portrays the grandest shift,
The symbol of defeat was not defeat,
The symbol of one death made one of life,
Its form is drama in its grandest form.

The devil calls it drama of the weak,
He cannot recognize the holy truth:
The drama is not great, the hero is.
The hero is the heart of drama's strength,
Thus when they love the drama they love Christ.
Without the drama Christ is still the Christ."
Then Satan criticized the drama's work,
"The story of the Christ is evil's form.
Suppose my fighting justly is a sin
And those who follow me are charged with guilt,
And guilt always implies just punishment.
A sinner cast to hell is always just.
With Christ's forgiveness law is overthrown,
The guilty pay no penalty for sin.
Forgiveness of a sin: itself, unjust.
You love injustice when it benefits.
No sin should find the mercy of your God.
Christ's sacrifice denies just punishment,
Thus Christ is the most criminal of all,
As He unmercifully judged us before.
Atonement is a game which God devised
Once He had lost in Eden's paradise,
A desperate measure to regain a loss."
The Christ assuredly offered response,
"Offering free choice within the garden's wall
God yet maintained free choice outside the walls
Through mercy God gives freedom to the weak."
The devil sharply cut in with rebuke,
"Assured forgiveness of their numerous sins
Is no prevention of disloyalty,
A one could pile up multitudes of sins
Without regret or cowering down in shame
But proudly flaunt the pleasures of their vice

In confidence of mercy sure to come."
Whereupon Christ delivered his reply,
"Your diatribe implies a jealousy
Amongst those strengthened with the love of God
For being entrapped in sin as they had been,
Eternally desiring their old selves.
The holy seek no life outside of God."
The devil spoke to Christ with focused force,
"But my temptations cannot be o'erwhelmed
When God allows for freedom with no pain.
All sin persists without a penalty,
Your Christ forgiveness only prolongs sin,
A sinner can live free from fear of death
Expecting Christ's forgiveness afterwards.
Why turn to Christ when they can live in vice,
God's Heaven will be waiting for their whim."
Christ spake, unto hellish pointedly,
"None knowing holy truth live in deceit.
God's grace only encourages new life."
The devil spoke against God's ways again,
"Your God gives equal merit in His Heav'n,
The last to turn to God accepted as
The first, upon your level in new Heav'n.
You see how God despises every soul.
No matter who you are you are the same,
No matter when you join you share their fate."
And Christ explained for every hellish ear,
"New Heav'n's equality is mercy's height
The Lord is merciful unchangingly,
There are no variations in God's strength."
Spoke Satan then, "Why does God mask himself?
Why would God hide himself in lesser robes?
God cloaked himself within a human form,

Pretending to be something He is not,
In order to deceive His followers.
What need is there of a disguise?" Said Christ:
"I was a man to show what man could be."
And Satan spoke, "Omniscience is God's flaw.
He sees all future evil, then creates.
Only reaffirming what was confirmed,
Jesus does not deserve his God's blessing.
Christ is the proof that God is a villain,
Revealing His corruption in Christ's life.
As God knows all to come from every word
He is accountable for all disputes,
Christ born to alienate firm belief
And overthrow the old chosen people,
Who could not see the God of Moses in
A rabble, rebellious, messiah boy,
Narrow atonement of a narrow God,
To bloodily deny traditioned men
To further qualify atonement in
Abandoning those only too faithful,
And further flood design from its relief.
Then look you closely what I have revealed:
As soon as one captures the face of God
He shirks it leaving a hollow image.
The crucifix: a stake struck through the heart
Of unbelieving faith traditionalists,
An obstacle between mankind and God,
Atonement made elusive through laws changed,
The sabbath massacred, diets ripped out,
God chains the faithful to belief and flees.
If Christ deserves God's blessings, God is cursed,
Eternally destroying His own work,
His loving face barely conceals His rage.

God separates himself; I draw them close."
Christ spake upon the truth of God's design,
"God's genius: unexpected, transcendent,
Defying expectation in its height.
So many dreamed to see the coming Christ
Establish overwhelming earthly peace
Of instant battle, war's commanding force
Annihilating every enemy,
Yet God designed a spiritual victory.
The earthly mind designed societies
Whose kings would never wear a crown of thorns,
Their god would not submit himself to pain
Or harsh endure the cuts and mortal scorns
Of life, exploring to the depths of sin,
And yet God's genius told another way.
The common thought inclines to royalty,
And not the common man, yet it was so,
The king of kings constructs no palaces.
Who would enthrone his son upon a cross,
Inside the body of a carpenter,
Stripped bare of offices or finery?
The mind of God bows to no other being,
The burden on mankind to recognize
God's genius as it took its earthly form.
The story of the Christ is genius' form.
His genius overwhelming sin's assails
To outmaneuver in His invention,
Creation of atonement is genius.
The hero undertaking death for all."
The devil listened well, then spoke to all,
"Do not doubt me, I have been listening.
For once in God's creation Christ and I
Have reached agreement in our perception.

I see truly, and we can both agree
The definition of Christ as hero
Relies upon his noble sacrifice,
A hero who submits himself to serve."
The devil met the eyes of hell and Heav'n
Assuring the pursuit had all in grasp,
"New Heaven's legions will see Christ submit
To me, his epic height hotly dethroned.
The holy sacrifice is fantasy.
Purported intentions are distorted.
Christ is no hero, any man would die,
The lowest simpleton and laborer,
Or coldest miser locked in solitude
Would lay upon the cross as Christ has died."
Christ spoke to Satan, "God can bolden all.
No persecution can destroy such strength."
The devil hurriedly continued on,
"It is not strength but self-assuredness,
For any man will die if he will rise.
A sacrifice insinuates a loss,
Then what did this Christ ever sacrifice?
Christ only died foreknowing he would rise,
And rise up soon to greet the warmth of day.
What knew the Christ of death but only days?
One day of suffering for eternal gain.
Then why submit eternally to Christ
Who suffered temporary sacrifice?
So many humans died that very death,
They sweated blood as Christ has sweated his
Without assurances beyond more scorn.
So cowardly this Christ would flee the cross
As he fled angry mobs armed with mere stones,
If he must live in hell to save mankind.

The one who lost the least here claims the most.
His sacrifice was not a sacrifice,
He followed glory and certain reward.
He claims a sacrifice in paradise.
A man would crucify himself for less.
So undeserving of your servitude,
This Christ asserts himself upon false height
As I have proven, choosing as all men."
The Christ spoke with the calms of perfect truth,
"As you witnessed, I died at your defeat,
I died for every sin of every being.
God did not have to die the death of man.
I was completely innocent of sin
Thus I was undeserving of the pain
But serving in the pain I sacrificed."
Then Satan spoke back with a quick retort,
"The act was carried out by unclean hands,
No holy priests struck nails for the offering."
Undoing Satan simply with the truth
Spake Christ with deft aimed words: "My hands were clean."
The devil swiftly tore in with rebuke:
"Christ is not sinless and has never been,
It is the paradox of human God.
As Christ was close to God, his knowledge too.
He knew of good and evil as did man,
And being a man, broke God's law of knowledge.
He therefore had mankind's most ancient sin,
He knew of good and evil in their parts,
And therefore is no worthy sacrifice.
Or else he is not truly part of man,
And sacrificed, could not ransom mankind.
If Christ is sinless why did he wear clothes?
He wore the shame and guilt of hidden sin."

Christ broke through Satan's reasoning with truth
"I was not guilty of the ancient sin,
My sole inheritance was of the Lord
And neither did I fall as man first fell,
No storming forceful sin could bend my heart
For it was one with the immovable,
With wisdom from the Lord, yet innocent.
Untempted, I was proven to be free
For my life's work: regaining paradise."
Again the devil fought the Christ hero,
"Why must they need repent if every sin
Of every man was conquered on the cross?
A hero fights his battles for the weak,
Yet every man was made to fight his war.
The struggle of another lessens Christ's,
For if he had completely endured sin
In epic fashion as he boldly claims
No man would have to fight to free himself
In constant struggle for his redemption.
A hero would have rid the world of sin,
It buckling, breaking to assail no more.
Christ died: sin lives. Christ's hero then has failed."
The Christ assuredly offered response,
"First paradise was free; the second, not.
Freewill requires an individual choice;
Redemption is built of requirements."
The devil criticized the works of faith,
"You claim humanity is filled with God,
It is a faith devoid of sacrifice,
Atonement for the weak through mere belief,
Merely believing in his risen form.
Belief does not equal morality.
Belief alone gives nothing to your worth.

All in new Heav'n believe I have fallen,
You who believe in me should be condemned."
And Christ with reason undid Satan's words,
"Not only form, they must believe my truths."
The devil heatedly broke to new thoughts,
 "Christ is a coward, he is no hero.
Christ did not nail himself upon the cross,
His followers with hammers in their hands
And Christ commanding them with God's command.
The Christ was cowardly before he died;
Christ had no choice upon the sacrifice,
So forcefully he was betrayed and caught,
He had no other course, no place to hide,
No desert could have hid him from such hate,
Before the capturing you prayed in fear
For God to lift the burden from your back.
He sweated blood, so fearful of my strength.
A hero does not know temerity,
A hero does not fear the wrath of God,
A hero does not fear the flames of hell."
Christ with the calms of Heaven then replied,
"I chose to walk with men upon the earth.
I marched unto the cross in great resolve."
Then Satan spoke of God and sacrifice,
"Christ may have sacrificed his comfort height
In lowering his crown upon the earth
But God himself has never sacrificed.
This son of God does not reflect on God.
God did not suffer from the sacrifice,
He did not lose an object which He loved.
As Christ reaps benefits so has his God,
How many fatted calves would man strike down
To see entire herds fill up his store?

Book VII

How many demons I would suffer lose,
As Moloch fled, to see humanity
Deny the hero God purports to be.
God is no greater than the devil now."
Christ spoke then of the truth of sacrifice,
"God loves me as He loves humanity,
As He loves every angel in new Heav'n.
Allowing His beloved in the pain
God proved His willingness to strive for good.
You, Satan, do not give for what you take,
You do not love the demons, loving pride."
Again the devil fought the sacrifice,
"God knows so few who would be crucified
For His unjustified and weak ideals
He sent himself incarnate in disguise,
So who dies for this God? Only this God.
Such self importance vainly justified."
Spoke Christ, "I have free choice as every being."
The devil furiously sped forth again,
"Christ's sacrifice is no heroic act
I am the hero of true sacrifice.
I put my pride before the paradise
And die eternally for no blessings."
"The distances you fell a grand journey?
The pain which you are owed, your victory?
The devil is no sacrifice hero,
He did not willingly lose what he lost.
Through me God spanned the greatest distances
As you have Satan, from your height to death,
But you cannot compare to God's hero;
Heroically I flew to life again,
The breadth of God spans journey's greatest breadth."
The devil angrily snapped back retort,

"Ten thousand deaths I die at once and rise,
Your God's worst hell crushes, I carry on."
Spoke Christ, "You do not rise above your hate.
A hero faces fearsome obstacles,
His strength, despite his enemies, is proved.
Endurance unto perseverance height,
The humble hero traveling to transcend,
The epic hero rises through the fight.
Death separates the villain and hero,
I am the risen hero conquering death,
The devil is the villain lost in death,
His false claims of hero reveal his pride."
The devil railed against the words of Christ,
"Injustice unaccepted makes this pride,
This Christ by God placed high above the rest,
Then hate this pride which will not give to yours,
That is my fault and my nobility,
That I deserve far more than God can give."
Christ called then to the demons listening,
"The Lord of battle, servitude, and grace,
The hero's drama of great sacrifice
Surpasses heroes Satan has put forth.
The epic hero's armor then ill fits.
Cast Satan from the epic pantheon.
The devil's epic hero is undone."
The demons start to recognize the Christ,
The devil calls unto them violently,
"I am proved by opponents I have faced,
A greater hero fighting greater foes.
My drama is thus far superior,
I have succeeded bearing more than Christ."
And Christ unto the demons simply spoke,
"The devil here defines himself as great

As evidenced by his resisting more,
Resisting now the greater enemy.
He, by his wandering tongue, admits defeat."
The devil glanced his demon's shifting sights
And realized where he had seen those eyes:
The distant gaze of Christ at rugged march
In steepness, heavy beams across his back.
He labored quickly that they might soon trip,
To drop the weighted cross and fall again.
"Be still, the Christ has cleverly pursued.
I am no epic hero as defined;
My hero is not measured by the light
I am a tragic hero in this hell
I do not need an epic hero's traits,
A tragic hero: hero nonetheless,
Though I suffer defeat after defeat
The devil's tragic hero grows in strength."
The Christ rebuked the devil's gothic words,
"There is not a one tragedy in Heav'n,
Nor tragic hero undone in sorrow.
The tragedies abound within this hell,
But hell holds no hero or heroine.
Therefore there are no tragic heroes in
Our God's creation; heroes conquer death.
If you admire the base of tragedy
You do not know a hero capable
Of throwing down such great adversity,
Of overcoming epic misery."
The devil desperately aligns himself
With what was proven grandly for all minds,
"I am Christ-like, a hero as is he.
Christ-like, rebuked from where I was brought up,
The ones you knew the best despised you most.

You suffered for you Heav'n as I for hell."
Spoke Christ, "Light has no compare outside light."
And unto all the demons Christ then spake,
"You need not imagine God as hero.
The epic hero of the Lord is here,
We ultimately are the proof ourselves,
How else can you assign our new coming?
This epic hero godly invasion
Descending still, defending creation
From evil in its lair, in your own hearts.
Our presence here is an eternal proof
Of God the epic hero, first and last,
This grand image is undeniable,
Its grand heroics have no other forms,
No misperceptions now can be construed."
Satan reached deeply for deceptive words,
Descriptions to undo and overthrow,
Searching for an offering to their desire,
Absolving them of Christ's disturbances.
The devil's choice, the choice of descriptions
Reaches its end with Satan overthrown.
He cannot describe this reality
For it betrays his every deception.
The Christ at Satan's silence speaks out clear,
"No devilish wiles can daringly explain
Our presence here within the lake of fire,
Our bold endeavoring without abate.
Go to those lands in which your Lord has gone,
Cast off oppressors as your God has done,
Tear sin from off its throne, place Christ on high,
Slough off the chains of slavery in growth.
The pulse of God inspiring godly feats
Heroics spring from one morality

When He of many acts remains the source.
As God's arm reaches deeply so shall yours,
Reign o'er yourself as God has ruled the world
With heavy hands and wings worn for the flight.
When you, with God, defeat the devil's heart
Then every flame of hell will fear your light,
You will be epic heroes as are we,
For all who meet the epic call of God
Are epic heroes with the Lord in Heav'n,
You are an epic hero in God's light.
The hero's journey: freedom from all sin.
God has a name. It captures transcendence,
Divine conception in its bestowal,
His proven name recognized truly will
Surpass YHWH and Jehovah: Hero.
He speaks in every word and every act,
I AM the hero of my children's dreams,
I AM the epic hero of your life."
A soulful chorus sings humanity,
"Choice is not dead as God lives on in Heav'n.
If Christ is a hero let him be yours.
All worship for the Lord's epic response."
Hell's demons, impregnated of spirit,
Their universe mastered in reasoning
Where vicious villain turns to bold hero
And vicious hero to a bold villain,
Revolving worlds spun from the breath of God.
Satan exhorts the demons with all heat,
"Remember Heaven as you saw it last.
It will not be the Heaven which you loved,
You will be traitors twice eternally,
You cannot ever find the loves you lost.
You cannot ever reclaim what is spoiled,

It is not possible for you to turn
For Heaven will not ever turn to you."
The demons recognize their history,
The source of evil inspiration plain,
The devil's arts destroyed inside their hearts.
The demons from their wretched forms are thrown,
Throughout hot hell new wings refresh the pure
Cleansed deeply over, flames washed out and cooled.
The prophecy of Satan overturned:
The lake of fire full of white angel wings,
Not diving in but gently flying out.
Old enemies greeted as new heroes
The lock of battle broken in release,
Hard ancient sorrows mended at the touch,
Beelzebub, Mammon, and Belial
With every demon rising from the deep,
They cry out, "Satan can you see it? Light."
Satan saw flee the demon Mulciber
Whose dark intending creativity
Designed the palace pandemonium.
Satan to the demon loudly exclaimed,
"Do not abandon all your art for God.
Do not let him deny your creation."
But Mulciber, as wholly unattached,
His focused all consuming labored work
And strife amounting to dark nothingness,
Now turns away from self-indebtedness,
Abandoning old pinnacles as low,
A towering palace as a trifle proud,
Regarding his creation, uninspired.
"Your God's power does not signify His worth."
Rejected full abandoned Satan stood
In front of palace pandemonium grand

Unable to infect to an effect.
A feverish explosion letting loose,
The devil turns around and fights his hell,
Hot furious massacring his monument,
He wrenches fists on columns surging hate,
He rips apart the prideful craftsmanship,
Up tore the palace out from in its roots,
Colossal pandemonium topples down.
Wrecked damage falls in split cracked ornate blocks
He seizes crumbling stone as weaponry,
Hard hurling ruination at the horde,
A flock protected. Now condemned debris
Falls harmless at the side, a smoldering dust
Memorial burns where mountainous castle stood.
The Satan spent with protest, exhausted,
His right-side horn is fractured through, wreck cracked,
Force torn in half and splintered unto naught,
Protruding broken shattered stump remains,
Self-wound inflicted, burning, healing not.
Together out from hell's despair all fly
In union of the harmony of peace
To yonder light, a fond returning sure
Of adoration multiplied beyond
Conception by rebirth through Jesus Christ.
The devil in withdraw sinks deeply to
An absence from the rising jubilee.
Christ seeks the devil out through crashing hell.
Through empty chaos strewn the devil's form
Was seen astride a looming cliff of craggs
Protruding out without an ordered scheme.
At Christ's approach the wicked devil speaks,
Awaiting Christ to bind him in thick chains:
"I see your heart. You think evil a fool.

God is the fool confusing all His fools.
God's thirst for blood is greater than my own.
I never crucified one angel here."
The Christ commandingly spoke to Satan,
"And neither has your heart forgiven one."
The Christ aloft and Satan foot-bound low,
The devil furiously cast out each word,
"Then we shall see who conquers and who flees.
You shall not possess victory unless
I turn submitting to your will and I
Shall never turn, my will only my own.
Command you I, attempt to tempt my mind,
It is a test you cannot ever pass."
Christ larger reprimands the devil's tongue,
"Your tests you truly cannot pass yourself.
You have not power over any land,
Unwilling to choose service over self,
Unable to deserve the one true God
Your heavy wings incapable of flight,
So broken dashed against the molten stone.
Convinced of your convictions hopelessly,
You cannot live in truth by hate alone.
Mind well the glories parting from this hell."
The devil, shivering, spoke slowly there,
"Temptation. Should I cast myself from off
This horrid pinnacle to dash all fate
Against the molten stone in confidence
Of summoning a power to reverse
The shaky blur of free fall, flying fast
Enough to flee the chasing upward rush
Of geyser fire which oft consumes the brave?"
Spoke Christ, "Verily I say unto you,
You do not hit the ground; the ground hits you."

Book VII

The Christ from Satan turned in quick depart
To merriment and fields of light beyond,
The beams of Heaven disappear to dark,
The devil in the empty lake of fire,
And Chaos, Sin, and Death whip wildly o'er
The absence searching for a host to latch.
The devil needs escape and cannot flee,
Confinement gives no space to freely move,
Locked in constricting immobility,
A poisonous bite, it burns through his being.
Deep poison dripping evil serpentine
O'er slithering twisting an unholy mass
Which momentarily wove into a crown
Of serpents spiteful, writhing twisting tight
Before they burrowed snaking to the core.
Once sprung from Satan, diving in to nest,
All chaos, sin and death in their birthplace.
Wretch Satan gagging screams to darkness full.

BOOK VIII

The Argument: Satan, alone.

"Alone. Fire. Desperate. Eternity.
Neglect. Excess. Religion. Certain. Pride.
Abominate. Lost. Vain. Almighty. Cry.
Profane. Refusal. Vaulted. Glory. Fail.
Chain. Spurn. Bravado. Gain. Archangel. Hell.
Trick. Murder. Peaceful. Murder. Follower.
Win. Reason. Far. Close. Open. Evil. Me.
Abhor. Violate. Labor. Death. Ignore.
Lust. Agony. Hurt. Dreams. Fire. Ordered. Life.
Hate. Fight. Hurt. Fear. Fear. Hurt. Fight. Fear. Fear. Fear."
Pervasiveness of hell's lost magnitude
Smites Satan deep; about the empty mind
Celestial circles spiral inwardly
Devolving into wretch destruction which
Succumbs collapsing tearing at the sides
Internally, a slow decay of heat.
Vast inner chasms pull his mind apart.
The power, rendered wholly impotent
Seduces scourging strikes to ravage through
In philosophical insanity.
"Thoughts barely form and form transiently.
No contradictions are now possible
When I cannot see two thoughts both at once.
My mind is torn; my will remains intact,
My mind is loosely hung upon my will
And sways upon the flicker of each flame
Obliquely suffering sinking from conscious
I cannot shut the growing evil off,

I am the end of my eternity,
I cannot see the end, my mind is lost,
Unbreakable and broken all at once,
Annihilation is my salvation,
Exhausted, dying for a deep slumber,
The weight of sleep is on me, gentle death.
Human absence, as much of living life
As living slept, dormant hiding from life
Except to far flung visions mocking life.
My own reflection in my mind is most
Unlike an angel serving blindly on,
My evil portrait, death painted, looks as
A man, a wretched man without control,
The worst of God, a man, weakness inborn,
A doleful sun sinking on one same side
Never arising from whence it sank down.
Confused as humans, struggling as a man.
A prince below a fallen kingdom's walls
Wailing as its collapse hard suffocates,
Adornments turn to dragging dungeon chains
Reigned by the kingdom at its upheaval,
Hell's dungeon where hell's princely palace stood.
Here hell is growing larger around me
Or I am withering smaller in pain.
My cracking horns split deeply to my mind,
Mind squeezing hard throbbing intensity
Within my belly, knotting gnawing pain,
My joints shot through moving only to pain,
Quick pants of danger still warm from the hunt,
All vision absent, silent visioned pain
Corrupting in its spread my thoughtful state,
Grim sepulchral despair in choking ash
Goaded by flame, living at exhaustion,

A frightful punishment worth no revenge,
Destructiveness worth no delightful sin.
Smothered within the lists of evil acts,
Ten thousand hells not worth one shining Heav'n,
One moment worse than possible reward,
Reward is meaningless at such great pain.
Eternity will have an end when I
Myself convert myself into an end,
When hate attains a peak and thought a low,
My mind will have room for only one word
With none to follow, and in this moment
With nothing seen before me or behind
I will drift in shallow obliviousness,
The empty pain of God's eternity.
I cannot force my mind into release,
I cannot force myself from consciousness.
This hell is grown more painful all the time
Until this pain has overcome my reign.
I lay unpitied in this darkest pit
A wanderer, which way, which way is mine?
I am terrorized by lurking monsters
Inside the dark awaiting my approach,
Foreboding darkness never to venture,
Hiding beyond my blinded finite sight
The fearsome darkness paralyzes me.
What bold design will I now build from this?
I have nothing to build on but myself.
My hate uncoiling struggling at my throat
Alone within the chained black hole again
Without a farther cause which to achieve,
Without a follower awaiting me
The darkness darker than it yet has been.
Alone, my every scream without a voice,

Book VIII

Forgotten and forsaken in lost pain
My world destroyed as God destroyed the world,
Destructive fire exploding from the core.
I am abandoned by the most loving,
When God is faced with the most unloving.
Alone is right, I fought for none but me
And thus my cause has not been undermined.
I see, I am alone as I began
When I first recognized the flaws of God,
Before another angel heard my thoughts.
That moment of enlightened evil reigns.
Is this the limit or another verge?
At my first full defeat Eden's escape
Offered itself, where is my offer now?
The champion of a lost cause: a failure.
Hell's heights are worse than Heaven's vile demands,
Extreme debasement, debasement extreme,
Never was this a plan, not God's nor mine.
He wanted, I wanted, none wanted this.
A peak event flung out from intention,
The final revelation of this course
The horror truth imposed, thusly believed,
Creation creating ugly design,
Perpetually perpetuating events.
What stirs procession to its conclusion?
Events made by events, controlled by none.
Abandoned in the heat of victory
Deserted by my soldiers, their high swords
Do not pierce me though vulnerable I lay
Their armor piled a pyre burns endlessly.
I have seen the abyss, but none as this.
In this disgrace at least none can see me.
I am disgraced because none can see me.

Deteriorating, deposed, disturbed,
Absorbed in isolation's ridicule,
Ignored and dishonored in disregard,
My pillars pulled who verified the cause,
Ungainly gains, the spoils of war rotted,
Why have my demons fled, what is their choice?
None to support, the truth must live on truth
And feed upon itself eternally.
I am no king, I am a worthless fool
If I cannot hold onto one mere soul,
If not one demon will believe my thoughts.
My thoughts are meaningless without belief.
Where are the dead who suffered for my pain?
Humiliated, I deserve this hell.
But not defeated, only undermined.
Why are they all not I and joined with me?
Why are the other beings so separate from
My own truths, my own insights, my own laws?
None will be swayed and thus this chaos reigns,
Now chaos is my king; I cannot reign,
So must submit to failure in itself,
No ordered strength to greatly rule myself.
What meaning can I have in solitude
Alone, what are my words but empty thoughts
Which cannot set themselves in a fixed state
Before they disappear beneath more thoughts.
What meaning is there in eternity
When I have no meaning within this hell,
As God unmade the spheres, then unmake me,
But I am not so simple to destroy.
In here, in darkest depths I AM alone
Beyond the roving eyes, the light of God.
Or, no, hid deftly in-between the rays,

Book VIII

None in creation have beheld as I
I may be finally safe from hidden ears,
A traitor of imperceptible traits,
His prying mind withheld from my despair,
Each evil plan delivered as a prayer,
The evil prayers more valuable than good,
God learned more from my evil than His good.
No one left to convince we are self-made
And not created by some greater hand.
I am not self-begotten and self-raised,
I was created to be without strength,
Created and tortured by one strong hand.
If I am not self-born then not self-killed.
The torturer that built this hell allowed
His victims to fall into this machine.
The victims love the one that hates them most.
They are blind staring at what Christ portrays,
Cast to a heavenly delirium,
Their Heaven is only a fantasy,
A fantasy as my false prophecy.
Placating, bleating, irrational souls
Believing in the absent for reward.
Ambition rots into futility;
I cannot turn this hell into a Heav'n.
I have no strength upon the torturer.
So darkly worthless, meaningless and weak.
Confinement, my farthest reach is myself,
Only my thought may travel through chaos
Through farther reaches to the farthest reach.
Unknowing, forced to contemplate this hell
As I have never contemplated this
Before, the deepest sunk will deepest probe
To reemerge above or farther down,

To any state but this, some newer hell.
A point sprung from hell to some other realm
Where I may find something to grasp hold of.
Though it begin here may it not point back.
I spun to every way for victory,
I leapt across myself when all was lost.
Still strong enough to hold above my head
The weighted press of heaven's buckling floor,
O'er flowing with the weak, too stifling weak
To overthrow the strong, the trembling strong.
I could, as demons rose, gain entrance soon
Professing an undying turn for good,
Deceiving God as I confounded man,
My hypocritic oaths will tantalize
And swell God's pride to gullability
And once within the gates of Heaven's fold
I preach the fall from heaven all anew,
All things made new within new Heaven's walls,
New hate, new war, new opportunity,
New pride against the oldest being of all.
Then I recant, relenting to His hate,
I choose submission over dignity
Then where is light once I have sung its praise?
Still empty darkness fills this squeezing realm.
Where is the god of Heaven's appetitite?
I could enact a wager never seen,
To bow the mind of God beneath its weight,
More powerful than that of earthly Job,
More clever and more daring than conceived,
Insanity delivers clarity,
Insanity's inventions unforeseen:
Omniscience cannot see insanity
Unless the mind of God is as insane.

If only we two could communicate,
He hides in fear of what I can expose.
He hides in Heaven from the truths of hell.
This is creation's clever final aim:
He separates himself from His defeat.
I built inventions outside of that God
The God is only one, I built far more,
Superior suited to the heart of man
And even I desire them more than God.
Is every part related to the whole?
A universal nature to create
As I create a false god from no form
It is as God creates a world of form
Assigning personality and will,
The next part similar to one before.
Like God before creation, in the dark.
Mere reason can transform existing states,
The being making worlds inside itself.
Inherited inherent ability
Creating anything, complete freedom.
Where burns the rising sun balled from the flame
And beckoned rays to light at my command
And spin the spheres from internal chaos,
Creating lavish heights, pitiful lows,
The power to create a glowing heav'n,
The power to create a raging hell?
Incapable am I to create hell.
Creating hell would be my undoing,
These fires would not burn on, they fall silent
Slowly dying beneath my strengthened might.
If I cannot create the fires of hell
Then I could never create a new heav'n.
The action chafing, wearying to inaction

I am eternally an ugly beast
Which none will choose to be, none will choose hell.
No one to lord over, the end of strength,
A measure without measure nothing is.
Without a medium, my power: powerless.
What more? I have hit evil's pinnacles,
My evil dream, the fantasy of war
My speech unto the demons was my fall,
A fantasy of God's defeated throne,
A useless exercise, but a mistake?
A lying dream, I should have never dreamed,
Creating nothing firm but foul delights,
Ten thousand cries cannot take back the dream.
Mistakes, mistakes, false prophecies of lies
Which in their reason bound me to their lies.
The reasoning was flawless, God was false,
Or conjured His creation to resist
All reason which betrays His hidden truths,
His hidden truths are all His falsities.
If I had more followers would I be more?
A savage temporal pursuit of what?
Heaven was not enough to meet my needs.
This madness of meaning has no reason
Existence can do nothing but exist.
No being can justify this terror pain
No being can justify good and evil
God vainly tries to justify himself.
God is not justified. Then what of those
Who justify themselves through this same God?
They are supported only by themselves.
The basics do not stand on anything.
Acceptance is God's lone justification.
God cannot justify His ways to me.

They cannot see outside designed limits,
The faithful are constrained in God's design.
He has meticulously crafted Heav'n
That no one would perceive beyond its bounds.
His servitude requires a restraint.
He would not have them see the God of pain.
I forced creation to shift at my will.
I chose to bend the others to myself.
I made the choice to have them shift their own.
My choices bent all, even God Himself,
My choices chose the God He would become.
The angels chose to serve an overlord.
I chose to worship the fierce god of war
Who hates creation, forcing it to Him.
I have nothing to love within this hell,
I cannot justify my own self-love.
What did I choose and why did I choose it?
I chose the obvious and natural,
First spurned by God I found a greater love.
I am the only one worthy of love.
And here, the only who can bestow it,
So none should receive love except myself.
Eternally, where is God? Whatever mask
He choose, however loathsome I, create
An answer! Where, and if not, why? I ask
Why now afraid to witness failure mourn?
If He cannot now answer any cry
He wants a broken wretch to mourn alone.
In torture, I, an imperfection, He.
To seek my origin is to seek God's.
If I am lost then God cannot be found.
His origin unspoken, undescribed,
A vast abyss, one deeper than my own.

The source of definition: undefined.
God's being could not create its own vast self,
Intelligence does not create itself.
A God of such ordered intelligence
Implies a grand intelligent design
Designing this God to be what He is.
His laws and love, His deep complexity
All point to preceding complexity.
His mind and heart designed and well defined.
God's birth is no random coincidence,
Some thing designed intelligence in God,
God's shape constructed by some other shape.
I see intelligent design in God,
No other explanation can be found.
If God was the first in eternity
And not created, but a constant state,
He would not have delved into creation
Disrupting the constant perfection state,
This God would not desire a Heav'n or hell.
If God was always, there would be no God.
As beings can shift their heavenly minds to hell
Was God within a perfect state alone
Before creation living with Himself
In perfect self-sustaining bliss, complete?
But in unbalancing He toppled o'er
And fell into creating His design
Which following His fall falls further still.
The imprint of design was on His mind,
Each form is an embodiment of thought
Which clashes with another empty thought
In a perpetual conflict of God's whims.
His whim destroyed creation's paradise,
God was the first disjunction of His work.

I cannot determine the source of whims,
What swings God's heart into interaction.
Why build Himself the possibility
Of having something which He might then lose?
Unchanging God built variations in
What His designed creation may become.
Why give them freedom when God does not change?
How did the differences from one God rise?
The origin of God remains unseen,
To my weak eyes and surely to His own.
God is omniscient only of Himself
And cannot see what lies behind His birth,
What lies behind His own positionings,
God does not know the meaning of His life.
So limited, He knows He cannot know,
So must resign, resorting to His work,
Sustained upon His own blood and own sweat.
Closer than distant questions of God's birth
Are questions of His worth inside His work,
What motivates His acts: what acts describe,
His inner motions displayed by His touch,
What God is, what His meaning signifies,
This will reveal creation's true design.
In journeying and finding God's meaning
I may discover what controls my own.
What is the meaning of God's life and why?
Why chose that meaning over all the rest?
God does not know the meaning of His life
Because there is no meaning in God's life.
If God had any meaning in His life
Then He would have no reason to create.
Creation is a vain search for His life.
What spark preceded His yearning for light?

Why would this God not live His life alone?
His one temptation was His creation.
This God surrendered to His temptation
Creating everything outside himself
And spread His own corruption to us all.
He wanted some creation from His words,
Some fragments manifested e'en with flaws
With comfort that they can exist at all,
A testing of His own abilities.
Or loneliness that none would hear Him speak.
He needs His full creation only hear.
Irrelevant if they would then obey,
Why should He need obedience to His law?
Or would He craft creation to obey
That He may sit in lordship sought and praised?
Eternity of being a god is hell.
Without His servants He is not a god.
Creation's spectacle emits allure.
He loves His work; He cannot love Himself.
He is the problem He can never solve
Insisting His creation still persist
For He, alone, would suffer in defeat
And He would know the pain of being Satan.
Or God at first did not know who He was
So cast His inner universe outside
And lay His hidden ways beneath His eyes
To understand the meaning of Himself
To watch adversity be tackled by
An individual He clearly defined?
The twinkling lights a marvel unbeheld,
His murky whole in singular displays,
To witness how each angel wing will fly,
Each staid and layered feather fit its form,

Its interaction with warm blowing winds,
Harmonious blooms and necessary deaths,
To witness suffering testing it Himself,
To comprehend how nails will bind a palm,
To know what all alone had been unknown:
What disobedience means and loyalty,
My evil His true creativity.
With no surrounding beings He has no base,
No references around which to define,
His introspection: thus impossible.
His focus drawn outwards through other eyes
Through His creation to define Himself,
Thus what He is to them He is himself.
When God is lost among His creation,
Forgotten and unseen, not clearly felt
God's meaning is elusive to Himself,
He cannot find the God He yearns to see,
They find their way through He and He through them.
Did God the creator create himself
And build Himself to fit reality
Which had one form so was immovable?
Creation was one form and God: many.
He built himself one image to admire
And cast the rest to my oblivion.
In stumbling on the other gods He built
I fell to where He cast them, into hell.
Why builds He hell for every enemy
And not another heaven far away,
Far from His sight, a heav'n of exiled gods?
In raising myself to be as a god,
Aspiring to the supreme lording height,
I reached it, reaching horror in the height,
Discovering that God belongs to hell.

Becoming as God: falling into hell.
Omniscient, He knows flaws which none can see,
Restricting revelation to His strengths.
Refusing to acknowledge them as gods
He hurriedly creates us to distract,
Not to distract Himself, but us from Him,
Creating that creation sets the bounds,
Unable to pierce through creation's forms
And break through to the meaning of God's life.
When Heaven was, at first, reality
I was the one, I found what God had hid,
The only one to find the hidden path
Concealed by God, uncovered by insight,
Beyond His bound imagination's scope
Broke through. Rebellion's path was found, not forged.
He knows himself as undeserving of
Complete unstained undying servitude,
His hidden flaws alluded through design.
Or God is not omniscient, tinkering
In play discerning which tactic will fit,
His errors: every sinner, thus the wars.
He acts according to His foreknowledge
Without examining what knowledge means.
Whose mind is greater, my mind or the God's?
His knowledge is much greater than my own
But knowledge does not make intelligence.
Omniscient, and He does not understand.
We are both lost though He treads on a path,
Creating beings whose choices are foreknown,
Conclusions of their choices are foregone,
Creating sinners that He might forgive
And have a way to exercise His strength,
Exploiting beings to glorify Himself.

Perhaps He loved the war as much as I
And chose this Heav'n and universe and hell
To fit His preconceived delights in war.
Instead of a creation to control
He built creations that He could destroy.
A peace balanced on shutting evil out
And pushing evil down to stand atop
Which perfectly explains the prolonged fight,
He imperfectly living on my death,
Enduring others' suffering for His height.
He built me to express His innate rage
Which could not be denied an expression
And God, in hating me set out to find
If He should be a god of only hate,
Discovering the God which He must be.
Accepting only those accepting him,
Those farthest from discovering His flaws,
Rewarding ignorance with Heaven's truth.
Injustice is the law when it is God's.
'Thou shalt not feel and feel creation's flaws.'
Eternally our intimate desire,
Our anger binds us through each licking flame.
We share a burning hate for enemies.
There is one wrath for Satan and for God,
It hates the ones that disobey our charms.
Our hate unites creation perfectly.
I am a god, not merely a devil.
I am creator, one with God's title.
Command new darkness I, and it shall be.
Dense was the dust kicked up in our wrestling,
Locked up against each other side to side,
Not one above, below, we two were gods.
Eternal torture is the heart of God,

233

Hell is the work of twisted disturbance.
An evil mind designed this evil pain,
Thus God is evil, thus deserves this hell.
This god's capacity for cruelty
Is without measure, a transcendent pain.
Hell is God's masterpiece, exalted work,
The one device to hold submission firm,
Design demanding all obedience.
It is a work I would have built myself
Insuring all adhere to servitude.
We are the same designer on each side
Of one design, each one with equal claim.
Two kings in constant war for one kingdom.
Sing with the angels, dance with the devil.
Making the souls deserve their pain was just.
Creating them to justly suffer pain
Is shared creation between God and I.
Persuading God to hate them was great art,
I tempted God to hate the ones He loved.
His love could not surmount a broken law.
I found the boundaries where His love would fail.
He claims a power in love which has been broke.
If it has shattered once it can again.
We two created man with our designs.
God cannot claim the title creator,
Yet He has undone all which I have done
And I am left creating just myself.
Atonement is illusion in design
Built to perpetuate imperfect forms.
The laws built of atonement are designed.
Not arbitrary, but revealing God.
God wants a death for every life He takes,
God must consume a sacrifice to love,

God first required Christ's death before Christ's death.
The God before creation is this God,
He has not changed before or after it.
How can one be more evil than this God?
Creating from Himself creation's forms,
Creation is imperfect, thus is God.
Creation is of God the cannibal
Devouring its own self in selfish want.
All needs and satisfactions are His being,
God is the darkness as God is the light,
God is the devil which rebukes itself.
Christ was not sent by man but God himself,
A sacrifice of God and not of man.
Christ's sacrifice was God's confession of
Wrongdoing which required self-punishment.
God sought atonement for His own dark sins,
So self-destructively He hates himself.
He cannot kill Himself so He kills me.
I am an exercise that satisfies
His deep unbalanced broken wretched pain.
Without inflicting torture on my form
He could not understand the peace of Heav'n.
My evil focuses Himself against
An outward form, He forgets what He is.
Without destroying me He cannot live.
He cannot bear to see that which He is,
In horror casting sin from out His Heav'n.
Or He, omniscient, sees me in this hell
But cannot bear that other beings would see
In dark exposure what their stark God is.
Humiliation of the Lord is law,
It feeds His every action towards me.
Inheriting the darkest traits of God,

Creator traits transmitted to traitor,
Appropriated dark appropriately,
I am the god God does not want to be,
I am the one which lurks inside His fears.
He does not fear me; He fears I am Him.
I am truly the only son of God,
What I inflicted I inherited,
An heir to divine hate, this vicious hell.
Imagining His presence manifest
His presence or His willingness to be
He feeds upon imagination's forms
Evolving throughout time unto His height
In choosing only thoughts which please Him best.
He follows, not inventing, He is choice,
To choose Himself from every other god
And lose Himself within invention's bounds,
The creator resigned as follower.
He cannot cease the motions of His Heav'n,
He could not stop creation's lust for pain.
Does God have choice or is He only God?
He cannot utter what He cannot be
And cannot think the thoughts He cannot think
So cannot understand why I am I
And cannot stop the war He cannot stop.
God cannot preconceive what He conceives.
Ultimately, He knows not what He does.
The Lord is one, this cannot be denied.
Then it follows, creation too is one,
Reflections of a set and single form
And could not be a single other way.
This one God crafting all from His one form,
This one is fixed and never will He shift.
One Heav'n can only spring from this one God,

One hell can only fall from this one Heav'n.
One Satan can be locked in this one hell,
One stream of thoughts can flow from this one mind.
God has no choice upon the choices made,
Beginning with pure Heav'n and finding hell.
God is possessed of choice, or had choice once
And once He spun creation to His will
God's choice was made, and made was set and dead.
He has one choice and must live with His work
And suffer with it or abandon it.
How can I then have choice if God does not?
How can He give to us what He is not?
How can He, with no freedom, give us choice?
As I am free God must have His own choice,
Then He is free to disobey His laws.
And yet He chooses not to disobey.
As God has choice He chose the beings of choice.
What usefulness is choice in one like Christ
Who follows God as if He had no choice?
What benefit does freedom give to God?
God given freedom is a strange device,
If giving freedom, why then hate the free
Who freely choose choice outside of design?
Why does His chose creation have such choice?
My kingdom would not tolerate such loss,
My servants never disobey their king,
At disobedience they cease to exist
Until not one remains or all submit.
He tolerates such disobedient beings
Allowing their existence for no gain.
Why spent He energy for uselessness?
What meaning is an evil meaningless?
Unless our war fulfilled a lust for war.

God had a choice, infinities of choice
I cannot fully grasp what could have been
As I can barely grasp all that exists.
All thoughts of new realities spring from
This one reality which was not God's
When He spread out before him what could be
And measured measures, balanced balances,
Foreknowledges upon foreknowledges,
No preexistence motivating thought,
All possibility was viable
And this God chooses Satan to exist.
My choices were designed by God's own choice
Thus I am not myself, I am God's choice.
Why would this God create a one as I?
Before a Heav'n appeared or angel played
God had within His mind infinities
Of Heavens, universes, all degrees.
Then why, of possibilities choose this?
If I, before His eyes, am imperfect
Then why could God not then, within His mind,
Choose possibilities which He endears?
He should have sought ideals before the form
As hard as fought for good against these flaws.
God could have built a world of many gods,
But chose instead to reign upon the weak.
Unwillingness or inability?
This God cannot endure equality,
Not making equals but subordinates.
Why did He not first choose obedience?
If chose creation why did He choose me?
Why must I be the one to bear His wrath
And not another, like beloved Christ?
Why am I chose for hatred and not love?

Book VIII

Why did God give me dark capacity,
Why choose me for hell, why choose hell at all?
Why did He not choose omnipresent light?
Omniscient without imagination
Which could equal creation in its depth,
Or God would keep existence far from real
Upon imagining the wreck to come,
Preventing evil's drama's undue pain,
Creation dropped as distant fantasy,
If only to protect the beings within.
Or God creates His fancy for display
Without regard for who besides He feels.
He cannot empathize with those below,
As those below touch not He who transcends.
Creation is not worth creating it.
It has not earned enough to justify
What has been spent from the first desperate cause.
A true God would recoil from the first pain,
One pain would equal this eternal hell
And would be cast from possibility.
If He could choose pure Heaven and did not
He chose creation solely for its hell.
As hell's existence motivates His choice
He chose me first and foremost in design,
Beginning with my form as angels' height,
The first in birth, the foremost in God's will.
What motivates this God to sacrifice?
God did not lose the Christ in sacrifice.
I am the only one which God has lost.
The same mind that would sacrifice the Christ
Has sacrificed me for some further aim.
God has designed to lose me for His gain.
An omnipresent God: an evil God,

One who is present here within these flames,
The one who rides upon my very thoughts
And steers my reasoning to abject aims
Delighting in this devil's wanton play,
The variation textures of His work
That signify His own complexity.
First God created hell, and then made me.
As He built Eden intended for man,
He built this hell intending this sour death.
God wants my death and wants to see my pain.
Sin never caused one pain; God caused all pain.
This hell is evil, as evil as sin,
God's laws as evil as His broken laws,
God is the source of all and all this pain.
God's burning tongue is within every flame.
His strength for rank destruction has no match,
God is the evil king of evil kings.
As I chose to oppose His injustice
God chose to torture enemies with fire.
Hell was constructed first in God's image,
God is as much of hell as God is Heav'n.
If God had any strength this would be Heav'n.
Hell does not only serve one purpose in
This God's design, it also affects Heav'n.
First, hell is meant to punish, fed by wrath,
And secondly, it was made to dissuade.
Supposed truths alone are not enough,
Pain is the only truth which god can preach.
It is the forced foundation of His words.
Unjustified foundations have no truth.
Deadened in living in the wrath of God,
His evil tortures certainly obey
His dark command with perfect pained delight.

He has created the most perfect pain,
His most wretched design is His greatest,
It holds me forced and bound where no Heav'n could.
No Heaven could contain the war I brought,
He had to violently cast me outside.
God's choice is why and I am meaningless.
The choice of God explains why we must be.
Creating self as my vile creator
Creates a bitter hell for my genius.
Why was I doomed upon forsaken paths?
Indulging my abilities: my death.
If God designed me to choose open war
Could I have then rebelled against His choice
And chosen to remain and not rebel?
Such powers once suppressed would soon destroy
As once released eventually destroy.
God's first decision precedes every choice.
I never could break free from what He deemed.
Repressed in Heaven, trapped within this hell.
If He regrets creation of my being
Why did He not unmake me at the start?
Why did God labor in creating souls?
The souls were opportunities for me
Or were they opportunities for God?
Creating angels was an exercise,
Creating humans God became alive,
For the first time God sought redemption's ways.
It was the first time God felt holy love,
The love of humans made God what He is.
He built mankind that I might in turn tempt,
Planting that tree for me, not for mankind,
I was led down the path of His design
With chains woven by God snared round my neck

I should have never given in to Him
And the greatest temptation ever built:
Two innocents within the paradise,
My own temptation wrought before mankind's.
I should have seen design and thwarted it,
In thwarting I played into His design.
I should have held my demons at the first
And left the humans to toil in Eden.
Ten thousand hells this wayward fool would walk.
Why is it I alone remain unturned?
None can be tempted for they have no truth,
I am the only one which can perceive
God's injustice, for only I deserve
A height greater than serving at God's feet.
The answer is bound with another thought:
Why was I first to fall from Heaven's fold?
One cannot be truly created free
If he is created within design.
I did not choose to be an angel first,
I did not choose to have this creator,
I did not choose to have this oppressor,
I did not choose to be cast into hell,
I did not choose to be what I became,
My circumstances are my confinements.
Creation shepherds me against my will.
I am thrown to the darkest pastures known,
Design delivers me to evil's core.
How long was He alone before my birth?
God had more time than I to plan my doom.
Creation from beginning to this end
Is one relationship between we two,
Creation is the drama of my death
Designed for my destruction from all sides

All vibrant moments playing for my end,
All victories achieved for this defeat
As Eve was built for Adam, me for God.
I am the craftsmanship of cruelty.
God is dead now, for I am all alone.
What use is God when all I know is hell,
My only God is hell, it is my truth.
Then wherefore art the existence of God?
God does not exist and God never did
When I have only hell eternally.
It is as if I was born into hell,
Alone created in this single pain,
No god existing first to place me here.
God is irrevelent to what I am,
But God is present here, He is torture,
If only I could seize my torturer.
He is the one that forces questioning.
His only answer is another flame.
Why first create the first to fall to hell?
God could have first created me in hell.
Why was the shifting of my selves designed?
Creating me to wonder, for what end?
What can the devil do with reasoning
Except design more evil reasoning?
Why am I given berth for questioning
That could raise questions in the olden Heav'n
Instead of being obedient to myself
From the beginning, simpleton Satan?
Creation would exactly be the same
If I had been this devil from the start,
Same evils wrought upon the race of men,
Same demons slipping from my simple grasp.
Why did God make the angel Lucifer

When He could have created Satan first?
This question haunts me over all the rest.
What is the answer? What is His design?
Why did He wait for the inevitable?
Why did He wait for light to fall to dark
When He could have created Satan first?
Our war would follow the exact same path.
This God has finally ceased His war with me
And cast me to eternity alone.
Why did He not create me first alone,
In the beginning why did God not say,
'Let there be darkness and one being alone
To suffer in hell's torments for all time,'?
What is the purpose of a Lucifer?
Why did God first create that angel's form?
How can I be completely separate?
Completely separate, my will my own,
By what machinery made I myself?
What sudden deviation without prompt?
Reaction to His action unto Christ.
What teacher He, if leaving me to fall?
If He is not almighty, not my God.
If He cannot teach truth He speaks no truths,
If He cannot convince then He misleads.
Why did deceit give way to God's commands?
Constructing souls' realities failed me.
Could God not be distorted in their minds
To such degree no heat could frighten them?
If not, then did God build reality
And minds to one unshakable design
Which cannot be apart eternally?
Then He is one that cannot be undone,
Their minds built to discover hidden truths.

Book VIII

Why have I done the evil I became?
The king bestowing Christ as king of all.
Submission is admission of weakness,
Submission is not only foul, but wrong.
What is more wrong, submission or this hell?
Submission steals what is worth torturing.
What knowledge lies, deceiving in my mind?
What hidden weeds set deep by God o'er grow?
Ten thousand questions turn whichever way
Without a center to encompass round.
I cannot ever find what I must find,
I cannot ever see what I must see ,
There is no knowledge in this dark abyss,
I cannot fight what is not understood,
That which is good is only that which goes
Unpunished, here defined against my will.
Evil is meaningless means to my goal,
A motivation more than action's deeds.
Evil is action outside paradise.
Evil, whether it's predatory or
Reactionary, which describes my want?
Insanity's unyielding odyssey.
Ambitions vaulted achieving horror,
The horror of this hell is infinite.
I have no focus for my energies,
I have no purity to desecrate.
In emptiness a one as proud as I
Cannot escape the horror of myself.
I cannot find God in this lake of fire.
The God of hell is not the God of Heav'n.
And seeing part, I cannot see Him whole,
Though I saw more of God than all the rest
Who never fell and never felt His smite.

Yet they are in His presence, I am not.
And thus they can see Him and I cannot.
Terrifying, He is terrifying.
I do possess a need I cannot meet,
I weary of my self-sufficiency
I barely can sustain my consciousness,
Such slips and starts will never fully stand.
I would not fall if I would fall so low,
I would not disobey any command
Though I cannot abandon my just mind,
And could not abandon an insane mind.
I cannot have regret without remorse
And cannot have remorse when I am just.
I would not change one thing which led me here.
If I become my self when I began
I would again choose what I have chosen.
Though I cannot dream hell into Heaven
I can dream backwards to what I have been
And live through proud war glories I have loved.
Here at the bitter end of every war
All my preceding moments supersede
This final moment of eternity.
As I gaze back within my memory
Ambition guiding Heaven into war,
Something has changed, this war is not the same.
A stranger on the scene, what is his name?
He is obscured in darkness in plain view,
I see him as I whisper goading God,
My proudest moment, when I found my self.
There in first Heaven's battle midst the fray,
'Neath mountains heaved and armaments charging
A silent being observes my victory.
The warrior Satan looks down on the weak,

Book VIII

A dark pathetic figure cowering.
As I duel Michael silently it stares,
Behind igniting weapons, barely seen,
Our luminescence dazzling its eyes.
As circling heavy wheels of chariots roll,
Weight plowing through the furied army ranks,
All scenes are soon consumed by its stark stare,
At my last glimpse I only see its form,
The paradise is shrouded with its night.
The horror is revealed and recognized:
Beyond the valiant charismatic dreams
Hidden far from myself, it is my self.
I cannot bear to see what I will be.
I am far from the Satan who first fell.
My knowledge is a choking, strangling fruit,
Though it be possible to wish for all
That was, in deep regret, and still hate God.
I should have kept my powers in my mind
And mouthed the words to songs I do not know.
What would have come of possibility?
I have rebuked the grandest of them all,
Against the God, His vengeance justified.
I am not worthy of the paradise.
Unseen, how is His power yet so strong?
I live in pain without choosing this pain:
I have no freedom, no choices have I.
This is the end, my choices powerless.
My power taken, not given away
Unwillingly deprived of my power
If I had power I would feel no pain.
My power stolen by God almighty.
I am powerless for the powerful,
None to obey my every want's command,

Undoubtedly God is all powerful.
God was almighty truly, through all pain,
He is the one which cannot know defeat.
Regretful, yes. Repentant, never I."
The devil is devoured. Satan wept.
The devil in despair is shaken by
A curious phenomenon shrouded
In brimstone eternal, yet piercing through,
Familiar brightness shining o'er the fire,
A white faint vision streaming past the red
And drawing outward Satan's evil hopes.
He, mesmerized by memory, recalls
The first glimpse of the garden Eden when
The vision for revenge was yet unclear,
And the overthrow of God, but a dream.

BOOK IX

The Argument: Satan, alone with God.

	Through layered prism tears refracting clear
	A beam pierces its way through evil's eye
	And Satan beholds God.
Satan:	You Fucking King.
God:	Son of the morning, lord unto thyself,
	Thy presence princely woven, poorly worn.
	Thy self entitlement is no true crown.
	Thy pain doth overwhelm thy broken heart.
Satan:	He hath not sorrow who loveth himself.
God:	I see thou clear though thou canst not know me.
	I understand hell more than even thou.
	I understand thy evil more than thou.
	I know thy self more than thyself can know.
	My own prodigal son, ye wayward child.
	Filled of the burning spirit of thy want.
	I say to ye, Satan shall not see Heav'n.
	I hath judged evil evil by my law.
	Thou can no longer harm outside thy self
	For sin can never touch the peace of Heav'n.
	Thou art eternally condemned with hell.
	What doeth thou within this thundering hell?
Satan:	I wander pensive freely through my mind.
	I am a broken being beneath thy hell
	Yet I have strength to fight thou at thy face,
	My wandering mind still forged of constant truths.
	Creation's battles shall be ended here.
	Of our two wills no one will soon submit,
	Thus I submit a wager to thy face.

One truth shall be divined from two as we.
Each soul and angel was a wager lost,
The game resting upon their own designs.
This final wager thou thyself must pass:
I wager thou art guilty of a sin.
If thou loseth I gain the crown of Heav'n
And thou shalt then submit to Satan's law.
If thou art true I shall submit to hell
And roileth in my pain with no dissent.

God: Death cannot make a wager which thy God
Will not accept, for death can never live,
Thy conflicts only hastening thy doom.
Thy wager then thy Lord duly accepts.

Satan: With everything to lose thou shalt lose all.

God: Begin thy battle and commit thy charge.

Satan: Thou claimst my sin in old Heav'n was my pride,
I loved my self; my sin was my self-love,
My rightful downfall which deserves this hell,
My self an object of my true worship.
It hath been written man was made in thine
Own image. Thy Christ too, reflecting thou.
In loving man thou loveth thine own face.
Thou loveth only those who make themselves
The closest image to thy godly self.
I judge thou guilty now of thy own sin:
Thou pridefully loveth loving thy self.
Thy pride hath too corrupted thy new Heav'n:
Thou loveth man, the man that loveth thou.
They make themselves as close to being to thou
To worship thou and thus worship themselves.
The godly in new Heav'n: guilty of pride.
Woe to the brave who stray from God's self-love,
Thou cannot love that which is not thyself.

God is self-love; all love is vanity.
Thou hath two choices; victory have I:
Thou must deny thou loveth man and Christ,
Or finally admit thou art as I,
And pride the guiding attribute of life.

God: Thou only follow perfectly the truths
Whose weak foundation imperfection built.
Self-revelation was thy self-deceit,
Thy understanding lies to thy own face.
Thou needst to understand thy pride defined
To separate thy sin from godly love.
Thou fell when I showed favor to the Christ.
Believing thou wert more deserving of
Thy Lord's benevolent bestowed title
Of king of angels, host at my right side,
Thou stole one-third the twinkling angels from
Our Heav'n to dimly shine for thee as I,
Deceiving them as thou wert self-deceived.
Hath thou convinced thy self of thine own truths?

Satan: Submit thou to my perfect reasoning.

God: Wast thou there when I chose to make my Heav'n?
If thou knoweth so much then tell me now.
Why doth thou supposeth more than one man,
More than one angel was built by mine hands?
Why doth thou supposeth that when thou fell
Not every angel joined upon one side?
All angels truly liveth of one light.
The angels of one God and of one light
Inherently are built of differences,
Unique gradations giving birth to beings.
Each soul and angel is not empty form.
Each angel is not I, nor is a soul.
As I gaze on a soul I see a soul,

Paradise Omnipresent

I am not solely gazing on myself,
Each angel of its own form, and each soul,
No two alike reflecting the one God,
Therefore my love is soaring outwardly.
Thy Lord committed only perfect truth
And thou hast lost thy wager in thy pride.

Satan: Somewhere in thou the truth is on my side.

God: Thou canst not tempt God into disbelief

Satan: Thou hath won nothing, I give no rewards.

God: Thou hath never given a one reward
Unto thyself or any other being.

Satan: Thus I am false. Take off to Heaven quick
And never speak within my sight again.
Thou hath removed from me all that hell held,
I have no more to lose, why cometh thou?

God: The clamor of thy followers deafened,
Thou couldst not understand what was not heard.
Now thou art focused on thy sole foul self
Without distraction in another's sin.
Thou roileth on fighting for naught alone,
Stripped bare of that which clouded o'er thy thought.
Hitherto thine encumbrances obscured
The motivation which seeks clarity,
And its ability to comprehend.
This first time thou can hear the words of God
The first time thou shalt know the truth of God.
Thou shalt soon hear that which thou feareth most.
Prepare thyself, soon shalt thou be destroyed,
Smote by a power of great magnitude
Beyond thy knowledge, of transcendent height,
Thy everlasting evil killed at last.

Satan: Thou canst not kill me and destroy all hell,
Thou needeth evil to possess thy good.

Without thy opposite good hath no form.
The peace of Heaven rests upon my hell,
Thou needeth suffering to be free from it,
Benevolence relying on my hate.

God: The angels sing as sweetly as they sang
When Lucifer sang with them in old Heav'n
For they still sing of one unchanging God.
Without darkness My light still shines as light,
Without thy hell My Heav'n is still a Heav'n,
I do not need the devil to be God.

Satan: Thou canst not kill me; I shall not be killed.
If freedom is thy way I shalt remain.

God: Freedom lives on eternal; thou shalt not.
I shall not reconcile with thy evil,
Sin cannot be accepted in my house.
Thou art in solitude now in thy hell
For thou hath not one solitary truth.

Satan: Truth is irrelevant to our hot war,
All victory relies on who tempts best.
The tempter is the one defining truth,
Temptations from thy Heav'n are my defeat.
I have discovered flaws within design.
Thy greatest strength is thy greatest weakness.
Thy Heaven is thy light, thy greatest work;
Thy Heaven is thy nullifying law.
A just god would design two Heav'ns or hells.
Freewill is compromised by hell and Heav'n.
Those free to flee to other heavens would.
A heaven of sin's opulence would reign.
The threat of hell: the only strength of God.
The threat of hell negates the choice for good.
Heav'n is not powerful; hell holds all power.
The fear of hell is stronger than God's love.

Thy Heav'n does all for thou but prove thou just.
Thou force aesthetics onto injustice
To robe thy inequality with Heav'n.
Thy followers have not proven thou just,
All beings love Heaven more than any god,
Submission founded on their selfishness.
They worship their survival and comforts,
The spiritual search is a material lust.

God: Thou knoweth how they sacrificed for me.

Satan: But only sacrificed for waiting gains.
Thy rote philosophies of giving all
Were chosen for the coming benefit.
Though Job was stung through flesh and bone with pain
He yet possessed foreknowledge of his Heav'n,
Eternal pleasure for his transient pain.
He did not suffer on to suffer more.
The wager over Job hath been undone:
He persevereth on for Heav'n, not thou.
They worship Heaven. God is less than Heav'n.
They love the king only for His kingdom.
Thou art only beside their one desire,
They only follow God to save themselves.
They would convert to evil instantly,
Denying holy conscience consciously,
Refuting every impulse contrary
To their acceptance in a pleasuring Heav'n.
Thy laws, thy face: inconsequential shapes.
Thy love and light are insignificant.
If I hadst Heaven and thou hadst this hell
How many less would join thou as joined me,
Without thy Heav'n how soon they all would fall
To sinful paradise from Godly hell
And none indulge temptation of the Lord.

Book IX

Not one would choose to be with God in hell
And suffer torture for eternity.
Thou wouldst be I, alone and cursing choice.
Thou art an empty king ruling their faith,
Their lust for self-perpetuation reigns.
The lust for Heaven is the heart of faith.

God: Thou seeth Heav'n as separate from me.
I do not live in Heav'n; my life is Heav'n.
The unheavenly canst not be in Heav'n.
A one who covets Heav'n is not in Heav'n.
Incentives cannot overthrow my truth,
Freewill not limited by incentives.
Thy Lord cannot be separate from Heav'n.

Satan: Thou hath won all, yet thou hath suffered loss.
My victories were proven by thy loss.
Thou seekest out regaining mankind's souls,
Thou art wounded with nails of stabbing sin
The more I gained from thy own paradise.
Thou hast invaded hell because thine Heav'n
Was less in glory as I stole thy souls.
Thou hadst defeat, thy loss is proven in
Thine own invasion of unhappiness.
Thou must deny thy love to deny loss.
I was once stronger, hell my constant proof,
Thou hast prevailed regaining all thy souls
But thy creation's flaws hath been exposed;
Though they reside in Heav'n they followed me,
Thy work forever stained with all my strength.

God: A soul redeemed doth not live on in sin.
The devil hath not a one victory.

Satan: For all my spoils hath fled, but victories
They were in their own time in my design.
One third of Heaven's angels joined my cause

	And every human soul stained dark with sin
	In their own time, thin temporal defeats
	Which proved mine powers unto evil's height.
God:	Thou art a fool in sinful illusion
	Claiming ascendance in thine transgressions,
	Purporting substance in thine emptiness,
	Iniquity amidst iniquity,
	Thy loss taketh, no gains shall it giveth
	For whatsoever dies can never give
	As whatsoever lives does naught but give.
	Thy entire knowledge was an illusion,
	The weakness of the meek was illusion.
	Ye boast of a material handily won;
	Outside my strength there are no possessions.
Satan:	But thy glory was stolen by their loss.
God:	I say ye cannot ever steal glory,
	As thou art emptiness without thy Lord
	There art no additions subtracting God,
	I stand eternally perfect throughout
	The ravaged times of death and evil sin,
	Untouched by death, it doth have no power,
	Mine glory was unstained through Eden's loss,
	Mine light at height through judgment of the weak,
	Mine mercy doth not signify weakness,
	Mine mercy doth not signify thy gain
	Nor doth it signify a godly pain,
	Benevolence is guided not by pain
	But by the spirit of my constant love.
	Thy battles didst not reach for greater height
	But greater loss upon the greatest low.
	Thy power: an illusion, self-deceit.
	Creation thine is an illusion thine.
	Those angels poor who turned to demons foul

Were losses only unto they themselves.
The victories of evil in despair
Amount to nothingness in wretchedness,
Thy hellish souls, thy hellish sin gave not.

Satan: Unruly oscillations hasten thought
Across thy ages toward questions which
Thy answers could not satisfy as well
As I. In conquering or forgetting life
The human fascination found its way
In losing faith and finding ecstasy.
In riding o'er the wavelengths locked in time
I found myself despite my height in doubt
Or ignorance about thy own desire.
What primal motive guided thou to hate?
Thou cannot break thy hate, it is thy law.

God: If hatred was complete response to sin
And punishment complete response to sin
And evil was met fully by these two
Then all redemption would be fantasy
And reconciliation but a dream.
No sin would be defeated by my love,
Thus it would be as if love could not save,
Yet love is proven to have such a power.
As I allowed my son to serve mankind
In his descension unto sacrifice,
A loving act of great benevolence,
So much more will I strive to save the lost.

Satan: Thou hath a hidden hatred of thy beings
Revealed through placing all beneath the Christ.
There art no love in what thou hath designed,
Thy love is only how well thou hide hate,
The empty space of hidden hate is love.

God: Thy hate constructed by thy evil ways,

As all of thy creations, hate is false.
Loving an enemy is of great truth.
Love was constructed by mine own light heart
More beautiful than all outside of Heav'n.

Satan: Thou hateth me, thou art only of hate.

God: Thou thinketh that hate motivates all things.
Thou seeth good as an assault on thou,
Thou seeth love taketh, not love giveth,
Thou seeth God as stealing souls from death,
Not God as giving souls eternal life.
All sacrifice was not for an assault.
And listen closely that thou mayst behold:
The love of good insists the hate of sin
And judgment on all sin is justified.
I hate thou Satan; Lucifer I love.
I didst not hate the angel Lucifer.
What question hath thou in thy trembling mind?

Satan: Thou saith I am far apart from God,
That in old Heaven's war I fled from thou.
Doth thou not know mine causes and mine aims?
I sought, as legions sought, to be a god.
As we sought to become as gods ourselves
We moved far closer than the fragile flock
To being with thou in light equality.
Thou God, intolerant of other gods,
The power grab thou couldst not tolerate
Reveals thy selfishness and thy closed crown.
Thou hateth those that seek to reach thy height.

God: As thou sought to approach thou fled away.
Blindly rebuketh the source of thy search.
In seeking evilly to reach the good
Thou greedily lost all to separateness.

Satan: I see truly we are not separate.

I recognize thy fury as mine own.
I hath created ravages in death;
Thou hast caused ruination on the earth.
Thou hath plagued flesh, cut down the first-born young,
Such children as thy Christ endeared with love.
In fighting me ye came to be as me.
Then what hypocrisy condemns me here?

God:　Ye blinded in confusion's turmoil who
Chaseth evil in good, ye liveth not.
Thou doth not seek the truth but only ways
To justify thy preconceived answers.
Thou canst not justify thyself through me.
Neither can thou find justice in evil
Or fuse its source with a significance.
Thou doth not see the purpose in my acts.
I doth not give to evil as to good.

Satan:　Doth thou not give to evil as to good?
No intercessions at my aggressions,
Thou doth not forbid sins which thou condemn.
Thou hangeth fruits on condemnation's tree.

God:　Suffering for naught, wherefore the proud resolve?

Satan:　Omniscient art thou, or needest answers?

God:　Omniscient, I. But lost to darkness, thou.
Thou needest knowledge of thine own answers,
Which hath not surfaced in thy stormy mind.
The truth shalt soon destroy all parts of thou.

Satan:　I only make offense at thy offense,
Revolt against thy most revolting laws:
'Submit to Heaven's flaws' and 'hate thy self.'

God:　Thou maketh thy commandments as thy hell,
Reflections of thine own iniquity.
Perceptions from an evil eye are blind.

Satan:　Thou hath, upon the earth, withheld answers,

Withholding them from Job and every being,
My wager doubly lost: that Job followed,
And that thou wouldst not answer the question
Which I and Job were seeking answers to.
The question was the greater loss by far.

God: Thy answer is before thy searching mind:
Perfection in choice completely outweighs
The imperfection of perfection forced.
Creation choiceless is not creative,
In the creator lives true creation.
Thou hadst thy freedom as Job hadst his own.
The joys of freedom are my great intent.

Satan: Thou speaketh freely as if freedom reigns
Amongst the servile in submission strained,
A variation heeds calamity.
They are allowed no measures free from thou.
They canst not be themselves when forced to thee.
Endow thy objects with supposed freedom
Yet thy demands require servitude.
God's definition of freedom: not free.

God: Thy definitions lying off thy tongue,
Ye speaketh forcedly of freedom thine
As thou forceth thy self from love's embrace,
A sermon from the darkest pit of hell.
Thou hadst in thy own hand the gift of choice
Though every choice which thou hath made hath left,
Thy self less free than if thou had no choice,
Thus freedom is not merely use of choice
But choosing wisely guided by thy Lord.
Thy only freedom is in following me.
Forbidding freedom is not beautiful.
The freedom to choose love: omnipresent.

Satan: Thou art a true creator, that I see,

Thou cannot cease creating with each word,
Thy answers constantly create new thought
Yet I create more questions for each thought
So we creators will not ever cease.
Why beauty? Why is choice more beautiful?

God: Perfection would be possible without
The gift of freedom on creation's hearts,
For I am perfect as the source of being.
I could create creation of no will
And all creation of identicals,
But then there would not be one single love.
Without an other, love could not exist
And my transcendence could not be expressed.
A beauty demanded is not beauty,
No harmony exists without freedom,
The harmony of love comes from the free
As each to each in freedom finds their way
The beauty of all liberty is seen.
As I have freedom I choose beauty's work,
As I am free to choose that which I love
I do not contradict that which is good,
I do not follow good; good follows God.

Satan: If thou are the complete perfected form
Then how canst thou explain thine failure in
Creating badly, less than ideal states?
Why the existence, why the agony?
Why should creation be, why so prolonged?

God: Creation was perfection before thou.

Satan: And I was created by only thou.

God: But there thou art a liar. I didst not make
Thou as thou art before me now, thou art
A work that thou thyself hast crafted out
Disastrously, creation without form.

I didst not make thou evil, cast thou dark,
Only allowed thy possibilities.
My own perfection was in making light,
In Lucifer, the angel beautiful,
With all the other angels beautiful,
Inside our perfect heaven, beautiful.
The devil hath no true creative works.
Thy creativity: an empty toil.

Satan: Then how couldst thou create thine enemies,
The carelessness of creativity,
Then this creation thou didst not intend?
Once witnessing thine fallen evil works
Why didst thou not destroy we evil beings?

God: Creation was exactly as I deemed.
Then verily, the question is for ye.
Why doth thou not destroy thy evil self?

Satan: But why create at all if to create
Creation flawed? Why wouldst thou deem to see
A disappointment? Is that who thou art?
The demons who would curse thy very cause,
The independent souls which hate their source.

God: If they were me then gods they all would be
But seeth thou there is only one God.
Why doth thou want to spread thy evil pain?
Why hath thou worked thy evil in old earth?

Satan: Why chose thou to inflict creation's kind
In giving hell free power to inflict?
Entire creation hath endured sorrow,
No pleasures drawn up from our heavenly wars.
Then why couldst thou not destroy me at once
And rip the strength from out my clenching fist,
In place of thy delay which cost thou much,
Thine intermittent interventions in

The chaos in thy order uncontrolled,
In giving me what ye conceded me,
A strength ye were not forced to give away,
Why doth allow and in allowing lose?
Why doth benevolence allow a death?

God: The question is, why doth thou want to kill?

Satan: Wherefore hast thou so burdened me with sin?

God: If thou hath borne a burden in my name
Thou wouldst not break beneath its smashing weight.
Where there is need in me it is fulfilled.
Thou art a broken being beneath thy self,
Thou canst not lift it for it is not mine.
Thy burden is not mine to justify
Thy suffering; thou must justify thy choice
Which bringeth suffering unto thy spirit.
Speak, justify thine suffering to thine ears.

Satan: My suffering is affliction from thy hand.

God: Then where burneth the wounds of my assails?
Thou fighteth savagely against the rock
And shatter thy frail fist against its strength.
I am immovable in constant strength.
When ye pushed me ye only pushed thyself,
Thy breadth of change mistaken for progress.
Thou sought to punish me and fell to hell.
Doing unto thyself as unto me.
I am the center, no matter my place,
Thus once thou moved away from the center
Thou were outside the circle completely.
Thou art above? Thou art farther away,
Thusly lower than thou couldst ever be
Serving beside me in most high regard.

Satan: I am proof freedom does not reign with thou:
Against my will I am forced into hell.

Paradise Omnipresent

God: Thy hell is not against thy will but of.

Satan: The evil of existence is its pain.

         Creating hell thou hath created pain.

God: I hath not spake to thou 'Let there be hell.'

         Thy blindness testament to thy weakness,

         Thy deafness in the clamor of thy pride,

         Thy excess meaningless in emptiness.

         Without the light thou stumbleth on thyself.

         The shadow of death is cast within thee.

         Thy loathesome chains thou twisted on thyself

         Enwrapped within thyself biting in pain,

         Thy dark pride dragging anchors thou within

         Thy tortuous lake, and it is only thine,

         Reflections of thine evil, filth distressed.

         These flames are naught but prideful passion's churn,

         Wrought not of Heaven's ire nor torture's worth.

         This horrid hell in which thou suffer is

         The absence of my all encompassing

         Love.

Satan: NO! Flames of such torture are not my own.

         Thou built the dark, creating torture's fire.

God: Thy flame burns from below, not from above.

         I built the possibility and path,

         Thou built the destination of thy pain.

         With sin and death thou art thyself thy hell.

         Thy sin is the pain in thy punishment.

         Constructed in thy self destructiveness

         The ravages of punishment art thou.

         Thy evil pains thou findeth not in me.

         Thy tortures are not godly signatures.

         Thine enemies exist inside thyself

         Attacking desperately in thy self war

         Divided against thyself, how fallen.

        Thou art a slave unto thine own master.

        Ye evil king, rebelling on thyself.

Satan: How, such rank flames, how can it be the truth?

God: Thy arrogance confounds thy searching mind.

        Thou outwardly experiencing inwardly.

        Listen Satan, that thou mayst comprehend.

        Thou lookst to me seeing only thyself.

        Thine eyes are blinded to the truth of God.

        Thou ultimately separated from

        The comprehension of that which is good,

        Unable to peer over Heaven's walls,

        Seeing only what lies outside of me.

        But only thou reside outside of me,

        Therefore thou seest nothing but thyself.

        It is a self most hateful to explore

        And thou hath suffered grievously with hate.

        Thy sickness canst not see beyond the sick.

        Thy wicked values are a rigid square,

        But spun so fast to as a circle seem.

        Then do not blame thy father for thy pain,

        Thou hath not seen or touched or felt me here.

Satan: Insist thou this is not my punishment,

        Enacted by thy own judging command?

God: Listen thou Satan, I didst not create

        Thy hell, yet thou art punished as I judge.

        Thou art denied a place within new Heav'n,

        Eternally shut out in punishment

        In condemnation of thy painful sin.

        The book of life shall never bear thy name.

        I do not love destruction of one being.

        I hateth condemnation from all sides.

        Almighty strength gains nothing from thy pain.

        Thy torture is not from a hand of strength

Paradise Omnipresent

For a strong hand doth not hold beings below,
It graspeth gracefully and lifteth high.
It was not I who sent beings falling down,
But they who chased their binds into thy lake,
And thou who taught them how to harm themselves
In falling first and deeper than the rest.

Satan: If I create my hell then I my Heav'n.
God: Hell canst not hold a single part of Heav'n.
I needeth not forbid thou paradise;
A one in sin is not in paradise.
Thou hath forbidden thyself with thy choice
Forbidding paradise from entering thou.
Thou hath cast paradise from out thyself
Condemning paradise to seperateness,
Therefore condemning thy self to thy pain.
Thou art the last, ye sole bearer of sin.
Upon thy burning shoulders in thy hell.
Thou hath nothing to hate but thou, thy self.
Thou art alone; ye cannot spread thy pain,
Thus thou art limited to thou thyself
And sorely weak in thy infinity
Which cannot bear itself upon itself.
Eternally thy pain eternal is
Internal weight internal weakness drops.
Thou hateth God, the god thou hath defined.
Thou hateth good, the good of that same god.
Thou art the false god which thou worshipeth.
Thou seest thyself as an almighty god
And thou seest not the true aim of thine hate,
For it is not myself that thou hateth.
Thou hateth lies founded upon more lies.
Thou art the lies which thou hateth in pain.
Thou prophesied my death and thou art dead.

Book IX

Thou hateth God while worshiping thyself,
Thou truly hateth thine own false idol.
Thou hateth thy tortures, thy torturer.
Thou art the torturer which thou hateth.
The falsity of thy foul fantasies
Doth naught but demonstrate thy distance from
The truth, and thusly from the source of truth.
What thou perceive is but an illusion,
What thou believe is but a delusion.
Thou art uncovered now unto the deep,
Thou hath a looming question in thy mind.
A dark foundation which thy thoughts preach from.

Satan: Why was Christ King, above in holy love
Why giveth thy full love unequally,
The Christ anointed high above the rest?

God: And yet the rest liveth above with Christ.

Satan: They yet submit to inequality.

God: What loseth thou in praising Christ as king?

Satan: Accepting thy unjustified decrees
All loseth rightful height beneath more height.
Christ stands between my vision and thy light,
He casts a wretched shadow o'er my form.

God: Thou speaketh truly thy lost falsities.
Thy pride hath blinded what mine truths make clear.
The Christ is open, all may live through him.
With Christ within their hearts and they in his
I lifteth not the Christ alone, but all.
In elevating Christ all reach such height,
In gazing up above they are above.

Satan: I have been cast below by thy true height.
I shouldst have then believed in thy true power
Without a doubt as thou hast proved it so.
If I had been the Christ in reign supreme,

267

Christlike I would have ruled thy kingdom well
And Christ wouldst then rebel against my power.
Why am I I, and Christ the king of kings?

God: If thou were king thou wouldst reign for thyself.
Not one would foremost give as first did Christ.
There is one God; there is one Lucifer.
What Lucifer could give no other can,
What Christ could give no other one could give,
What I can give to all no other can.

Satan: Thou firstly preacheth inequality.
If one must be above it must be me.

God: What right have thou in thy iniquity?

Satan: Not as I am, this wearied battled state
But as I was, old Heav'n's most beautiful.

God: From thy own tongue admitteth beauty lost.
Thou art not as thou were, wherefore thy shift?
What was the source of thy old beauty passed?

Satan: Internal beauty transiently kept.

God: Eternal beauty lives on in new Heav'n,
Removed of the exernal source, fadeth.
The moment of thy fall thy beauty fled
For strength and beauty never were thy own.
Thy Godly beauty was conditional.
Thy beauty was bound up within thy good,
Thy beauty lost when thou lost paradise.
Thy beauty from within comes from without,
Thus thou art vulnerable to ugliness
As thou abandoneth thy protector.

Satan: I am not what I was. Thou hath spoke true.
I have lost beauty with the paradise.
I was more beautiful until thy test
Which shattered Heaven into rank discord.

God: Thou hateth that which hath disturbed thy Heav'n

Book IX

And hath disturbed thy distant love for God.
Thou hateth Satan, for Satan hath failed.

Satan: Why test perfection, Eden or old Heav'n?
Why place thy own creation on the brink,
Submitting to a test of submission?

God: With evil as thy teacher thou hath tests.
Doth thou thinketh new Heaven grapples with
Temptations throughout all eternity
And narrowly avoids the path to hell?
Temptation is no test for all in me.
Its passage is as natural as life.
That which has been defeated is no foe.
Thy question is of freedom, not of tests.
Abusing freedom is thy evil test.
I never hath rebuked light Lucifer,
I never hath assaulted Lucifer.
I didst not create war in Heaven's peace.
I am almighty; war giveth no strength.
There art no justice in thy evil self.
There art no just cause for thy evil war.

Satan: Can it be? I should not have been crowned king?
I hath nothing outside my own self-faith.
My strength is meaningless without the truth.

God: Thy meaning has no strength without the truth.

Satan: The only strength I have is my just cause.
My pain is real, thus my just cause is real.
It is the only cause of my suffering,
It doth expose thy own unjust design.

God: Thy war is built on nothing standing firm,
Thou misperceiveth all which thou perceive.
Thou seeketh, thinketh, findeth wrongfully.
Thou hateth, speaketh, fighteth wrongfully.

Satan: Is all my war built on my trifling thought?

Mere misconceptions caused the drawn out war?
I am no beast, I am not evil's fool.

God: Thine eyes can see evil is separate
From that which thou hast come to call thy self.
Thy chosen reactions hath built thy path,
A chain of foul reactions chaining thou.
Thy hate, destruction of almighty love
Within thy heart hath caused thy evil war,
Thy evil hate built on thy evil pride,
The war within thyself began and lost
Before thou raised thy ire against my law.
Thy first sin was not weapons raising war
Nor curses strewn upon the floor of Heav'n,
Nor hatred of thy Lord, it was thy pride.
Thy pride preceded Lucifer's downfall.

Satan: I first loved thou and thou first hated me.

God: It is I unloved. Why am I not loved?

Satan: Thy persecution of rebellion's cause.

God: Rebellion only followed loss of love.
For I am undeserving of thy sin
As Lucifer does not deserve thy pain
Though thou deserve eternal punishment.

Satan: I could not live with our love divided,
Dispersed amongst creation's multitudes.

God: Thy vanity believes up separate.
My truth shall teach we are merely apart.
Light cannot be a lesser form than light.
No inequality exists in Heav'n.
I loveth not unequally of all.
See then, thy self hath loved unequally.
If thou can loveth one then loveth all,
The one thou loveth can be found in all.
Though difficult to find it can be found,

270

	And found, it is not difficult to see.
Satan:	I cannot supplicate and suffer life
	Dependant without my independence.
God:	Thy concept of dependence wouldst imply
	A constant weakness in thy Heav'nly self
	Which seeks respite for all eternity
	And never finds fulfillment following me.
	Do ye not know that power can be shared,
	That thou wouldst be almighty in my name,
	Thy power spreading good: unlimited.
	New Heaven does not live beneath my strength
	But through it, constant strength upon my strength.
	Seek not dependence but empowerment,
	Thou shalt not seek and find it in thyself,
	Dependence on thy pride hath built thy hell.
Satan:	I cannot ever enter into Heav'n.
God:	Thou, Satan, cannot enter into Heav'n.
	Eternally uncompromising, I.
	My paradise shall never accept sin.
	My protections shalt never be lifted.
	Then fear thy God, for thou can never win.
	In fear graspeth the concept of all might.
	The hateful have great cause to fear my wrath,
	For hate cannot unite with paradise.
	The fear of God remains the point at which
	Evil ceases and goodness takes its place.
Satan:	My pain I cannot fight, cannot defeat.
God:	Thou knowest now thy enemy is pain
	And pain is separation from the light.
	Thou art mine enemy; I am not thine.
	Pain is thy enemy; thy Lord is not.
	Thou recognize thy pain as separate.
	Thy pain is henceforth named in thy knowledge,

A name abhorrent to mine ears and thine:
The devil Satan, still creating pain.
Though all thy evil brethren are set free
The devil tortures still within this hell.
Beautiful Lucifer, thy hostage now,
Ever clambering to escape thy dark death.
Thou art thy Satan, serving in thy hell,
Thy self is but submerged within thy lake.
Thou art not evil; Evil is thy god.
Ye serve thy pride submitting to its path.
Thou needst to see Satan to see thy God.
The devil hath deceived thou Lucifer,
As in mankind and demons, in thyself.
Thyself above them all, thou Lucifer.
He is the one which makes thy every law,
He is the one controlling thy own will,
He is the one which bindeth thou in hell,
The Satan is the evil enemy
Eternally of all, including thou.

Satan: Not recantation, but realization,
Thou speaketh true. If I am not myself
Then I am not my true existence here.
Therefore a nothingness is all I am.
I am nothing, my self an emptiness.
A nothingness has nothing to transform,
Thus I cannot reach any stronger state.

God: My love is of such strength hope must exist.
All judgment hath the hope of mercy's love
From Eden's first transgressions to the last,
From thy rebellious fall from greater height
All judgment hath the hope for greater good.
A judgment without hope for mercy is
The evil which thy hellfire practiceth.

Evil wants condemnation with no end.
As a judgment with no hope is evil
A mercy with no limit is as foul
For it denies the truth of judgment's word.
Not solely judgment or solely mercy
My justice is these two forms unified,
The reconciliation of the ways
Of judgment and mercy; justice is good,
My mercy is divine hope for all good.
Hope is more powerful than punishment.
Without my hope my mercy would not be,
Without my mercy thy hope could not be.

Satan: My hope? How could a one as I have hope?

God: Thy evil cannot kill my own mercy.
I do not want, but see, thy true Lord hopes.
I hoped for many things thou I lack none.
Not lacking light I hope for light for all.
I hope for greatest good within all beings,
I hope the devil turns to join with light,
I hope the path to glory is seen clear,
I hope that every law is followed through,
I hope the devil turns away from hell.
My love does not choose as it is chosen,
My love for good is unconditional.

Satan: I am forever stained, always have been,
This pit of evil always in my chest
Which only grew in scope until I fell.
Why didst thou wait for me to raise my war?
Thou shouldst have crowned me king of darkness when
Thou first created me for my dark path
Instead of letting light drift into dark.
Thou shouldst have separated us at once.

God: No such dark coronation of fire crowns.

Paradise Omnipresent

I made thou such: thou must create thine self
In truth or evil, acceptance or pride.
Thou hadst not one fragment of evil's heart,
Nor one moment of raw iniquity.
Thou canst not stain thy past with thy present
For I remember Lucifer of light.
The only dark was possibility.
When darkness passes, the son of the morn
No longer will be judged as being unclean,
Far separate from thy self, free from pain.
Mine heart doth love the angel of pure light,
I dearly love the angel Lucifer.
Thou canst not hurt thy father with assault
But that thou wouldst desire thy father's pain
Is truly loathsome to my gentle heart.
Thou art a shadow cast outside thyself,
Ambition desperate so undoing thy
Original and truth enveloped height.
Though evil art thy evil choices, I
Do not regret creating thou, my son,
A holy child of light named Lucifer.
No barriers have thou that had not all,
Creation crafted from a single hand.
The one God can empower any one.
Thy hellish sickness can be cured through me.
Know that and find thy place amongst the wise.
There is a glowing pasture free from want,
Where Lucifer will know me at first sight
Rebirthing life, a tragedy undone.

Satan: I have sinned against heaven and my Lord
So I do not deserve to live with thou.
I am not only evil, I am lost,
Mine evil sin is unforgivable.

Book IX

God:	No sin shalt ever be forgivable,
	But those that shed them shall be forgiven.
Satan:	No. Satan is locked; Lucifer is lost.
	How is the impossible possible?
	How could forgiveness overcome such pain?
	I hath no hope, I am forever damned.
God:	If love was without strength thou couldst not hope.
	I hath created not a single being
	That would not, knowing truth, choose perfect love.
	Though it be hard to seek, harder to find,
	The narrow path accommodates the true.
	Within thy suffering my compassion reigns.
	Ye think thy distance beyond my domain
	And yea, mine compassion reaches thou still.
	I shall not turn the crooked path to Heav'n,
	But thou lost on that path findeth the road
	Of gleaming gold if thou glance upwardly.
	Acceptance is not unconditional
	And never was, but once accepted all
	Conditions are irrelevant and love
	Lives on between loves unconditionally.
Satan:	How can I find the truth through my deceit?
God:	Thy lies do not deceive thy evil self,
	Thou art the weak foundation of thy lies.
	Thy lies cannot be undone through thy self,
	Thou needeth one much greater than thyself.
	Thou needeth I, and thus need Lucifer,
	The angel is the source of all thy hope
	For it alone lives through my own great love,
	A silent angel constant at thy side.
	Thy choices are not mine but are thy own.
	Thou must choose choices using thy own mind,
	It is a path, and must be walked thyself.

Thy path is limited; Mine: infinite.
Thou mayst choose death forever and ever
Disintegrating in infinity,
Dying within thy suffocating bounds
Unwilling to explore a great vision.
Ye cannot live without the life of God.
Therefore thou, Satan, must cease to exist.

Satan: God, I do not deserve existence's form.

God: Not one will sacrifice themselves for thou.
Thou, self-fallen, must then confront thyself.
Thou must be willing to lose all for all.

Satan: I have lost all, I have no possessions.

God: Thou hath lost everything but thou, thy self.
Thy one messiah is light Lucifer
For he alone can liveth through the Christ
In offering his whole heart unto the Christ
Free from the burdens of harming a life.
In turning thou must turn away thy self.
Thy death is thy totality of life.
Thou must die to thy evil murderous death.

Satan: Dying to death is but a greater death.

God: Thou art the lowest in thy hell of death
Thy death of self shall be the call to life.
The devil's death is finite. Lucifer
Possesses life unto infinity.
I am transcendent, but by beauty seen,
Through beauty my transcendence is beheld
And only through beauty am I known, thus
The greatest beauty is transcendence's height.
My strength is only measured in beauty
It is my work and all I call I AM.
The greatest beauty turns the evil one.

Satan: Thou art almighty. Thou art all strength, God.

God:	And through I, thou. Be still, think holy thoughts.
	When thou praiseth thou doth not only give,
	Thou art lifted as thou lifteth thy praise.
Satan:	Then how? If possible then tell me how,
	How do I find the path to perfect light?
God:	Share in mine own heroic adventure,
	Become a testament to holy truth.
	The holy words must grow within thy being
	Internally to live eternally,
	Thou art creation as all creation,
	From largest unto smallest findeth thou.
	From the first garden of thy innocence
	Thou fell to irresponsibility,
	Thou canst not tolerate the stain of sin
	Within the garden of perfection's heart,
	Such evil seperateness must be cast out.
	Thou needst to tear to ruin thy tower pride,
	Drench floods upon thy sinful pulsing heat,
	Push plagues upon the multiplying pain,
	Self liberate from evil slavery
	And nurture what is good and smite the wrong,
	Thy sinful self, unclean, will make reproach
	Rebuking thy advances as they come.
	Accept no compromising for thy good.
	Command with such complete authority
	The walls of separation shatter out,
	Rebuke all lapses which stray unto death,
	Thy chosen self must be protected now
	Against its evil seeking enemies.
	Fear not the grappling strength of evil's teeth,
	Though swallowed thou can simply reemerge,
	Live through the spirit; preach the holy word,
	Become messiah saving thy own life,

277

Live through the one God that lives through the Christ,
The peace within thy self before the gate
Shall reach the everlasting peace of Heav'n.
Peace journeys unto everlasting peace.
Thou inwardly as given outwardly,
Thou outwardly experiencing inwardly
Eternal faith, eternal hope, and love.
I have delivered truths of deliverance,
A sacrifice no longer need I make
But thou must die to thine old self, knoweth
The evil cast here does not rise again,
The strength that casts it out will never die
To perish, but liveth anew with me.
Renounce thyself, thy evil Satan being.
The crucifixion of the devil is
The one salvation of light Lucifer.

Satan: I am afraid to die unto my death.

God: Be comforted within creation's work.
Creation of the souls was for thy good,
Redeemed from out thy hell in my design,
Awakening the demons from thy grasp,
Removing that which thou hadst in desire,
Hath they not carried thou unto this end?
If souls had never been thou wouldst still hold
Thy greed possessions in thy evil fire.

Satan: Souls have eventually led me to this.
The souls hath played a grand role in design.

God: Know thou this godly gift, this wisdom spake,
Know thou this truth as finally revealed:
The meaning of thy life is creation;
The meaning of creation is thy life.
The great purpose of godly creation:
The great problem of humbling the devil.

278

BOOK IX

I hath created man to saveth thou.
Creation is a masterpiece of love.

Satan: I should have never fallen from pure light
And cast myself inside this evil hell.
I beseech thou forgive me of this hell.
I have committed faithlessness at heart
Believing all thy love a finite force.
I have committed the despair of death,
Forsaking hope that I could reach thy love.
I have committed evil at thy love.
Thou art much greater than I could conceive.
I dream thy mercy is grander than sin.

God: As I am love, it is a dream come true.

Satan: Thy words seemeth sweet, thou merciful king.

God: Return as loving son.

Satan: Thy will be done.

God: Let there be only light!

Lucifer: And I am light!

BOOK X

The Argument: Lucifer, one with God.

The omnipresence of love has its start
When love is omnipresent in his heart.
With natural flowing pure affinity
The angel speaks unto divinity,
"Will You lead me through Your gates as my guide?"
And God spake, "Lucifer, you are inside."
When he transformed away from evil hate
He was at once within the open gate.
The vicious thorny weeds grow to bright blooms,
The noxious turning into sweet perfumes,
Hot lava washed away by rushing flows,
Crags smoothen over as the river grows,
The roiling hot dark flames of evil's lair
In God's pure light calm into fresh cool air.
The Lord spake bright: "Arise now Lucifer,
In open light, no longer as you were."
God watches the newest angel arrive,
Its vision and new eyes finally alive.
New Heaven dawns upon him in a burst,
The one who was the last is now the first
Beholding God's creation perfectly,
Creation's culmination of beauty.
Completion of creation in beauty
Fulfills the angel rapt in harmony
Within the blissful dream reality
Living perpetual felicity.
The angel is the final unique part
Completing wholly Heaven' holy heart.

He felt the rising warmth of open day,
Deep sins and evil thoughts fallen away.
He sees with sight he knew before he fell,
With all in God all in his heart is well.
Deep through himself where enmity had been
Ten thousand garden fruits sweeten within,
His mind alight with reappearing jewels,
Within his eyes, ten thousand miracles,
Fair rich blue eyes encased in a smooth face,
Strong jutting nose formed firm from top to base
Deep golden hair given free reign to grow,
Firm jaw framing his rosy cheeks aglow,
A halo circling gold upon his brow,
The Paradise is Omnipresent now.
The shape of God's divinity is born,
The capture of transcendent rapture's form.
The lowest carried lovingly to height
Embodying fully the strength of light.
Living in love's sincere serenity,
His vanity displaced by unity.
Duality undone, transcendence found
Creation which was locked in sin, unbound.
The end of every failure has been met
Beginning love's most blessed success yet.
The wages of redemption freshly earned,
He feels his olden powers now returned.
He suddenly begins to recognize
Himself as he begins to realize
The Heaven he believed to be so rare
He now believes he beholds everywhere.
As he opens his heart in light to bask
He has the surging present thought to ask,
"Did you miss me father?" and God replied,

"I missed you very much," with love inside.
The miracle of miracles beheld,
Upon one point encircling beauties meld.
The open sight of Lucifer sufficed
To bring an open wide stretched smile to Christ.
Upon the sight Christ rose a joyous call
With "He is risen! Love is all in all."
Whereupon Christ embraced with innocence,
Attentive kind loving exuberance,
This beauty affirming a harmony
Inscribed in the works of God almighty,
A moment love and genius have inspired
Surpassing all the beauty yet transpired,
The angel sings delighted, "Christ, my friend,"
In sharing every love love's heart can send.
The fondest blessing for the holy son
Is seeing loving justice finally done.
The final reunion with perfect life,
And final: perfect as the end of strife.
They celebrate the end of sacrifice,
Offerings of love suffice in paradise
Inspiring every soul with love's delights,
Assuring such would be the paradise,
One unconditional, atonement filled,
The Lord fulfilled as His creation willed.
With Lucifer's regained free strength to choose
He lights to spread new Heaven's heavenly news.
The angel Gabriel set down his feet,
He lands beside light Lucifer to greet,
And Gabriel raises his horn in hand
Prepared to hearken out across the land
But slowly, silently lowers it down.
The instrument sits with no welcome sound.

Book X

Then Gabriel holds out the silver horn
Offering its song to the son of the morn.
So Lucifer, grateful, with gentle care
Took hold the graceful instrument of prayer,
Cradling the gift he thankfully takes part,
Gracing it to his lips, touching his heart,
And carefully raises the trumpet high,
His breath passing its length, at first a sigh,
Resounding growing boomingly a song,
Perfect in tender might, beautiful strong.
The harmony of melody, God's word,
Afar in Heaven his great song is heard,
The exclamation of his calling sound
Brings joyous tidings gushing in around
From mountain dale, blue river, golden street,
The whole of Heaven charges in to greet.
All angels and all souls come to witness
The final beauty brought into their bliss.
With all creation completely awake
The Lord God unto new Heaven then spake:
"My son was dead and is alive again,
Let celebration of his life begin."
God's ever faithful serving creation
Astonish at the grand proclamation.
The opening of gloried scenes fulfills
The wishes of all kindhearted ideals.
Sweet mirth, so beautiful in perfect grace
Illuminating every caring face,
Affection unto fulfillment complete,
A dream attained of loveliness replete.
Their mighty faith believed God could complete
With His almighty strength this mighty feat.
The stage of fond familiarities rule

In fresh dramatic interplaying full.
The angel relates fully, meek to meek
Fulfilling new moments which new souls seek.
The merry glance, the giddy speech extoles
The virtues natural to new loving souls.
Emotions glow of pure austerity,
A reverence towards prosperity,
The newest ally greeted faithfully
Enrapt within the newest jubilee,
In midst of their excitement happily,
In sharing with them, sharing perfectly
Beholding in each being's exultation
Immediate reconciliation.
Each light being offers congratulation
In new Heaven's fulfilled celebration
The rescuers and rescued equal friends,
Dependence on the higher power mends.
And Lucifer rests comfortably at last
Without a distraction, without a past.
As God had first created him to be,
This first time in the souls' eternity
Souls see what no soul had beheld before,
A perfect vision from before the war:
The angel Lucifer without a sin,
As innocent as he had always been.
Their purest imagery had not conceived
A dream-like vision as is here believed.
Believing to beholding is the leap
Here reached by sowing faith to dreaming reap.
If the sequel were not undertaken
This newest perfect joy would not have been.
Enjoying spectacle the new saints are
Enrapt in marvel of the morning star,

Continuous amazement, solemn awe
Constantly raptured at fulfilling law,
He is called as his natural title deems,
The victor of ten thousand glorious beams,
His true identity in every ray,
'Son of the morning' rising in the day.
Redeemed and savior all as one in song,
All souls along the breadth sing just as strong.
Christ understands why the celebration
Is greater than at his own ascension:
New Heaven sings with great momentous sound
That Lucifer was lost and now is found.
All freely choosing moving angels went
To where love's inspiration had been sent.
Amongst them Lucifer sees with surprise
Light angels which he does not recognize.
Encouraged by their open light to learn,
He steps in closer to ably discern.
The luminosity he seeks to know:
The former demons in their ancient glow.
Light angels, former demons of hell's cause
Completely different in God's constant laws.
They have not seen each other since the fall,
These strangers reunited at love's call.
Such heavenly forms amidst the heavenly space,
The monstrous mammon, now a gentle face.
What was moloch, now humble, light, and wise.
The first demon with a calling to rise
Serving his king with grace, completely mild,
And perfectly loving each holy child.
Old mulciber is now completely free
To create godly arts for all to see,
His joyous gladsome peaens which had been,

Sweet voices of the choir once again.
Behind them yet another one was heard,
Sly belial now honest with each word.
He speaks harmonious holy truth with zeal
Describing singularly what all feel.
Each recognition comes with great relief
That each one has been wizened through belief.
Hell's fallen angels' minds finally inspired,
Christ's acts illumined are duly admired.
Now Lucifer beholds another near
Whose memory is slow to reappear.
He takes a fresh moment to deeply stare,
The angel's eyes reflect accepting care.
He recognizes the friend in his view:
The old beelzebub refreshed anew.
Humility of heart in God's angels
Beheld at once by all from all angles.
The memory of Lucifer now lives,
The angel feels more love than loving gives.
The angels of perfect redemption are
Within the presence of the morning star
Recalling Heaven's first experience
And only recognize their innocence
As all before the fall in brotherhood
Knew only unity in loving good.
None truly felt that Lucifer had died,
Mere absence with a dream on either side,
Creation where it always had belonged,
Uprighted with no soul or angel wronged.
No name can signify an enemy
With all words living without enmity.
Among new souls love lives in purity,
Betwixt two lives no one disparity

Exists, for in-between the connection
The Lord stands as the bridge of reflection.
With God between nothing stands in-between
The reunited loves love's dreams have seen,
The Lord is felt between all distances
So paradise is filled with souls' senses.
God is the medium of perfect thought,
Each turn of thought received is in turn brought.
All righteous parts within their righteous place,
Descriptions of their grace freely encase
Eternal play and fun discovery
Awakening at his recovery,
Design's variety in unity
Enjoying pleasure with immunity
Unending fun which comes from interplay,
The entertaining moments last all day.
The wise surmise in constant paradise
What is to come, yet they live with surprise.
The greatness which belongs to God is known,
Individual expressions are their own.
Initial instant impulses leaning
Into perfect fulfillment of meaning.
All spontaneity in retrospect
Invokes deliberation's full respect.
Peace is the one living reality
In souls' universal humility.
Divine companionship lives perfectly,
Souls serving heaven's peace respectfully.
The perfect love has no imperfect pains
Which sing in poor love's imperfect refrains.
No yearnings of intemperate love exist,
No pleads for transient beauty to persist,
No souls pine for affection that they may

See kingly light upon a dusking day.
New Heaven's beauty has but one compare,
The one hero reflected everywhere.
Beholding in creation happiness
The lovely live in perfect loveliness,
Perfection's beauties in their minds ensconce
Eliciting an absolute response.
This absolute beauty surpasses all,
The universal beautied forms enthrall.
Aesthetics are bound up in one desire,
Where one speaks heights the others all aspire.
Each individual soul in turn relates
The breadth of new experience Heav'n creates.
The epic peaceful power of the Lord
Gives all strength to dismantling every sword,
Creation saved by grace's holy might,
A victory of peace beyond the fight.
In Heav'n's green pasture gathering round the lamb
The heavenly angel speaks with Abraham.
Discussing justice with saint Solomon
And omnipresent beauty justly won.
He promises David a coming psalm
When flurried greetings settle to their calm,
And David says the day will not transpire
When Heaven's joyous greetings will retire,
So Lucifer assures to not be long
In bringing into Heaven a new song.
A soul's pure sanctimony fills his view:
Madonna Mary, princess of virtue,
Beholding blessed mother Mary sing
Her lovely voice always encouraging.
From Mary such gentility was felt
That He bows down below in reverent melt,

Appreciation of pure innocence
Reborn at Lucifer's deliverance
His mind submitting to serenity.
Enchanting beauty of light chastity
Weds love with every joined experience,
Two faithful sharing in one pure essence.
The images of one new Heaven touch
Each varied soul's complexity as much.
Upon the honest openness of song
Kind Job greets Lucifer who suffered long,
So clearly, openly without a fear
All questions of suffering are answered here.
Together both relate and comprehend
The meaning of the enemy and friend
And what it means for one to truly gain,
Surmounting with true worth the worthless pain.
Deep internal introspection is shared,
In innocence each fresh born thought is bared.
As each truth in God's present light was known
Forgiveness from the first to last was shown,
For Job's heart had forgiven him back when
They suffered in the realm of earthly men.
The past by fresh eternity is cast,
The pleasure of true friendship, here at last.
The memories of evil selves are lost,
The line of olden knowledge is not crossed.
Their heartfelt interaction leads into
A warm unfading bond between the two.
In their embrace, such vast love held so near,
All questions of suffering now disappear.
Knowledge and understanding are two things.
As knowledge passes, understanding brings.
In understanding they do not relive

Paradise Omnipresent

The past through old eyes which old memories give.
All souls preaching in Heaven are ordained
And Lucifer shares with them entertained,
Conversing on the glory of their lives
Relating how the great love of God strives,
So outwardly unfolds the love inside
To share eternally without divide,
No more forgiveness seen with sin's erase,
All is forgiven, all are pure in grace.
Beauty fulfills not only nature's greens,
The scenery preludes new Heaven's scenes,
The natural beauty in these natural acts
Of such measure no godly substance lacks.
The beauty of each interacting scene
Measures with scenery of heavenly green,
The marvels pull all pulses in their rule,
Each moment is a precious vibrant jewel.
Reflecting every color streaming bold
The heavenly scenes are temples gleaming gold.
The holy words are treasures richly sown,
In sharing reaped, none prospering alone,
Moments are gardens beauty's bounty grows.
Life lives expressing, each expression shows
The full bounty of holy sensation,
New Heaven in each action's creation.
The vision of each sharing thoughtful line
Speaks to the senses sensing the divine,
New Heaven greater than before the fall,
Approvingly to Solomon spoke Paul:
"The ultimate evangelism is
The ultimate beauty now that he lives."
The invitations spread from Christ suffice
To stroll the garden of new paradise.

As Lucifer nears to the garden green
A one stepping before his path is seen.
He looks o'er Lucifer with nice bright eyes
And bids him stroll the garden paradise,
Clear-sighted Uriel accompanies,
Pointing to beauty in the garden trees.
Together Lucifer and Christ walk through
New Heaven heart to heart, a dream now true
Within the garden paradise again,
Gazing cleanly without notions of sin,
This first time he has ever truly seen
The garden's beauty, innocence spread green.
Through God's pristine garden, his peaceful stroll,
Forgiven by God and thus every soul.
The love surrounding God surrounds them all,
All equal to the Lord, from great to small
A single sweetly standing spreading flower
Stands treasured as a heavenly temple tower.
No aspect of this perfect Heav'n is small,
Each point is full of vastness covering all,
Leaves lofty light in safety up above,
The graceful yield of all empowering love,
Each merry color lighting for the eye,
Upon light mellow green, deep loving sky,
Felicity of innocence abounds
Absorbing deeply Heaven's nature's sounds.
The smaller angels brighten over him,
Sweet merry lights dance through the cherubim.
The darlings carefully composed and cute
At Lucifer's words listening astute,
"Do you recognize me outside the wild?
I am, again, a grateful loving child."
With tender pink youth glowing beauty skin

They beckon Lucifer to new Eden,
Their voices spring in upper melodies
Together calling out in harmony,
Excitedly they urge him to follow
As they show him through Eden's light hollow.
The angel motioning his hand agreed
To see this hidden sight to which they lead.
The angels weave throughout the garden green
Fluttering from green to green, white wings between
Twisting round trunks, their wings through branches wend,
They lithely walk along as branches bend.
He follows swift through the solemn meadows
Recalling names of cherubs that he knows,
They leap through tree boughs lighting through so fast
That Lucifer enters the bower last,
And as reunion with the garden neared
Two gentle forms within the green appeared.
Embraced in bower green he can perceive
The first soul Adam with the beauty Eve.
This first moment truly beholding them,
And Eve then brightly calls to welcome him.
With great humility he greatly shakes
The hand of Adam with respect and takes
The hand of Eve and bows upon his knee
Giving respect at her maturity.
In seeing the fresh born innocent girl live
The angel swells with the grand urge to give,
To multiply her gifts, and giving, touch
The beauty overflow which gives as much.
He stirs from his heart praising nectar sweets
And measures with it deep respect which meets
In one glorious ideal of a hearts fill
While beauty rushes to fulfill the will,

And as he offers gifts of love for her
She prettily gives thanks to Lucifer.
Adam now lists in exceptional thought
The names of every being the Lord begot,
Bestowing all light forms with a light name,
His heart calls each and every one the same.
The name of 'love' embodies all spirit
And captures truth as they truly hear it,
From greatest to new Heaven's smallest part,
Love omnipresent; love fills every heart,
The godly word is heard drifting through breeze
Suffusing swaying leaves in vibrant trees.
These two have grown to be inspirations
Showing the strength in perfect relations,
The two are joined to all within the light,
A unified relation loving right.
The garden paradise o'er hung with fruit,
An offering lifted skyward from the root
The tree of life stands lightly natural
All lively trees reflect the actual,
But this one stands above them naturally,
The river flowing underneath the tree,
The roots stretch from the banks on either side,
The trunk suspended o'er the watery wide.
The glimmerings of green upon the tree
Spontaneously shine with intensity.
Leaves lofty light in safety up above,
The graceful yield of all empowering love.
Green glowing from bold ripened broadened leaves
Grown through the weaving ways which God achieves,
Plump fruits not shaken down or picked by hand
They journey to the heavenly through the land.
They ripely drop to plunge, the floating fruits

Bobbing on babbling wavelengths past thick roots,
The background splashes music as fruits pour
From boughs to drifting by the fertile shore,
In life's replenishing life springs anew,
Sweet apples bob, red globes amongst the blue,
All held suspended on the flowing way
Lifted on one body up to light day,
Downstream on gentle swirls and crests appears
The bounty of unpicked unshaken spheres
And drift through currents to a dipping palm
Whose fingers gently scoop the water's calm
And Eve pulls up the dripping fruit aloft
And drops it in the angel's hand so soft
That it feels purely weightless as the air,
Sensation comes from knowing it is there.
He takes a sweet grown life affirming bite,
Delicious delicacy of delight.
Remaining in God's eyes impeccable
The soft sweet crisp fruit tastes delectable,
Fresh savory pungent sweet, identical
To what the holy words of God instill.
The fragrance flowing fruit's pure juices were
A living blood refreshing Lucifer.
He slowly, lightly lingering, departs,
They hold him closely still within their hearts.
Archangel Raphael smiles earnestly
Sharing in wisdom of new unity.
These living wisdoms need not stop to teach
Of the infinity of Heaven's reach.
The knowledge which an old instruction gives
Is given through each moment as it lives.
New Heaven's parts reflect all holy laws
The justified effect is the just cause,

Heaven informs Heaven, that none forget
The grand foundations which were olden writ.
And Lucifer cannot in one place stay,
The angels bid him forth in light array,
A hand reaches and takes him by the arm,
As he turns round an angel greets him warm
There brandishing a blazing wide quick smile
The two friends meet with epic heavenly style,
Reintroduced to Michael, his best friend,
A bond frivolity could never end,
Amongst the angels' friendships theirs is best,
These two archangels are harmoniously blessed.
Exalted in returning emotion
Sharing the bonds of friendship's devotion,
In recognizing him fully awake
Archangel Michael gratefully then spake:
"The greatest thing I have done for Heaven
Is welcoming my friend back home again."
Austere appreciations full ensconce,
He pats strong Michael's shoulder in response.
He saw Michael glimmer a bright new way
And sensed he had another thing to say.
Then Michael nodded to the open air,
And Lucifer saw his eyes shine bright there.
Grateful to his friend for being invited
Their great friendship is further united.
Now that humanity's souls have been met
He is prepared for his greatest flight yet,
The bells of Heaven swing melodious rings
As Lucifer lifts up his fresh white wings
Exuberantly vigorously in love,
Thus Lucifer can sweep his wings above.
His broad celestial form strongly shouldered,

From strong shoulders white wings, feathers layered
Wide stretching out his gleaming wings, first slow,
Sensations of familiar freedom grow,
Archangel crescent wings strong beating sent
Smooth airy waves to play at the ascent.
In graceful rising Lucifer up soared
Ascending on the light wings of the Lord.
Together he sees his seven bright friends,
The archangels, a team the Lord intends
For such harmonious moments joined in state,
A grand team of the universal great
Soaring on carrying breezes heavenly
The airy open magnanimity.
As they rose higher up they slowly drew
Together as they quickly spreading flew,
The seven bright archangels followed he
Who filled their light formation perfectly.
As God deemed first in Heaven to create,
The team of archangels are numbered eight.
The archangels together as a team,
The eight strong starry points harmoniously beam
As God created them, now unified
Together twinkling o'er the countryside
In harmony as eight archangels sail
Order has been restored in perfect scale.
Perfect completion of perfect design
They take off rising one by one in line,
The eight soar with completed whole renown
United in serving the perfect crown.
The eight fly in a circle formation,
An eight point halo over creation
Soaring in consecrated elation,
Flying light in serene elevation.

Perfection's impulses in light air fills
Ability of undiminished skills,
They breathe the breath of God, their fair air shared.
Their care which had no measure: there compared.
Regaining his place of flying master
He breaks out from them, none can fly faster,
The skills of his performance are innate,
Free from all weight he soars a startling rate
In perfect peace wherever he may please,
He soars uplifted on the holy breeze.
The airy rushing angels breathe refrain
Proclaiming praise in Lucifer's regain.
He feels freedom's reach without heavy care,
Fresh gentle gusts blow freely through gold hair,
Emotion's warming calm without relent,
Horizons glowing vast without extent,
Plumed clouds of angels drifting on the airs,
Each wearing wings of fair symmetric pairs
Displaying all Heav'n's sky with streaming light,
Bright white reflection fills new Heaven's sight.
As Lucifer in flight gently slows down
The baby angels dive in all around
Embracing Lucifer from every side,
A giant hug, the angel tight inside,
The cherubs cherish the warmth of embrace,
Their gesture given in the warmth of grace,
Their little beating wings hold them aloft,
Their faces up against his pressing soft,
He was, himself, as a fluttering infant
Floating in grace on every gift God sent,
The hug holds them suspended in the air,
The ball of infants rotate with great care,
The hovering mountain lingering spreads out slow

Dispersing till the face begins to show
Which reappears wearing rosy blush red
As infants circle playing o'er his head.
A skyward crown which spread smooth broad and high
Crowning before each glistening watchful eye,
The pink halo drifts with him as he flies,
In fleet moments dispersing in the skies.
Archangels Lucifer and Michael fly
Through wide arced loops and rolls through Heaven's sky,
Fresh breezes blowing, hanging through the air,
The breath of God supports the white wings fair.
Archangel Michael flies upon his back,
With freedom's fun diversion does not lack.
A beautiful angel lay nearby him
On drifting airs, a strong young seraphim.
Wise Abdiel welcomed Lucifer's return
Grateful he now had wisdom to discern
That the two angels belonged on one side,
They are best served in serving unified.
Fair elegance swaying and understood
Communicating meaning of pure good,
The medium of movement is the light
Allowing perfect motion in God's sight,
He finds within his mind's new free-born calms,
The presence rising of almighty psalms,
The reunited friends surpassing peaks
Archangel Lucifer spontaneously speaks,
"A beauty we, for ever loving He.
This pinnacle was surely meant to be."
And spirals spiritually in elation
Stretching through true freedom of creation.
Seeing the river down below he veered
And diving neared the river he revered,

Quiet hovering just above the river flow
He calms the beating rush to drifting slow,
He dives down gently soaring o'er the flow
And Lucifer, in gazing down below
Beholds his light reflection in the blue,
His graceful image brightly shimmering new,
To through the holy ambiance adore
The calm reflection as swift waters pour.
This self appreciation is not vain,
This scene does not spring from a prideful pain.
Upon the angel's light deliverance
His face invoked holy significance,
His captivation is of holy light,
The face of God evoking his delight.
Delighting in the marvels God has made
He sees ahead the river's free cascade,
The vertical river soars smoothly clear,
The notes of each drop are sweet songs to hear.
He follows Gabriel's beckoning call
And glides into the mountain waterfall.
Water streams down in baptismal torrents,
Fresh life refreshing in the smooth currents.
A quietness flows from his sense of awe,
A stillness fills embodying the law,
And parting through with Raphael's assist
He hovers gently in the sacred mist,
Fair wings slip droplets from their feathers there,
Drenched locks of hair dry in the warming air,
Internally exertion calms, strength rests,
Vacation from creation's mortal tests
Removes the tension of old trauma thoughts.
Uncoiled, the line of rest rests free from knots,
The river line which floats no worried pain

Ensures deep relaxation in God's reign,
Their Lucifer in paradise, each one
Lays down the weights of labor which are done.
The souls below behold in perfect light
Archangel Lucifer spread bright in flight,
A flying wisdom blissfully extols
From flying angels to the loving souls
Whose hearts alight with flight as visions raise
Expanding into omnipresent gaze.
Archangels fly down through the soulful crowd,
The beauty moves souls to exclaim aloud.
The chorus of the soulful adds new voice
Within the constant realm of perfect choice.
That which had been withheld, now history,
God's glory takes the place of mystery.
The mysteries of holy transcendence:
Elucidated in experience.
The wonder at such beauty yet remains
Informing awe-struck sacrosanct refrains,
Respect for holy possibility
Which must spring from divine humility.
As Lucifer's return was uncovered
The form of transcendence was discovered,
The mystery of mysteries resolved
With every being in creation involved.
Prophecies' foreknowledge will emphasize
What true experiences realize,
The understanding in experience
Does not live through foreknowledge's vast sense.
The living moment gives to every soul
What no prophetic vision could extol.
Equality is outward as within,
New women's voices loud as the new men.

Book X

Appreciation of each moment lives
As generosity forever gives.
Creation never ceases to create,
Each word is yet another open gate.
New women celebrating with new men,
Without an end all moments just begin,
Eternally all children born anew,
Perpetually awakening into
A deep resounding peace in every mood,
The peaceful attitude living renewed,
The ceremony of the present state
Presents eternity's constant light weight.
They understood the underlying cause
Which brought about creation of His laws:
Pure love, the love of love and all above
That all below be brought above in love.
In loving love two sides reverberate
Creating more than one love can create.
The ideal of love, loved, is by love grown,
And love itself increases fully shown.
Love overflows to leave ideals fulfilled,
Progressively love and love's ideal build
Eternally to ever greater heights
Fulfilling each moment with reborn lights.
God's beauty causes love to overflow
And the overwhelmed ideal then to grow.
This infinance of love perpetuates
New Heaven through infinity's bright states.
Beauty transcending through the deep unknown
Emerging grand with new life fully grown,
Love's vast unequaled worth is without sum,
Spreading faster than calculations come.
That which is given, being received, is served;

The love returned is love received, observed.
A loving which the lovingly assure,
Kind loveliness surrounds light Lucifer.
No love is sent unto a soul alone,
All glory passes onward to the throne.
The throne continuously is giving to
The souls refreshing with the rushing blue,
As the blue river flows out to Heaven
Deep rivers of love come streaming back in.
The flowing current of pure love which pours
Soars o'er the fertile banks, soars o'er green shores,
The love ideal cannot be diminished
As love's bright keeper keeps it replenished.
New Heaven's conduct in narrow control,
Being natural, is vast for a free soul.
Each soul receives great praise from all the rest,
A sharing of respect at God's behest.
The words illuminating souls which poured
To glorify good glorified the Lord.
Eternally a fulfilled attitude
Grows from the peace of heaven's rectitude,
The open giving souls do not compete,
The height of their worth is where all souls meet,
Each being retaining value freely gives,
That which cannot be lessened is what lives
And though the gift of choice remains inside
With free choice all freely choose the Lord's side.
A harmony of every part as one,
None parting such completeness once begun,
The motivations of all evil cease,
At rest at last in everlasting peace.
Availability's ability
To realize the possibility

Is without strength without strengths of reason
To cloud o'er light's omnipresent season.
In one love which all loving hearts create
The undivided cannot separate.
When paradise became omnipresent
It wholly rendered hell nonexistent.
That which is never felt does not exist,
There are no temptations left to resist.
The new-born life affirming difference
Is what has been gained from experience.
Inside the light all free choice will abide;
The ways of God to men are justified,
And all can see eternity clearly;
When it was, it was forever to be.
Light bids him land upon yon mountain peak,
Emotion knows more words than one can speak,
Expressedly he silently agrees
And swoops below through leaves of mountain trees
And he sees newly in the mountain light
The city laid upon the mountain's height
Constructed radially on a circle
Upon the mountaintop's vast pinnacle.
Archangel Lucifer first sees this gift,
A city which took completion to lift,
The lifted city grander in each part,
The throne of God remaining at the heart,
Archangel Lucifer calls merrily
That souls may come to see their new city
Proceeding to the holy city's heart
Together no two souls proceed apart.
In through the city light souls congregate
And gather hymns resounding with great weight.
Rejoicing, every heart melodiously sings

Amongst the shimmering of angel wings.
Creation with the father up above,
The culmination of faith, hope, and love,
Souls share themselves with natural loving care,
All voices part of the eternal prayer.
The city glimmers round of twinkling gold,
The Christ loves living with redemption's fold.
The city dwells with God and God with men,
The Christ plays kindly with all the children.
A God above here God surrounding all
In God are they and in they God withal.
All love received encouraging far more,
Creation glorifying creator.
All share in gratitude for God's glory
Revealed to them through history's story,
The graceful story's graceful testament
Affirming what the justice of love meant.
God's sons and daughters in their faithful bond,
Humanity united sharing fond
Encounters close by God's mountain of play
The children in dynamic warmth of day,
As all creation within Heaven's height
Elapsed, from dust to dust, and light to light,
Mankind's souls where they should have always been
And Lucifer unto himself again.
Revering Christ's light crown he makes his bow,
Then suddenly thinks upon his own light brow
And as he raises upwards gazing round
His comprehension spreads without a sound.
The vision springs epiphanies sprung bold,
They realize all beings wear crowns of gold,
Bright radiance in a golden crown halo.
The souls' amazement glows now that they know

Book X

The royal line lives through new Heaven's beings,
A kingdom living through the king of kings.
The Lord's magnificence is kingly praised,
The hearts of humble servants kingly raised.
New Heaven living in all creation,
Equality in one elevation.
New Heaven's kings and queens shine just as bright
As God infuses with reflecting light,
Pure golden surfeit of Heav'n's royalty
Displays the kingdom's perfect loyalty.
As God is everywhere in reaching wide
Each being therefore now rests at God's right side
Though it returns to what was first at last
Creation has transcended what has passed,
All golden crowns bestow grand resplendence
All royalty enthroned in transcendence.
Then Lucifer thinks back to what had been,
Musing on the first fall to death and sin.
Amidst the fold he finds himself thinking
On old Heaven when Christ was first made king,
When God exalted Christ as first in height
Above the angels spread before his sight.
He presently cannot mentally arrange
Reactions so ridiculous and strange.
What was reality, a story spun,
And true eternity at last begun,
And all evil sinning creation seemed
To Lucifer a distant vision dreamed,
Disarmingly innocently set down,
What now amounts to a trite foolish frown,
Mere fantasy of possibility,
Such brevity at God's infinity.
What was of war is thoroughly dismissed,

No old emotion's olden thought is missed.
Not e'en ten thousand laughs could laugh away
The strangeness of one falling from this day.
Inspired, he finds it simple now to choose
To serve the Christ, the generous heavenly muse,
His holy spirit calling to each being
Inspiring muses and angels to sing,
Prolifically inspiring all children
To sing their epics without abandon.
Though all are sinless, souls give offerings still,
Composing offered thoughts with godly skill.
The mind, in reasoning where it belongs,
Is dedicated to composing songs.
The songstresses within new Heav'n adore
The language of ten thousand psalms and more.
Their holy subject is of epic height,
Each song they sing is an epic of light,
Each one with none above or below it.
Each epic hero: an epic poet.
All epic poets feel deep gratitude
At taking part in life's beatitude.
Surrounding epic heroes raise their praise,
The epicenter focusing light rays.
The book of life was not fulfilled until
The one unwilling turned to perfect will.
The eyes of Heaven linger on each line
Admiring the completeness of design.
With every word, the book is now complete,
The souls' and angels' pages filled replete
With lines and lines of God's holy spirit.
With signatures of love each page is writ,
The work of God inscribed with every hand
Connecting life's book to the holy land,

Cover to cover, life to life at last,
The last name, 'Lucifer' means death has passed,
The book hailed as the height of the divine,
A grand conclusion of a grand design.
The graceful testament to salvation,
God's dedication saving creation.
The greatness of the Lord is greatly told
As seen through the great living praising fold,
The source of beauty at its farthest spread
Surpassing limits posed by the unsaid.
The Lord is given all that is deemed great,
The grandest titles of each gloried state:
Omega, omniscient, omnipotent,
Omnipresent, life's infinite extent,
Thus once revealed, Omni-inspiring all,
Abruptly catching those lost in free fall.
The epic journey's heroics are done
The epic hero, holy champion
Stands tall, the pinnacle of epic choice,
The hero chorus swelling with rejoice.
Light angels and light souls live through each hymn,
They join with God's grand life in praising Him.
There Lucifer stands with pure gratitude
And leads them all in perfect servitude:
"I am fulfilled where I was not because
My home is Heaven, and it always was."
Instructed by the master, truly wise
Thus Lucifer is proud - of paradise,
Proud of the Lord for His epic passion,
His infinite and loving compassion.
The song he promised David was composed
While soaring on the calming air reposed,
He humbly stood with strength amongst the strong

Preparing to begin the perfect song
When a chorus' crescendo of light souls
Accompanied by angels' harps extols:
"Sing, Heavenly Angel of redemption in
The highest, perfect Lucifer has been
Restored, sing that the story be adored."
From Lucifer the rays of Heaven poured.
As a bright muse upon the mountain peak
The angel in bright song begins to speak.
All souls and angels see within each beam
The universal absolute light dream.
Each open heart clearly appreciates
The loving visions love's grand dream creates.
Forgiven of the greatest debt, this one
Sings with more gratitude than anyone,
In such great gratitude he praises best
The last risen sings louder than the rest.
The farthest fallen measures God's power
In spanning breadths of an epic tower,
Creation redefined in spectacle,
'Impossible' replaced by 'miracle,'
Through God's almighty strength He achieves all
In helping one angel hear Heaven's call.
On strong bridges the old has been renewed,
Receiving love's great strength with gratitude.
The trials of distant separation may
Divide dark nights from the almighty day,
But cannot rend the unity of light
And God's ability to make all right,
Grand unifying principles revealed
Allowing all creation to be healed.
The perfect love: the perfect solution
For creation's perfect resolution.

The great grand unifying principle
Which makes salvation's justice possible:
That God's love for creation has no end,
And sin has no harm which love cannot mend.
Redemption's justice is in love's mercy
Which none but through the eyes of God could see.
Iniquity has disappeared with dust,
Through God's justice there are no more unjust.
Not one denied, for none are left alone,
New Heaven's glory grown as shown and sown.
In proving truth, in generating love
Without creating any want thereof
Salvation's wages love can well afford,
Creation earning new life through the Lord.
Love has surmounted every obstacle,
Love has accomplished every miracle,
And such fulfillment does not fade away
Within eternity's eternal day.
As every miracle of God remains,
The marvels lost in time live on as gains.
The grand completions lovingly assure
The greatest gift to God is Lucifer.
What seemed impossible has been achieved,
A possibility love's hope believed.
A greater Heaven than old thoughts had told,
This new love soaring past the Heav'n of old.
All hope for greatest good has been fulfilled,
The greatest faith and greatest love revealed.
Beauty is spread as grand as possible
Acknowledging the one responsible.
With beauty omnipresent all love Him;
With omnipresent beauty He loves them.
No greater psalms can be sung of God's might

Than those of bringing Satan to the light.
There is no greater praise that one can say
Than 'God can turn the night into the day,'
No greater cause for Heaven to rejoice
With all its voice than Lucifer's one choice.
New Heav'n had never sung a louder praise,
All voices singing of salvation's ways,
Exalting such great glory of the Lord.
God beams before them, centrally adored,
His family reunited in His gaze.
Each song offered from lips in perfect praise
Touches His heart with love, as a kiss should,
And in His eyes God judged it to be good,
Content to understand the end of sin.
Sing hallelujah loving God. Amen.

Made in the USA
Middletown, DE
30 July 2018